Beyond My Wildest Dreams

by Albert "Al" Rayl
for those dear to me

IF YOU CAN DREAM IT –
YOU CAN DO IT

*FAILURE
IS NOT AN
OPTION*

Dedication

This book is dedicated to my parents and to my children, their children and future descendents of mine.

To Mary – my Sweetheart who has supported me in everything I have attempted. I can only wish the ride has been worth your time since we met. The years with you have also been "Beyond My Wildest Dreams."

My wish is this chronicle is used to realize there is NO obstacle too big; NO dream is unobtainable so long as you never give up.

Dreaming is the foundation for success. Success can come in many ways and not just monetary. I am a **Billionaire** of my dreams, my children and their children and the friends I have made.

Dad   Mom
Harold   Mary Susan

Purpose

Why would I attempt to write a book like this? First, I learned to dream as an escape from reality. I wished for things that I thought were never or could never be in "real" life. Money isn't everything but it sure helps get you some places and do a few things. Growing up as I did there was not a lot of money in the family. My parents taught me if I wanted something, earn it.

As the years passed I never gave up on my dreams. I think that I have been so blessed in many ways. I wanted to get some of the dreams, accomplishments and funny tales down on paper so that they might be entertaining to future generations.

I have tried not to and would never bring up any of the controversial times in my life that would hurt anyone. There are always two sides to those kinds of stories and they are never interesting.

The primary reason is to pass on that dreaming is great and you too can accomplish "Your Wildest Dreams" if you NEVER give up.

"Failure is not an option"

If I have accomplished "my purpose" then my dream of this book creates another success for me.

Forward (October 2005)

Where to begin…Have you ever sat down and read a book, finished it and felt like you were there the whole time? Well, you won't in this book. Have you ever felt like you knew what was coming next? Again…not in this book.

What you will feel and realize in this is a man who worked hard and made his dreams come true. You will see a bit of "Sgt. Bilko" here and a lot of sneaking around, but you will also see a man that made things happen. As I read over Al's life, I don't see merely a dreamer, but a go-getter. And because of that, here he is at "almost" 70 accomplishing one more dream.

In the past eight years that I've known him, Al has helped me realize some of my dreams, too. Al has been very diligent, especially the last four months, to get this done. Even to the point of letting his "household" chores remain undone. But that's okay, because the gleam in his eye as he shared "just one more chapter" was all worth it.

Al will never become rich off the book…probably because it would not be for sale, but he will be rich in Spirit and soul as he shares his memories, good times, bad times, and awesome life with the ones he loves, both family and friends.

As always, I am so proud of you, Honey, and I love you with all my heart.

Mary

Al's Sweetheart Mary

Table of Contents

Beyond my Wildest Dreams
IF YOU CAN DREAM IT – YOU CAN DO IT!

Looking back a long time ago to my childhood I realize what a wonderful ride I have had. In my early years growing up as part of a family that had a roof over our heads, food on the table, milk delivered but not much else I learned to **DREAM**.

Fantasy and dreams were a big part of my early childhood memories.

These wild dreams gave me a reason for living. The lessons that I learned were so valuable. If you never give up or quit, you can never fail and ***"FAILURE IS NOT AN OPTION"...***

If I were to leave any king of a legacy behind it would be that every child MUST Dream and set Goals and then be willing to exert the effort to make those a reality.

I have been so blessed and the greatest satisfaction is not "money" but it is seeing the results in helping others accomplish their goals and know "I have made a difference"…

Money provides luxuries but not wealth. Wealth is what we have done with our lives and those that we have led, steered, directed and prodded to accomplish their "dreams".

- -

The primary book was written 2005 but it is now updated to the end 2008. I found I wanted to elaborate on some subjects and add a lot of photos to the basic book. My thoughts are there will only be an occasional update after this…

Over the course of the past four years I have learned a lot about book printing and have assisted in almost a dozen books being printed for family and friends.

A lot has happened over the last four years and I wanted to include the happenings into this ***"ride down life's highway"***.

Chapter 1 – My Early Years

My father worked in the steel mills; mom was a stay-at-home mom, as were most in those days. My older sister, Barbara and younger brother, Jim made up the rest of the family. In the mid-1930's when I was born the Country was just coming out of "the Big Depression" and there was not much to look forward to. Having a house to live in and food on the table was a blessing. Clothes were often made from old flour sacks, which in those days were made with pretty prints. Mom was a great seamstress and some of my earliest memories are watching her sew clothes for my sister.

During the days before starting kindergarten there were not many things to do. As a youngster I enjoyed watching my mom cook and sew and I was always full of questions. This would pay off big-time in later years. I think every child should be taught to cook and to sew.

In those days there was no TV to watch, no calculators, no computers & Internet and no Cell phones. There were no CD or DVD's to rent but radio had great programs in the late afternoon and evening

There were a few friends named Attilio, Jack, Eddie and Billy who were all a couple years older than me. These were the only boys in the neighborhood and when they started school I was pretty much left to my own imagination. What an imagination I could conjure up.

During that period there were Tarzan movies at the local theater. Once in a good while I was privileged to see the movies and seeing Elephants, Lions and such thrilled me to no end. When I was lucky enough to come up with the ten cents for the movies, my friends and I had to see the latest ones. I knew that I just had to go to deep dark Africa and hunt me an Elephant.

My quest for becoming a *"Big Game Hunter"* started at my earliest recollections. Partly due to the Tarzan movies of those days and primarily because it allowed me to dream, the unimaginable, yet conquer those dreams within another dream.

Some of my earliest recollections were of *"our gang"* going over behind the golf course and watching the mail plane pick up mail. I had to be about five or six years old at the time and the rest of the gang would have been about seven or eight.

It was so neat to see the biplane come in and drop a big rubber tube full of mail from maybe 30 feet above the ground. Then we would watch as he would make a second pass and pick up mail that was going to Pittsburgh. It was awesome to watch, as he would come in, snag a rope strung between two poles with a hook and reel the outgoing bag of Airmail into this small plane. The poles were only, I am guessing, about eight or ten feet above the ground. One of these bi-planes is now in the Pittsburgh airport. I knew right then and there that *I HAD TO LEARN TO FLY.*

Clifford Ball started flying the air mail between Pittsburgh and Cleveland in 1927 with 2 Waco 9s in an operation that became Pennsylvania Air Lines and, later, Capital Airlines. One of the Waco 9s, Miss Pittsburgh, survived, was beautifully restored, and can be seen today hanging in the Pittsburgh airport terminal

As time passed and we went to the golf course to watch the mail pick-up we started exploring the woods around the golf course. We were sure there were Elephants, Tigers, Lions and all kinds of other wild animals in those woods.

As I look back at the world I grew up in, how nice it was that children could be safe and trusted to hike so far from home and parents never having to worry about their coming home. In those days we were safe to go almost anywhere. If we got lost all we had to do was to find someone and they would point us

4

in the right direction, No one was interested in hurting young children.

That golf course was a good mile from home, and today you would never think of letting kids go off that far without being with them. We went to slay dragons or make believe we were in Deep Dark Africa.

Becoming a "Great White Hunter" at the ripe age of five or six was really living the dreams to the fullest. My buddies and I would hike the mile or so from my house on Oregon Avenue to the wild woods behind the golf course at LaBelle Park.

With our stick or wooden big game rifles we would search the thickets for those all elusive trophies. Seldom did we come up empty handed because we dreamed it up as we went along.

Once in a while we would have to act as cowboys and chase the Indians from our African hunting grounds. Little did we care about mixing cowboys and Indians with our big game hunting, we were having fun.

My father had quite a wood shop in the basement and we fashioned some guns for our hunting trips. The first ones were pretty crude but as time went on I was able to con my father into cutting us some out of wood that really looked liked "big game rifles." The fun we had coming home and telling of our exploits of shooting all of the big game and fighting off lion attacks and such. My mom never made fun of our wildest tales but would sit and listen. She knew it was all in our minds but we were having fun and living what we could only dream.

During those very young years of dreaming it never seemed within the realm of possibility that the dreams could or would ever come true. We thought of the "darkest of Africa" as almost being on another planet. All of our excursions started before we even were exposed to school. We had no concept of distance and had not even had a geography course in school. By the time we really knew that Africa was half-way around the world; the expense of going there seemed like it would take "all the money in the world."

I figured I was just dreaming and because we were so poor I would never be able to live my dreams for real. Little did I know that it could be accomplished? I knew there would never be that much money in the world to let me learn to fly and also go to deep dark Africa and be a "big game hunter", but time and age would show me things "***Beyond my Wildest Dreams***".

Kids and Their Dreams

I think that it is necessary for little kids to have dreams that seem unimaginable **because THEY CAN COME TRUE**. Had I not had those dreams to set goals for the future I might have ended up working in the steel mills like my father. Not that there is anything wrong with working in the mills, but having those goals led me down more exciting paths.

As I mentioned earlier there were great radio programs. Many years later I was to hear the phrase "*Theater of the Mind.*" That is exactly what those old programs were. From the Lone Ranger, the Squeaky Door of Intersanctum, Dick Tracy, Amos and Andy, Fibber McGee & Molly, Our Miss Brooks, The Shadow, Superman and many more. If you allowed yourself to listen you became part of the story. You were right there hanging on every word that was spoken. You knew everything would be all right in the end but you couldn't figure out how they might pull it off. Some of these old programs can be purchased on EBay today.

I started school in 1941 since my birthday was on Labor Day. I didn't know how to read and learning to read didn't seem fun to me. I remember being a very slow reader. I am now a strong believer in parents teaching children to read. (Lesley learned to read at just under 5 years old). I just thought school was a necessary evil, and was really not enthused. I now wish my parents had made me look forward to going to school. I remember getting some new clothes for school and a pair of shoes we called, in those days, clodhoppers. They were like an ankle work boot of today and for us kids they were really cumbersome but would last a year.

I can also remember sitting on the floor in front of our floor model radio, with a pull out record player, on Sunday, December 7th, 1941. Even though I was just a little over five years old at the time, I remember this day as if it were yesterday. I remember President Roosevelt saying that Pearl Harbor had been attacked and even though I was young, I guess I could tell from the tone of his voice that President Roosevelt knew this was serious.

Photo of Navy ship sunk by Japanese at Pearl Harbor

We never again will see a country so united as it was at the time of Pearl Harbor. The brave military and civilians at home all worked together to defeat both Germany and Japan.

World War II Begins

A short time later the government had a call for everyone to save his or her bacon grease. We could turn it in to our local market, (no supermarkets in those days) and we received ten cents a pound. My mom would let my sister and I take turns getting the rewards for the bacon grease from Stanley's market up by our grade school. We were told that the grease was to be used to lubricate the launching of boats and ships for the Navy. Heck, we just wanted the money because we could not comprehend being "at war."

Rationing came soon thereafter and families got a book for each member of the family. There were stamps to buy flour, sugar, gas, tires and other necessities of life.

War Ration Book #3 when I was 6 years old

War Ration book #4

It is very hard for the people that did not live through the times of World War II to comprehend the sacrifices that were made. During the war everyone did their part and all of the Military were our Hero's – they were maintaining our Freedom – Lest we never forget our Military.

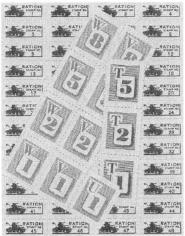

Ration Stamps

Ration Tokens used alone or with the needed stamps

BUY WAR BONDS

"When you buy that Extra Bond today think of your boy or your neighbor's boy." This was one of the slogans. We would get ten cents sometimes to buy the stamps.

Booklet for holding War Savings Bond stamps

We soon were introduced to the "Civil Patrol" which came around and talked about blackouts and how to cover the windows so that enemy planes could not see the light. These people took their duty serious and patrolled the "hilltop" where we lived, as did their counterparts over all of the country.

This 1942 Civil Defense Index booklet offers advice useful to civilians on the home front. Information is given for air raids, blackouts, bombs, poison gas, as well as first aid situations.

As the days and months passed into years we learned more and more about how terrible war could really be. My Uncle William went into the Navy CB's (Construction Battalion) and was sent off to North Africa and then Italy.

Uncle William in Navy was Chief Petty Officer when discharged

After the war I would always try to get Uncle William to tell me "war stories." His favorite was while he was in North Africa. His battalion was short shoes and a local Arab had some military combat boots. They tried to work a deal and when they got together with the locals they were going to exchange blankets for the boots. The locals said there was not enough blankets for the number of boots they wanted, so to solve the problem they went around the corner and cut the blankets in half to have the required amount. They went back and made the deal thinking they had boondoggled the locals. They opened the bag of boots to find out they only had left foot boots. They then had to set up a meeting to get the right foot boots to make a pair. Uncle William used to laugh about the story and how they thought they were smart only to find out they had been outsmarted.

My father's wood shop in the basement would prove a valuable asset during the war. Plastics were just invented and my father would make initial pins for ladies to wear and sell them for $3 to $5 each. My Dad had beautiful penmanship and made the pins drawing the letters on graph paper and gluing that to the plastic. He would then cut them out on the jigsaw. I would sit on the workbench and watch him work. He might rough cut three or four one night and sand and finish them the next night.

An initial pin my dad did for Barbara but it is not finished as some were

As I got interested in the tools he became a real stickler. I wasn't allowed to touch a tool until I knew the proper name, all of the features, how to safely use them and pass his test. As

11

you can imagine I wanted Dad to be proud of me, but I also wanted to use those tools, so I did what it took to "pass his test."

More of my early memories were visiting my Grandparents. One time when I was about five years old and at my Grandparent's on my father's side, I was told there was a lady coming in the afternoon to help around the house. My grandmother got me aside before Marie arrived and told me her name and the fact that her skin was black and not to mention it. I guess I had never really paid any attention because we had black people where I lived. Anyhow, when she told me not to say anything, I took that as something I must find more about.

I remember very clearly being in my grandparent's bedroom, lying on the floor with my elbows propping my head into my hands looking out the window, and asking Marie "why are you black"? Marie came over to me sat down and said that God had created some people white, some black, some yellow and some red. That was a good enough answer for me and I just stayed in the room till she was done. Marie thought it was so cute she never forgot the story or me. I saw her many times while a child and then at my Uncle's funeral when I was grown. She always had a great big hug for me and had to tell anyone that would listen about the story. She was working full time for my Aunt in the dress store and made a little extra money doing some housework, which she used to put her children, she put through college to become a doctor and a lawyer. Marie had goals in her life and she worked hard to accomplish them.

My friends and I continued to go over behind the golf course to pursue our "African Adventures." We even ventured to the far edge where we could look way down at the Ohio River. We were not only hunting we now became real explorers.

Dreaming of a New Bicycle
At the age of seven I wanted a bike. Some of my friends had bikes and I can remember that late in the fall of 1943 the Pittsburgh Press newspaper had a special promotion to get new customers. The special was for their carriers to get a new customer every week and to pay $1 every week and at the end of 26 weeks they would give you a Roadmaster bicycle. They thought they had a sure thing in that most kids couldn't or

12

wouldn't keep up with such a task. There was a local newspaper but it did not print on Sunday so everyone got the Pittsburgh Press at least on Sunday. The Press was a bigger paper with more news and lots of big store ads. People would drive the 40 miles to Pittsburgh for shopping adventures.

My buddy Attilio and another friend Joe already had a newspaper route and were excited to get started. I had to get in on this deal because to get a new bicycle at that time was impossible at any price. I pleaded with my father but he had a friend that had a bike in pieces that we could have. That excited me and we went and carried home all the pieces and put it together. Dad impressed on me to learn the serial number in case it was stolen. B23609 was the number. However, it did not fill the place of a brand new Roadmaster.

I begged, and begged, pleaded, cried and did every tactic I could think of to get my parents to allow me to carry the Pittsburgh Press so I could get a new bike. Dad's remarks to me were "hell you are seven years old and you can't count and make change and I don't have the money to make up your losses." I said, "You can teach me." I must have put on one heck of a show because I convinced my dad that if he taught me, I could make change. Dad thought he had a sure thing in that I was not going to be able to learn to make change and get to carry the paper. He finally consented that if I could go a week without a mistake in making change he would let me have a paper route. This was the first necessary part if I was going to be able to learn in time to get in on the bike deal.

Because we did not have financial holdings of such, my father showed me each bill up to a $20. Then he cut up pieces of paper and made the amount in pencil on it. Every night for a couple hours we sat at the dinning room table and we would go through the drill of making change. We would sit and he would tell me the cost was such and here are the bills that he was going to pay with. For example he might say the order is $7.64 and here is, and hand me a piece of paper with a $10 bill written on it. I had to make the change with other pieces of paper that had amounts, using the least amount of coins and bills possible.

Well, to his dismay and disbelief the second week I did it error free and he said I could have the paper route. The next problem was to get some customers. My buddy Attilio and I talked to the newspaperman and he was allowed to give me 13 of his customers to start my route.

My father came up with his own set of rules for me to be allowed to carry papers. I was told in no uncertain terms that if he ever got a call about a paper blowing away, getting wet or on Sunday being delivered after 6:30 am I was done. I had to put the papers in the screen door, under the mat or somewhere out of the rain or snow. These things proved to be a blessing because later I made more in tips than I did on the paper route.

As the months progressed, my buddies and I became very business minded. Attilio, Joe and I got our heads together and we decided that if we worked really hard we could all get the new bikes. Our plans were that if we got two customers for the week we would only turn in one and hold the other for the next week and pay that customers paper out of our profits. If we got say three or more we would just hold back one. This worked like a charm and in some cases we even gave a customer to each other if they didn't have one for the week and we had an extra one. So it was all for "one and one for all." As I look back on this today this was really something for seven and nine-year-old boys to think up.

The time now was 1944 and I was not even eight years old yet. I remember like it was yesterday coming home from school and there was a great big cardboard box on the front porch. I had to beg my mom to let me tear it open. Inside, there it was MY Roadmaster bike but only partially assembled. This meant waiting till my dad came home from work in a couple hours. I was off up the street to see Attilio and he had gotten his and Joe got his too. Three young entrepreneurs were on the go for great thing ahead in our lives.

Little did we know or realize how much of a great learning experience this would be for each of us. It proved right then and there that if we really wanted something bad enough and willing to work hard and not let obstacles get in our way; we could meet the challenge and the goal. I carried the papers till I was almost 13 and always made more in tips than I did for

14

carrying the papers. I even had one customer that brought me a shirt and a menu back from Hawaii.

Jim's Wagon

Looking back it must have been the Christmas of 1945 and my paper route had grown to over a hundred customers. The Sunday paper was a very thick paper, about three or four times the size of a daily paper. The newspaper printed some of the non-news sections during the week and then the real news sections were printed on Saturday night. When I received my papers I had to assemble the two big sections by putting the non-news inside of the news section. This took close to an hour to do. I was up a 3 am and with the number of customers I had I would have to make four or five trips home. This was because I couldn't carry but twenty to twenty five of the papers because of their weight. What I needed was a vehicle but at nine years old I was limited to something like a wagon.

My parents came up with a plan. Santa Claus would bring little brother Jim a wagon for Christmas and I could use it on Sunday. The catch was I had to take Jim with me. This wasn't all bad since I could use him as a paperweight. The bad part was he did not like getting up at 4 am to be pulled around in the wintertime, but we survived. My parents just felt it would not be right for me to use the wagon without Jim along. I am not sure but I don't remember having to haul Jim around the second winter, so by then the wagon was not the most important thing in Jim's life and I was probably free to use it.

My buddy Attilio was of Italian descent and his mother was a great cook. She would make pizzells which are like a waffle cookie and really delicious. There were no electric makers in those days. She used the old-fashioned hand cast iron model and on the stove. It took about two minutes to make them and Attilio and I could eat them as fast as she could make them, washing them down with some milk. We would finally get cut off from eating too many and told to go play. I can never remember her being anything but a wonderful lady.

My sister's best friend next door, Ruth Ann had a brother, Don who joined the Air Corps at only 18 years of age. Like all families that had a member in the service they displayed their flag in the window with pride. I can remember Ruth Ann coming over one day and saying that her brother's plane had been shot down while flying a bomber mission. He was not declared dead but missing in action.

Don was flying as a bombardier on a B-17 and on Nov 7, 1944 his plane was shot down. With the help of Yugoslav partisans he made his way to Italy and was reunited with his group to fly more missions.

Then almost two months later Ruth Ann came over to say that he had made it back to his base and was fine. She found out after New Years, January 1945 that he was alive. What a great present to have your brother still alive. This brought the war close to home.

As I would later learn, as a military photographer, there were many raids over Europe and we lost thousands of airplanes, many of which were B-17's & B-25's. On a raid on the Polesti (also spelt Ploesti) oil fields in one day we lost over 300 bombers.

As the war ended in 1945 the rationing ended and things seemed to be getting better. I always had a few coins from carrying the papers but I wanted more. In those days most all of the houses were heated by coal. The steel mills of the Ohio Valley used coal or coke (a coal derivative) to fire their big blast furnaces.

Our house at 1524 Oregon

The houses all got covered with a black coating. I was required to carry out the furnace ashes in the winter and in the summer I was required to scrub the front porch with soap and water. This was a four to six hour job. It meant cleaning the underneath roof of the porch on a ladder, the banisters, the walls and floor. To do the job it was clean a little area a couple feet square with a brush and soap then rinse till it was all done. Cleaning the underneath of the roof meant getting soaked while scrubbing and rinsing. Some of the neighbors either felt sorry for me, or were too lazy to do it themselves, so I would do their front porch for $5. This was a lot of money in those days but doing several of these each summer gave me spending money.

One of the sad times of my life was when Attilio moved to Arizona about 1947. We had been very, very close and it was like a part of my life was taken from me. We wrote a few times then lost touch for about 57 years before we made contact again thanks to the Internet. Off and on I had tried to find him by calling information in different area codes in and around Arizona, but no luck. When the Internet came about I used People Search but could not find him, partly because he had moved to California. I had Googled his name before but one evening in 2004 I tried and low and behold his name came up in a newspaper article. From there it was a piece of cake to get a phone number and in fact I got two. The only thing wrong was when I tried one I got no answer and the other number I got an answering machine which I left a message on. I tried a couple more days to no avail. Then about two weeks later I get a phone call and it was Attilio and he and his wife had been gone for two weeks to some art classes.

The ironic thing was how our lives paralleled each other in certain areas. While kids, I would have never imagined Attilio in the Military. However he is now a retired Naval Captain. He got into Information Technology about the same time I did. He was blown away with the fact that I had joined the Army and had actually gone to Africa and fulfilled some of my dreams. What a joy it has been to hook back up with him.

I remember the old push lawnmower we had. I can remember pushing that thing when I was not tall enough to get the proper angle of push to really cut the grass. When I would push the front end would lift a little so I had to learn everything there was about the lawnmower. I had to learn how to adjust the back roller to change the angle and depth of cut and how to sharpen the blades. After I kept our yard cut, I was off to cut anyone's grass that would pay twenty-five or fifty cents. I had a great Aunt Lil way down on the other end of the block that had a huge lot for her house. She would pay me $3 to cut it and it was a full day job. It is the only sight that still looks big in my old stomping grounds after all these years. It is the equivalent of four house lots today. Aunt Lil was my Grandmother Hooton's sister and also the sister of the mother of Cyrus Vance (Secretary of Defense/Secretary of State). Don Knotts (the famous actor) is related through Grandpa Hooton.

Aunt Lil's house big side yard between houses

Barbara and the Furnace

One of the fun things I did, as a kid was to go in the basement and put my head in the coal furnace and make ghost sounds while Barbara baby-sat me. I must have been somewhere about eight to ten when I did it and came up the steps and Barbara had a hatchet and chased me out into the backyard. She swung it like a tomahawk and let it fly. Needless to say, I hit the ground and it ricocheted off the big pole in the back yard used for the clothesline. Had I not "hit the ground" it would have surely hit me. When mom came home I was the first to run up and tell her what Barbara had done. To which Barbara got a spanking then told mom what I had done and it was my turn to get my bottom beat. I don't remember doing it any more but it was sure ghostly sounding coming up through all the registers in the house.

18

Chapter 2 - Parents Family

Grandparents - Rayl

On my father's side Grandpa and Grandma Rayl lived in Clarksburg and had a big old house on the corner of Broadway. Grandpa worked in the steel mills and when the Phillips sheet and tin mill moved and became Weirton Steel, Grandpa went to work there and would come home on the weekends. He worked there for many years and rode back and forth with John Pepper (Ruth Ann's cousin) who also worked in the mill.

The Rayl Grandparents house 526 Broadway

Grandpa had invested heavily in the Stock Market and when the big crash of 1929 he lost most of everything. I do not know exactly how much he lost but I have always heard it was sizable.

Grandma pretty much stayed home and Aunt Frances also lived at home. Grandpa Rayl was an avid stamp collector and would spend hours and hours on the sun-porch working on his stamps and "first day covers." I was later told he had one of the best collections of the covers that existed. Grandpa Rayl was also a 32-degree Mason.

Grandpa and Grandma Rayl celebrated over 60 years of marriage. I remember the 50th anniversary and a lot of relatives from all over came for a big picnic. I had never met some of those relatives that came. I was overseas at the 60th.

Grandma & Grandpa Rayl

(Front L-R) Linda, Mary Beth, Doug, Janice & Eddie
(Back) Jim, Linda, Carol & Susan (Chuck and Ruth's girls)

Grandparents - Hooton

Grandpa and Grandma Hooton lived in Jordan, WV all the time that I was growing up. Jordan was a small town of about 125 houses and the living was in the mining company owned houses. There were no indoor toilets and the outhouse was at the top of their lot by the street. It was what we would call a "four-holer" and had two sides one side for each of the families in the duplex. Mr. & Mrs. Hixon lived on the other half of the duplex and were very nice people. Grandpa eventually got "black lung" from inhaling so much coal dust that and had to retire. That's when they moved to Uncle Charlie's, at Lost Creek. Grandpa and Grandma Hooton also celebrated over 60 years of marriage. More about them later on.

The house in Jordan with the mine across the river

Grandpa & Grandma Hooton

Aunts and Uncles - Rayl
On the **Rayl** side of the family my father had one sister and two brothers, Aunt Frances, Uncle Linzy and Uncle William.

Front – Grandma, William, Grandpa
Rear – Linzy, Frances, Harold (Dad)

Aunt Frances had been engaged and her fiancé drowned. She then married in 1926's to James Noon who was a State Trooper and Motorcycle Officer in Virginia. He was killed chasing a violator on Christmas Day 1927. She had only been married less than two years when the accident happened. James Noon had been her fiancé's best friend.

Frances and Dad as kids

Photo I took of Frances

As I looked at some of the Websites for "Fallen Officers" in Maryland, I noticed that there was an extremely high loss of the Motorcycle Officers. I had known of her marriage as a child but it was something that was not discussed, I am sure because it was such a terrible thing to happen.

Aunt Frances put herself into her work and became a manager for Lerner Shops women's clothing. As time went on she became a partner with Mrs. Haught in the Clarksburg store, then later buying her out. When Mrs. Haught retired Frances purchased the store in Shinnston that Mrs. Haught owned. Frances maintained the store for over 20 years before retiring.

Uncle Linzy worked for the Tuller Corporation and was married to Aunt Fountain. I remember that early on Uncle Linzy was living in East St Louis and working with the Tuller's. A group of the guys he worked with purchased some land on a lake and built a cabin to get away on the weekends. The lake was full of fish, frogs and snapping turtles. I visited when I was about 11 or 12 as the cabin was just about finished. They were working on the porch and Uncle Linzy had driven a nail into the decking and it bent over so he just smashed it into the wood in its bent condition. I told him that was not a professional job and that I was going to fix it. He told me that I couldn't do it because it was into hard wood. He couldn't get it in and now it wouldn't come out. I was so determined to prove him wrong I spent several hours prying the nail up, straightening it out, holding it with pliers and driving it little by little. If I was getting paid anything that would have been the most expensive nail ever put into wood, but I finally got it in and he was impressed.

One of the other funny things that happened at the cabin was the time Aunt Fountain went into the "outhouse" that had been built she started to sit down, when she saw a big black snake curled up on the back of the bench. She screamed and ran out pulling up her pants and the guys just broke up.

Uncle Linzy and Aunt Fountain on a cruise round the world

Uncle Linzy was a fantastic cook and loved to cook fish. While I was spending the week at the cabin with them I got to wade in the lake pushing the boat and also got to be in the boat to shoot frogs on a couple occasions. On the weekend we were going to have a big fish fry and some of the guys would go up to the Illinois River to get some "spoonbill catfish." I had never heard of them but they can get up to a hundred pounds. Also they had set turtle hooks around the lake for some of the snapping turtles, which they caught. One of the turtles was at least three feet across since he wouldn't fit in a #3 washtub. On Saturday they had the fish, frogs, turtle, and invited some friends. It was pretty neat watching all of it "come" together. For many years I felt I was pretty much like the son they never had.

Uncle Linzy was also a collector of stamps and coins, which he left in his will to a friend to dispose of and give the money to his favorite organizations. The friend turned out to be a greedy character and sold them for nothing near the value. What he did was to get paperwork showing what he sold them for to satisfy the Executor of the Estate, but really he was getting the difference on the side so as to make a lot of money for himself. We all knew what happened but there was nothing that could be done.

I remember Uncle William was given an ultimatum about marriage. Aunt Marge wanted to get married rather than just dating as they had done for some nine or ten years. She wanted to have a child so she said it had to be her way or the highway. Uncle William had no real objections since he cared for Aunt Marge very much. He was a very laid-back kind of person with a great personality. As I mentioned way back in the beginning, I loved to get Uncle William to tell me stories of when he was in the CB's in North Africa and Italy.

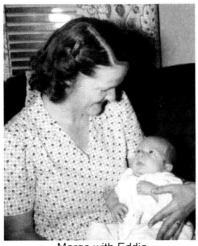 

Marge with Eddie   Mary Beth & Uncle William

I remember going with Uncle William on his route when he worked for Pepsi Cola. I couldn't have been very old but I got to ride with him one day to make his rounds. He later went to work with Fairmont Foods and he and Aunt Marge purchased some five acres of land by Aunt Marge's parents which was not too far out of Clarksburg. It was always nice to go visit on the farm and when their son Eddie was born he got a pony to ride. We came back from overseas to have Laura's feet corrected and the girls loved to go visit so Uncle William would walk them around the yard on the Pony.

Uncle William passed away at the early age of 52, leaving Aunt Marge with a young son to raise. Aunt Frances did everything imaginable to help Aunt Marge and Eddie. In later years for whatever reason Eddie turned against Aunt Frances. After all she did for him and after Uncle Linzy passed away Eddie was no longer in the good graces of many of the family.

Aunts and Uncles - Hooton

On my Mom's, the **Hooton**, side of the family she had one sister and two brothers, Aunt Margaret, Uncle Charlie and Uncle Bernard.

Aunt Margaret had a son, Charles Woody by her first marriage. Charles's father was killed in a mine explosion. Aunt Margaret then married Wilbur "Bud" McCartin and they left West Virginia to move to Baltimore where Aunt Margaret worked for the Social Security Administration. Later Charles would work there after being discharged from the Navy. Charles flew in Blimps out of Georgia that were used for sub-chasers in the early 1950's. Charles married and had a set of twins, later divorced.

Bernard, Margaret, Grandpa, Grandma, Charlie, Mary Susan (Mom)

Uncle Charlie married Aunt Velma and he worked for the Union Carbide Carbon factory in Clarksburg. They owned a small farm in Lost Creek and raised two sons, Tommy and Bobbie. I always enjoyed going to visit them but Barbara and Jim would rather not go out there for more than a few hours. In their later years Grandma and Grandpa Hooton would move to Lost Creek in another house that Uncle Charlie had on the farm. Uncle Charlie was a 32-degree Mason.

Uncle Bernard married Aunt Hazel and worked for the B&O Railroad as a design engineer after moving to Baltimore. Uncle Bernard assisted in drawing plans for the "Cincinnatian," a crack B&O passenger train between Cincinnati and Baltimore. He was an avid photographer and when I was very small and they still lived in Clarksburg, I would visit and he would take me to the darkroom and let me "watch" him process prints. I am sure this early introduction to photography is when the "bug" bit me. They had two daughters, Lois who was close to Barbara's age and Charlotte a year younger than me. When we would all get to visit Grandma & Grandpa Hooton in Jordan, WV we would play until we dropped. There was a big croquet field that Grandpa had made to the side of the house and we would play it for hours and hours. Of all of my cousins these two remained the truest and dearest.

Now here is the part that is hard to keep up with….. Uncle Bernard passed away in 1973, which left Aunt Hazel a Widow. Shortly thereafter Aunt Velma passed away leaving Uncle Charlie a Widower. Uncle Charlie and Uncle Bernard had both been married to their respective wives for over 40 years. Uncle Charlie was not in the best of health and Aunt Hazel having known him for all those years decided that she would help take care of him and so the two of them got married. Aunt Hazel moved back to Clarksburg from Baltimore. When Uncle Charlie passed away his two sons, Tommy and Bobbie did not do right by Aunt Hazel, even though Uncle Charlie's wishes were known. I have not had any contact since that time with either of those cousins.

Cousins
We had a lot of cousins and quite often got to see them at our grandparents. On the Hooton side of the family there was Charles, Tommy, Bobby, Lois and Charlotte. On the Rayl side there was only Eddie.

There was a man named John Pepper that worked in the steel mill with my dad and grandfather. John had his family in Clarksburg and drove home on the weekends and my grandfather would ride with him. He happened also to be my sister's best friend Ruth Ann's cousin. During the summer we would get to go to Clarksburg with John and spend time at the Rayl house and my Uncle Charlie would usually come by and take us to Jordan to spend another week or so. I remember the charge was $3 to take us down there. We would come home a couple weeks later with him late on a Sunday so he could go to work on Monday.

Me – Lois – Barbara – Charlotte (f) – Tommy – Charles

Barb & me with mom

me at age of going to golf course to hunt

When we would go to Grandma/Grandpa Hooton's down in the coal-mining town of Jordan, WV we had lots of fun. There was out-houses, baths were in a big wash tub, chickens and a big croquet field to play on. The trains went right in her front yard;

the river was just beyond that and the coal mine where grandpa worked was across the river.

The mine from Grandma's house – RR track and River

Being a miner was absolutely the dirtiest job I have ever seen. Mining is also a dangerous job considering the mine cave-ins. Grandpa took us kids over to see the mine one time. I thought it was funny that the miners would wear one kind of clothes over and change clothes in the shaft and put their clothes on a hook on a rope tied to the top of the mine and then pull it up and lock it. It was to protect their valuables such as wallet, jewelry or anything of value. When they came home they changed back, left their helmet and light on the hook with their old clothes. They used the same clothes to work in for two or three days. They could only hold so much dirt.

The coal from the mine was loaded into the trains and also into barges that were pushed up the river to Pittsburgh by tugboats. There were some that were paddlewheel boats. I remember one time we got to go on the tugboat and get a tour of it and it seemed like an exciting life.

When we were visiting in Jordan sometimes grandma would send us to the "company store." It was a store owned by the mine and was just a little general store. We would walk down the railroad tracks and listen for trains. It was about a half-mile down. Also there were times when my parents were there and then it was time to go out to the "beer hall." There was music and everyone would dance also our cousins. We always liked to go to the Bowman's beer hall.

Another great memory of Jordan was the haunted house next door across the creek from my grandparents. The houses were duplexes and then room for a garden between each set of houses. The Hixon's would go to bed and in the middle of the night there would be doors slam, lights come on and the piano play. Kind of spooky but they lived there without any problem. They always told us it was a good ghost.

In the winter the only heat was from the two fireplaces and when we visited in the cold weather we piled up on the blankets. The coal stove that grandma cooked on had no regulators other than moving the pots or skillets around to a hotter or cooler spot. Grandma was quite a cook on this stove. The side of the stove had a hot water tank that held three or four gallons and when we took a bath that is were the hot water came from. There was only one cold water faucet in the kitchen.

Uncle Hayward Snider was married to one of Grandma Hooton's sisters. He worked in Steubenville for the Carbon Company owned by George Rogers (also married to Grandma Hooton's sister) Hayward was a very dapper guy and always drove a new Buick. He loved mom and would visit once in a while, we loved him to come he always gave us some change.

Chapter 3 – Growing Up

School Time

School did not excite me much so I was a less than average student. It was not a big requirement at home to spend the time studying that I would try later to instill in my children. Sometimes we "**get too smart too late**." When my mother would ask if my homework was done I would say sure and be out the door to play with my buddies.

In the mornings when my mom tried to get me up she would go to the bottom of the steps and holler for me to get up. I would tell her I was up, the next few minutes she would say she didn't hear me and I would tell her I was in the bathroom, then roll over and try to sleep more. When I heard her coming up the steps I would jump up and try to play awake before she got to the top steps, seems like this was almost an everyday occurrence.   Once I was up and had my breakfast I would be off to school. Of course there were no school buses, but grade school was only about ten blocks away and it gave the gang a chance to throw the football or baseball on the way to school.

Hunting Rats

After my very best friend moved to Arizona I spent more and more time with other good friends Jack and Eddie. By this time I was about 12 years old and continued the desire to hunt. Eddie was 3 years older and Jack was 1 year older than me. We all were into the hunting experiences and Eddie had already gotten a .22 caliber rifle.

Right behind his house and across the alley was what we referred to as the dump. Just a half a block to the right rear of Eddie's house the ground started with what was a gorge and as it went down the hill it widened and got the equivalent of several blocks wide about a hundred feet deeper than the side streets. Near the beginning of this depression people in the neighborhood where Eddie lived used the "dump" to throw trash and old junk.

This was an area about a block long and made for an ideal place for rats to live. When I am talking about Rats I don't mean little field mice, I mean big Norway Rats getting nearly a foot long, not counting their tails. Some of them were as big as a small cat. With our vast hunting experience we had to work on the population of these rats. We would all take turns with Eddie's rifle and shoot at the rats. When we didn't see any we would throw a big rock down and that would make the rats scurry for us to get off a shot or two. A box of fifty .22 caliber bullets cost about forty cents, in those days.

As time went buy I was able to come up with a .22 of my own. Keep in mind this dump was right in the city, and in a better part of the city, but we never got in trouble with the cops for shooting within the city limits. Over the years I am sure we made a big dent in the rat population but we never ran out of candidates to shoot at.

I remember one **STUPID** thing we all did as a break from the rat killing. The cartridges for the .22 are what are called a "rim fire", and that means the casing is made with some powder under the rim of the cartridge, and when struck by the hammer of the weapon it would light the rest of the powder in the casing and cause the bullet to go. One particular day Eddie came up with the idea of shooting the .22 bullets with a hammer. We would crouch in his garage and at the open door place a brick, put a .22 bullet on the brick facing the other side of the dump. Then we would close our eyes, reach around the door and hit the bullet with a hammer and it would fire. It is a wonder that we never got shot from doing this as the bullet could have easily spun around as it went off.

Shooting City Busses
Also about this same time and through Jr. High School, the gang Eddie, Jack and I would shoot city busses. Not with our 22's but with a canon. Being skilled in the art of woodworking, and having access to lots of equipment, I would make the cannon holders. What we did was to take the wooden frame, shaped like an old canon and using wire we would secure the Drano can where the actual cannon would be. The can would end at a slight upward angle just as the cannons on the old pirate ships. We would then, with a nail, punch a small hole in the rear top of the can.

We bought carbide crystals to use as our powder. When carbide is mixed with water it forms a gas. On the warm summer nights we would take turns shooting at the big city busses with our cannon. The "hilltop" where we lived was serviced by three busses. We could shoot at three different busses from the same location then we would move several blocks one way or the other so they wouldn't know when they were being shot. It took one hour for a round trip for the same bus to come back. The carbide cannons would make the noise equal to the loudest rifle I have ever heard.

As we watched for the bus coming down the street we would prepare the cannon so it would be "ready to fire" as it approached our position. We would put on chunk of carbide and a few drops of water and wait about 30 seconds and hold a match to the hole in the rear of the can and it could blow the lid clear across the street. The gang was always hiding behind trees watching and ready to run if the driver stopped. When we timed things right and the lid hit the bus it would be with such force as to scare the people on the bus. Oh! What fun hunting days.

Jack and the snakes

My buddies Jack and Eddie and myself liked to walk down Paddy Mud road from around the golf course which took us clear down to the Ohio River. When I was about 12 we went on one excursion and decided we would capture some copperhead snakes and keep them as pets. We knew they were poisonous but we were invincible, so we thought. Anyhow we did manage to catch several of the critters and bring them home in a bag. Jack's mother Teresa was not too keen but allowed us to keep them. We made a pen from a wooden box in Jack's basement and put wire over the top with a brick on it to hold it down. The next morning Teresa went to the basement and the box was empty. She ran up the steps and got Jack to see if he had let them go.

It didn't take long for Jack to realize they had gotten out on their own. The box that held the snakes was located near the coal bin so Teresa made the three of us shovel all of the coal out of the bin trying to find the snakes. The coal bins held about two truckloads of coal but luckily it was summer and they only had a half a bin of coal. We didn't find the snakes and we searched everywhere so Jack had to do the laundry for the next six months, as Teresa would not go down to the basement. We guessed the snakes had gone down the drain or maybe got out under the door, but we never found any sign of them.

Gone fishing

My Dad really never did much with us as children. There was a time when a bunch of us went fishing at a lake located near East Liverpool. We went with Jack's parents, Doy and Teresa along with their other son Dick, my mom, dad, sister, brother, Eddie and me. The car was an old Hudson Terra-plane and all ten of us in the car. As I look back now we had to be crowded but we were all young and small. The trunk was full of the fishing tackle, coolers and other necessities. Our cane poles were tied to the roof.

Things were going well until we were about a half-mile from the lake. At time a rear tire blew and Doy just kept going since he didn't want to unload everything and reload to change the tire since we were so close. Since the tire was blown, it was not of any value, and being so close we just headed on to the lake at about a fast walk pace. After we had gone maybe a hundred yards Eddie came out with the phrase *"if your car rides like this it is time for a Marfak Lubrication."* We all just about fell out of the car laughing and it made the half-mile go by fast. Texaco oil was using the phrase to promote their oil changes and lubrications.

Since times were rough with the family, I never really felt much self-esteem. I remember many times my father and an uncle calling me lazy or the word lummox. I thought I worked pretty hard. I do know I pushed the limits quite often and by today's standards was probably an abused kid, because I got my butt beat an awful lot. As I look back on it today I see a lot wrong with the way my parents raised kids, but you learn partly by your parents and partly by winging it. I really don't have too many regrets for the whippings I got even though I think probably only a third were justified.

Chapter 4 – My Teen Years

The schoolwork and I never had much of a love affair, which I really regret today. My biggest thrill in school came in September of 1948 when I started Harding Junior High School. I of course wanted to take wood shop since I felt comfortable with that and you really didn't have much homework. I went to the first day of class in wood shop and the teacher, Elmo McBride, started taking the class around and showing the equipment we would be learning to use for the year.

Elmo McBride ended up being a great teacher but on that first day he made a big mistake. We had just gotten to a big floor model lathe when he picked up one of the tools and said that this is, and gave the wrong name of the tool. Having been required by my father to learn all of the tools for his little tabletop lathe I felt I was an expert at 12 years old. I immediately spoke up and told him he was wrong. He asked me what the name was and I correctly gave the name of the tool. He asked me if I knew how to run a lathe and I answered that I did. He directed me to the wood storage room and told me to pick a piece of wood and show him what I knew.

I went back and found a piece that would make a baseball bat and in about 15 minutes turned a baseball bat that didn't even need to be sanded. It literally blew his mind. His next question to me was "what equipment here do you not know how to use"? My answer was *"that glue pot"* since I had never made my own glue before. Mr. McBride then told me I could make anything I wanted, and use any tool I wanted, but if some of the other kids were having a problem to lend a hand if he was busy. I had lots of self-confidence in that class.

We had a geography teacher and a history teacher that got my interest. The history teacher had been off to the war and as he taught he told war stories and made it interesting. The geography teacher took a boring subject and made it fun. I did pretty well in those subjects and got decent grades as well.

One of the funny things I remember about Junior High was a bunch of us took the shop teacher's (Elmo McBride) car, which was a Crosley and put it in the coal bin of the school. The

Crosley car was a really small car and weighed almost nothing so about 10 or 12 of us picked it up and carried it into the coal bin. The car sold for five or six hundred dollars and got about 50 miles per gallon. There are some on EBay today. He didn't find it for two days and none of us admitted to it for fear of being in real trouble. One of the janitors asked him what his car was doing in the coal bin, to which we all played dumb.

One sad thing that I remember was during the seventh grade about 1948 at Harding Jr. High. We were sitting in class when there was a loud explosion. Everyone wondered what could have happened. On the way home we found out that a guy that had been in WWII and had been having problems adjusting to civilian life had taken his life by putting dynamite around his waist and ending his life. Having been intrigued by the war, and following it closely, I had not been aware of the mental problems our soldiers experienced on their return. We would later hear that this soldier had terrible nightmares and did not know where to turn. Many soldiers really had this problem and even today's soldiers suffer from Post Traumatic Stress Syndrome.

About this time girls were becoming young ladies and I noticed them for the first time. The lack of self-confidence in most areas and not having as good of clothes as most kids, I just stayed in the background. It was in the 8th grade that I started getting interested in photography and learned to make a few black and white pictures. I must have inherited this from my Uncle Bernard who was quite an accomplished photographer.

It was at this time, I must have had visions of Playboy magazine because I conned a girl into allowing me to take some revealing photographs. I didn't show her face and sold the photos at school. I sold hundreds and then another guy said he was going to copy them and sell them also so I decided to stamp the back of the photos with the name of my "company" which got me into real trouble. My buddy in on the deal with me and helped print and sell the photos. My other trouble was the girl was the daughter of one of my Dad's Bosses.

Roller Skating

During the first part of summer 1950 I found a job helping put a portable roller skating rink floor together that would have a circus tent over it. The pay was $1.00 per hour since it was really hard work. It took a couple weeks to get the rink open and Ray Keys, the owner, offered me a job as a skate boy but I thought roller-skating was for girls, so I turned him down at first. On opening day my sister and her good friend Lois were going to go. Lois lived downtown and caught the bus up to our house to go with Barbara. When Lois got off the bus there was a really cool younger girl with her that I thought was the right age for me. I changed my mind and decided to try my hand at roller-skating. I thought Peggy was really a neat girl and she was an accomplished skater. I split the seat out of my pants and had to run home and change. I ended up tearing several pairs of pants that night. But I had a reason to learn to skate and that was my new goal. What an incentive!

The next morning I went back to see Ray and try to get that job he had offered me. I got the job at $.50 per hour and started really learning how to skate. Part of the job required me to spend the night sleeping in the tent and watching everything. Ray had allowed me to skate after all of the paying customers had left for the evening. I was permitted to let a couple friends stay and skate from time to time. But for now this was my time to lean, learn, and learn.

I spent as much as 80 hours a week on the skates and became very proficient. This was to set my confidence level up a couple notches. I became very good and was able to overcome my shyness of girls in comfortable surroundings. This would prove to come in handy later on.

When school started it was time to take the portable tent roller-rink down. The sections of the floor were four feet by twelve feet and weighed about four hundred pounds each. The weight meant that it took from six to eight people to move a section. Ray had the idea that he could design a floor that would take only four people to move. I was offered a job at his roller-skating rink over in Follansbee, WV for the winter.

On the holidays of Christmas we started building the new floor. Ray had designed a jig to construct the sections on and the first

37

section took us about eight hours to build. After double checking all the measurements and being sure it would work we started building the sections needed. The second section took about two hours and then we got the hang of it could turn out a section about every forty-five minutes. We finished all of the sections needed and Ray ordered the tent to come in for late May. I continued working for him on the weekends until I finished High School. What fun memories remain of those times at the roller rinks?

Me – Judy Myers & Dick Meadows   -   Me and Marlene Beagle

Hannah and myself skating to the Collegiate

During my High School years Dick, Jack, Kirk and myself roller-skated all over the area from Akron to Baltimore. There was a small town south of where we lived called Tiltonsville where we really liked to skate since we pretty much had our pick of the girls. There were lots of really great-looking girls our ages that were good skaters. Hardly any of the local boys skated and thought skating was for sissies. After we had been there maybe a half dozen times some eight or ten of the girls asked us to go to the confectionery after skating. Naturally we were not going to pass up a chance to really get to know the girls.

When we went to the confectionery some of the girls that we skated with were there to meet their boyfriends. We quickly learned who had a boyfriend and did not hit on them. The other girls enjoyed the time with us but trouble was brewing. Shortly before we were going to leave one of the really hot girls that had a boyfriend, told us to stay inside for a few minutes and she and her boyfriend went outside. The next week when we came back we found out that all of the guys were going to jointly whip us for being friendly with their girls. The girl that had gone outside with her boyfriend stood up for us and told him that if he ever let anything happen to us she was done with him and that he better tell the rest of the guys that we were cool guys. From then on the boyfriends treated us as part of the group.

I went to see Ray in 1960 when I came back from being overseas in the Army and he had passed away. His wife Sally went and got those original plans we built the portable floor from and told me that Ray had wanted me to have them. They remain in my possession today.

Off to High School

September of 1950 found me heading for High School. I was one of the youngest in the class because of my September birthday and getting started earlier than most kids. The subjects started to get intense but I got a little help in that I was able to take Printing and Woodshop. The printing class would be invaluable in later years. I really enjoyed working with my hands in the Print Shop.

On the first day I went into the Wood Shop classroom and handed my attendance slip to Mr. Fenske. His response to me was "so you are Rayl, just do what you want and make whatever you want, I have had reports about you." He asked me, again, to help out other students, and that made me feel pretty good in that class. I made quite a few things, such as a big fruit bowl; I took Walnut and Maple strips, glued them together and crisscrossed the layers. It was about 18" in diameter and turned out pretty good. Then I made a really nice pair of end tables of my own design. It was then that I realized I could come up with some pretty good ideas, if I just thought them through.

Going to High School was quite an experience for me since it was a compilation of all of the areas of town. There were kids that were from well-to-do families as well as the less fortunate. I was ashamed of the clothes I had to wear since some of the kids had really nice clothes, but my parents just couldn't afford anything better. I found other odd jobs in addition to the roller-rink, and helped to buy some of my own clothes. You tend to take better care of the things you spend money on, and these were valuable lessons I would be learning to help later on.

School was still not the hottest thing in my life but the in printing and shop classes I got A's. I did pretty well in math and history, but could care less about diagramming a sentence. It made absolutely no sense to me. Oh, how I wished I had been inspired. What I didn't realize then, and took me 40 years to realize, is those teachers and current teachers put the information out and you are supposed to grab it. The thing that was lacking is a *reason* for learning the material. The teachers never really taught to the slower students, they just gave them bad grades when really they were having problems.

The problems can range from lack of study to not understanding what they are studying. In my case I was not inspired as to why I needed English in the future. I had a good vocabulary but I did not always construct the sentence correctly. Still do not do a great job, but people can usually understand what I am saying.

First Family Car

During the fall of 1952 while still 16 years old I had saved the $100 I needed to buy a 1939 Packard. It was an awesome car, and proof again that if you can *dream*, and are willing to work hard and never give up, **your dreams will come true**. This was the first car our family ever had and I brought it home from the car dealer and parked it in front of the house with pride. My father asked me as I was getting out "who is your insurance company"? I said you don't have to have insurance and his response was "**YOU DO**". This meant not moving the car until I saved the needed $50 for my insurance. That would take me another whole month to save the insurance and I didn't dare drive MY car until it was insured or that would mean a trip to the basement for swats.

I guess you could say "With pain comes smarts" and I was learning. It was nice to be able to take my mother to the grocery store, as walking for her was always troublesome so she usually called orders in or gave us a list for grocery shopping.

I loved my Mother very much and was so proud that she could rely on me for this outing. We found out when she was about 45 that her hip had been out of joint since she was a baby. Mom had been born with a lot of foot problems and I guess they never checked her hip. She was able to walk and as she got older she walked with a slight limp. Such pain she must have been in, but she never really complained.

About this time I decided I was going to teach my sister Barbara how to drive. We got into the car, a stick shift on the column, and she started it. I was trying to explain to her where the gears were and what to do, when she promptly backed it up a few feet into the telephone pole. It never even dented the bumper; it just stopped and scared Barb, and I don't remember any more about the driving lessons (must have scared me too).

Driving to school was so cool for me at the time. I guess I felt I had come up from the poor background and thought I and was really hot stuff. Not everyone had a car back then so this was quite an accomplishment.

In February of 1953 I decided to quit school, work full time and save some money. What I didn't expect was to have to pay rent at home, but I did and am better for it. I had been working after school, since school started that year, for a machine shop and ornamental iron works. I made parts for the fancy ornamental iron railings and corner posts. As time went on I learned to weld, again something that would be valuable later.

I thought of joining the Army and talked to the recruiter and was sent to Pittsburgh for the tests and physical. The trip would be an all day event, spending a couple hours taking the tests, then getting a complete physical. At the end of the physical my name was called and I went to see a recruiter. I was asked if I would like to be a pilot in the Air Force instead of the Army since I had scored a 99 on the test. I was really excited and answered a big Yes. He talked a little more and then found out that I had not completed High School. He told me I had to be a high school graduate and suggested I go back to school and come back. He said with that kind of score I would probably have no trouble being accepted. I thought I would still make it into the Army, but then had to see the Doctor where I was told that my ears would keep me from being a candidate for the Army. So it was a long day with a lot to think about. I went home kept my job at the machine shop and made plans to go back to school. I was able to purchase clothes I felt good about.

I still worked at the roller-skating rink on the weekends thru the winter. Ray had sold the portable to a group from Amsterdam, OH some 26 miles away. It would be too far for me to work full time during the summer, but with the experience I had I did get to skate for Free by being a floor manager. During that summer I met several different girls who became short-time girlfriends. My real first experiences having real girlfriends. I was growing up!

Death of the Packard

One of the girls I liked very much named Hannah lived in a small town half way to Amsterdam. One day on the way home, after driving the Packard out to visit her I started home and had not gone a mile when I heard the biggest noise from the engine. I checked the oil and it was dry. I left the car there and hitchhiked home, got my buddy Eddie, a mechanic for a Pontiac dealer, and we went back to retrieve the car.

Eddie put a gallon of oil in the motor, started it and headed the 12 miles home. By the time we got close to home we had to pass the Pontiac dealer, where I had bought the car and where

42

Eddie worked. By that time I was using the windshield wipers to get the oil off the windows and was driving by looking out the side window. The motor was smoking like it was on fire but Eddie told me not to stop till I got home. As we passed the Pontiac dealer Eddie pulled over and one of the salesmen was showing a car to a customer. Eddie said, *"There goes one of our Goodwill cars"* pointing to mine that I am sure was a site to see as a ball of smoke. Eddie almost got fired because of his remarks, which he thought were hysterical. I then junked the car for $15.

In between cars, I decided to ride my Roadmaster bike to Amsterdam, not smart, but I was young and untouchable. Keep in mind it was a single speed bike and the trip was 26 miles. By the time I got there I was so sore I could hardly walk and had to get friends from Steubenville to bring me and the bike home.

My next car was a Dodge about the same age as the Packard. I bought it from a guy down the street, brought it home, and cleaned it all up. I got the insurance and decided to take it for a test ride. I loaded up my brother Jim and his buddy Dick. We headed out Sunset Blvd and having gone about four miles a woman decides to make a U-turn right in front of us.

Needless to say, there was an immediate joining of the cars. Jim went into the windshield and had a cut nose, while Dick, in the back seat was thrown forward but was unhurt. I was probably going 30-40 mph. I only got bruised and sore but it was death for my week old car. I was found at fault even though she made a U-turn in front of me, because I rear-ended her. The cars back then were built like tanks but even a tank can become a pile of junk and mine did.

I saved my money and when school time came around in September I had some nicer clothes, and had become a lot wiser. I would be repeating part of the 11th grade classes and starting some of the required classes over from the beginning. That's okay because it gave me more time to pursue my passions.

Because of my desire to always have some spending money I got a job at D'Carlos bakery working the 4-12 pm shift. The only bad thing about this job was no matter how much I asked they would not let me leave 15 minutes early to catch the last bus home. This meant walking up Angel Trail through the woods and home, about two miles at midnight. That's something we would not consider letting our children do today.

I also decided to get a little more serious about schoolwork. I started paying attention and trying harder in English class, but I had missed out on so much in my first ten and half years it was impossible to catch up.

We had school buses that were really local city buses but went straight to the high school. They also took us home at lunchtime, if we wanted, and back for afternoon classes and home again after class. As I remember a pass was just a couple dollars a month. The hilltop bus was known to get rowdy so there was one bus for the girls and one for the boys. The boys would sing songs, pick on each other, talk about the girls and just be teenagers. I guess the girls did Foo-Foo stuff and talk about the boys.

On one occasion a boy by the name of Brooks got on the bus at lunchtime to go back to school. I promptly asked him if he had been picking on my brother, and he laughed and said yes. I then hit him in the face and broke his nose. I had never seen so much blood. He ran the couple blocks home. My brother Jim is five years younger and Brooks had been picking on him for a couple weeks. This was the first time I had seen him since Jim told me.

When I got home from school and we sat down for supper, my father promptly asked what had happened in my day. I commented that I had taken up for Jim and broke Brooks' nose. My dad said he had already heard about it since Brooks' father was my dad's boss. My Dad had to pay the $50 to get his nose set but told me he didn't mind it since I had taken up for Jim. I was sure I was going to be in big trouble. That $50 was about an eighth of my father's monthly income, so it was a hardship on the family. Needless to say Jim never had any more trouble. My Buddy Dave started calling me "one-punch Al".

I didn't like Algebra, partly because of the teacher. With repeating the 11th grade I could choose a different Mathematics requirement. They had something called "Shop Math" put out by Ford Motor Company. Since it had the word "shop" I thought it would be a piece of cake. It wasn't, but the one thing it did do was to make Math all come together, **A REASON FOR USING MATH**. I thought when we got the book on the first day of school there was no way it would take a year to complete the book. It was a hardbound book about seven by nine inches and maybe three-fourths of an inch thick.

As the year progressed I learned that we were going to have a hard time completing the little book. We learned everything about math, geometry, algebra, trigonometry, and much more. We would be given a set of plans for a house and had to figure the costs for the entire project. We were given costs for materials individually. We had to figure how many cubic yards of cement for the floor, the plumbing, how much wood it would take, the amount of wire required for the outlets, how much sheetrock, how much paint would be needed based on a paint coverage supplied. If we were more than $100 off we had to go back and redo it all.

Remember NO calculators in those days, just a pencil and an eraser and paper. I learned to appreciate Math because **THERE WAS A DEFINITE REASON** for all of this. When students can see a practical reason for learning it becomes interesting and fun. Just teaching so students may be able to pass a state test is SO wrong because the students don't retain the data.

Going into my last year of High School I had some extra credits because of the previous half-year attendance. I decided to take Distributive Education where you went to school a half-day and worked a half-day. I got a job at Kinney shoes as a salesman along with another student in my class named Sam. The store was a training store for future managers. The boss had very definite rules on selling.   We always had to sell polish and socks or hose with each pair of shoes. As I look back at this, we made a lot of profit for them in selling the extras.

Some of the most amusing times at the shoe store were when some *"Ladies of the Evening"* would come in for new shoes. Steubenville was well known for the houses of ill repute. These "girls" were beautiful girls in their 20's that worked in these houses. As most women, they had an affinity for shoes. When they would come into the store before Sam or I got there they wouldn't let anyone else wait on them. They would simply say they would be back. I guess they enjoyed giving Sam and me a thrill when they came in, and "boy did they ever."

Update – Sam and I got together again at our 50th HS reunion. (pg 292)

As the senior year progressed I met the girl that would become my first wife. I was also selected by the Distributive Education class to seek the office of State President. I had never had any type of public speaking and had no self-assurance. I was just roped into this because the class voted and I had to do it. I had to learn the speech I would give at the convention in Columbus.

The entire class as well as our teacher had written the speech. We were trying to come up with a great slogan for the speech and we needed a lead in to the slogan. So as part of the speech we said, "We put our heads together" and came up with this slogan "get on the right track and Go by Rayl" and it was really the best part of the speech. I practiced it and had it down pretty well. Then on the ride to Columbus my friend Dave the other guys helped me to practice the speech. When I would get to the part of the speech where "we put our heads together" they would butt-in and say "came up with a rock garden." They did this maybe a dozen times and when I had to get up in front of a thousand students at the convention that almost came out.

I was not elected and my speech was not very good because of my worry, but at least I tried. This experience also proved to be invaluable later in life.

My grades for my senior year were pretty good with wood shop, printing, DE and an English class. The English class was actually an 11th grade class even though I was taking it as a senior. I needed it to graduate. The English teacher thought I worked so hard that she told me she wanted to nominate me to attend Boy's State during the summer. However she realized that I was not a junior and thus not eligible but it was a good feeling knowing that I did well in her class.

In June of 1954 I had joined the Ohio National Guard. The unit was 191st Combat Engineers and had almost been called up for Korea. They had been on alert but luckily things had settled down before I joined. We went to summer camp at Indian Town Gap in PA. For two weeks the unit would build Bailey Bridges, take them down and build again.

After the first week, at a morning roll call they asked if anyone knew how to run a chain saw. I had never seen one but with all of my shop experience I figured it would not be too difficult to figure out. I volunteered and was led over to this long box that had a 12-foot long, two-man gas operated saw. A Sergeant was instructed to steady the one end while I operated the saw. I looked it over, figured it out and we got it started. For the rest of the week we dismantled an old firing range, cutting the telephone poles used to support the bunkers and all around it. I had it pretty well made, got to stop for drinks or rest whenever I wanted and I didn't have to make formations. I had only been in the Guard two months and most everyone knew me by the time we got back.

As I grew older and went into high school I learned the valuable lesson that ***"Dreams can come true"*** if you work hard and never give up on your dream.

A way to get to Africa – Go join the Army
As the school year progressed several guys from the class started talking of going into the Army upon graduation. I had a great-renewed interest in going into the Active Army.

When high school classmates of my sister Barbara, Lois and Bill whom I had known, came by to see her after returning from overseas I almost became obsessed. A bell, lights, whistles and rockets went off in my head. Wow! What a chance to fulfill that dream I had as a little boy of going over behind the golf course and hunting big game. I quizzed Bill and found that the Army had a base in Asmara, Eritrea and yes there was good hunting over there. When I found out that after Bill had been drafted into the Army and got sent to Africa, I had to corner him and get all of the details. This was fine since Barbara and Lois were busy gabbing about life.

As I drew the details from Bill about how he got stationed in Africa he sort of thought it was the bad luck draw. He just got sent there and had not asked for it and at first thought it would be a terrible assignment. He found out he really enjoyed it. He was only a low grade enlisted person but was allowed to pay to have Lois come and live there. He told me that after he had arrived at Kagnew Station, Asmara, Eritrea, and Ethiopia it really was a pretty neat place to live.

In the meantime I had joined the National Guard and was a tiny bit familiar with some of the Army branches. Bill explained that Kagnew Station was a radio communications relay station and that the Army Security Agency was the main unit at the base.

Me in a company photo in the National Guard

When I talked further to Bill and told him I wanted to go to Africa he explained my best bet would be to get into the Army Security Agency and try from there. A plan was developing in my brain.

Some of the other great memories of the high school were all of the proms I went to. Ten proms in all and the band that played for all of the proms was Bobby Vinton. This was just before he became the big hit and idol that he has enjoyed. Our graduating class had 265 students. I had not done as bad as I expected. I thought I might be last in the class but actually was 168th. This was not really bad since I had such a poor study attitude.

During my senior year I had also gotten very serious with Joy, my first wife. At this time she was a freshman and I was a senior. Of course we were very young and didn't know much about life. However, like most teenagers even today, we thought we knew more than anyone else. At one point in the year we decided to run away and get married. My buddy Dave and his girlfriend, with Joy and me skipped school and drove to Kentucky, but we didn't get married and were back home later in the evening. Our parents never knew what we had been up to.

Chapter 5 – You are In the Army Now!

Joining the Army

I now had a plan. The recruiter promised all of the guys "one choice" to get us to enlist. In 1955 it was possible to join the military and be guaranteed either a school or branch of the Army such as the Signal Corps, Paratroopers and the Army Security Agency. However the ASA required a security clearance and only if you meet those requirements would the guarantee be valid. If you failed to meet the security requirements you were at the mercy of where the Army wanted to put you.

There was a bunch of my buddies talking about going into the Army. Dick & Bob chose going into the paratroopers and I chose the Army Security Agency. I knew if I could get into the ASA there would be some way to get to Asmara. I could think of little else then as high school came to an end.

The plan to join the Army was to go into the service three days after graduation. We all went to Pittsburgh for our tests and physicals. This time I got a 98 on the test but no offer to go into the Air Force. That was OK since I was going to figure a way to go to Africa. As we took the physical the doctor got interrupted just as he was about to check my ears. We were standing in a line and as he checked someone they took a couple steps forward in the line. Another doctor was checking something else at the head of that line. While he was talking to another doctor for five or six minutes, I just stepped forward as though he checked my ears. When he got done talking to the other doctor he turned to me and said, "I checked you didn't I" and I answered yes.

I really had some doubts about being accepted but I guess the Lord was with me and it was meant to happen. Again one of my dreams would come true. After we got done with the physical, the doctors all sat at a table and signed everyone's medical records. I was in the Army now.

Next stop was Fort Jackson, SC and basic training. The summer is not the time to go south for basic training because it is really hot. When we got there we found out the Army was reactivating the 101st Airborne and we would be taking basic training as part of the 101st. As I remember we were the first company going through basic with the Screaming Eagles. There were still some officers and non-commissioned officers that had been with the 101st years ago and they had the opportunity to get back with it. The unit had some really memorable events during WWII and was much respected. We were told in no uncertain terms that it was going to stay that way.

It was really hot and I was not use to getting up at 4:30 am, long hikes, KP, physical training and all that goes with basic training but I took to it and did my best. About five weeks into the training there was a request at morning roll call if anyone knew how to hang Sheetrock. The Army is notorious for asking things like that and then giving you some real crappy detail. I just had a good feeling so I volunteered. I was told to report to the supply room. A couple other guys were selected to help. I had never hung Sheetrock in my life but understood the basics of how to do it and with all of the shop experience I figured I could do it.

For the next two weeks the only training I had to do was the rifle range, where I really did well. We got to go to the supply room at 8am and worked, had coffee and lemonade and a noon meal. The unit was in the field eating rations. One day the rest of the unit had a 25-mile march. I had been on one and glad I did not have to do it again. As the unit came back we looked out the window with a glass of lemonade in our hands waving at my buddies. I thought they would kill me that night.

We got the supply room done and the company commander, Captain Nunn, asked if we could put fold down stairs in his quarters. Again, never having done it I was sure I could do it. He purchased the steps and a Sergeant and I went and did the work. The Captain's wife fixed us lunch and snacks. Luckily there were instructions packed with the steps so I didn't have to do much but read and install. We finished basic training and got home for Labor Day weekend for two weeks.

During my junior and senior years in school, a bunch of my buddies and me would sometimes go to the Musical Bar downtown where a sister of one of the guy's in our bunch played the piano. None of us were old enough to drink but they served us beer because we acted like adults and they didn't realize we were so young. We thought it would be cool to go to the bar in our uniforms so we did. There was a new bartender and he carded us. Darrell was at the end of the bar, and when the bartender said he needed our cards, Darrell said "they're all right I have been serving them for years." The bartender looked at the first ID and said, "This one just turned 18 the other day." Darrell came over and said he would have never guessed we were all so young. He said we always had behaved and never caused a problem. He then said he was thankful he never got inspected while we were there.

After the fourteen-day leave, I was assigned to Fort Devens in Ayer, MA. I rode the bus to Ft Devens and while going from NY to MA I got to witness the devastation of a hurricane. There was a bad hurricane that had hit Connecticut, Rhode Island and Massachusetts on Labor Day weekend. Even though it was two weeks earlier there were still trees down, houses tore up and debris everywhere.

When I got to Ft Devens I was assigned to a replacement company for tests. There was a lot of scuttlebutt about the type of tests and where you might get assigned. I could tell there were some things I did not want to do. If you did well in the Morse code test you were definitely going to be a Radio Intercept operator. If you did well in the language test you were going to be headed for California and the Army Language School and come back as an interpreter.

I also was not in a position to go right off to Asmara, since I had no military schooling. I thought that maybe I would like to be a Company Clerk. I did well on the typing test and I was offered the chance, and took it, to go to Fort Dix for eight weeks to the Basic Army Administration School to become a Company Clerk. I knew a company clerk would have "connections".

I was then off to Ft Dix for eight weeks and then back to Ft Devens to be assigned as a Company Clerk. I understood enough about the Army that a company clerk interacted with Personnel Section and that could lead to being assigned to Asmara, Eritrea where I wanted to go. Ft Devens was a training center for radio operations as well as some other things.

Little did I know at the time just what a blessing this would be? The company clerk can really be a powerful individual in the Army. As the time went on I changed units and got into the Headquarters Company at Fort Devens. I got to know the soldiers that worked in the Personnel section since they were part of this unit. Fort Devens was one of the main ASA training bases and assignments were made to places all around the world as well as where I wanted in Africa.

While I was in the replacement company and also when I got back from Ft Dix I hitchhiked to Ohio every weekend to see my girlfriend, Joy. During the winter months there was a lot of snow and it took about 19 hours each way. I would leave right after we were released on Friday and get back very late on Sunday night. It was totally against regulations to go more than 50 miles but young love does all kinds of things.

Roy (Buddy) Williams – me – Joy – Donna (Roy's wife) on Wedding Day

In March of 1956 I went home one weekend and brought Joy back to Ayer with me planning on getting married there. She was still only fifteen. It took a week of her talking to her mother about getting permission and her mother finally gave in and we got married the middle of March and the next morning woke up to almost three feet of snow. We rented a little apartment on the third floor of a house on Main Street in Ayer for $40 a month. It had a kitchen/living room and a bedroom with bath down the hall. I had a friend with his wife on the second floor who was also a company clerk.

While being the company clerk we had a couple soldiers that had some importance. One was named Curry and his father owned a company that made military soft headgear called Louisville Cap Company. When the Army allowed the wearing of a "blocked soft cap" rather than a Beetle Bailey type soft cap, Curry's father started making them as well. We received several large boxes one day and in them there were enough hats for the entire company. When the company marched to school they were always inspected and having the new hats really made the troops look sharp,

Another soldier was named Gould. Ed had been in the unit for several weeks and was going to school but had not brought any attention to himself. He came in the orderly room one day and asked about getting a three-day pass to get married. This was standard procedure so I started filling out his papers. When I asked him where he was going for the wedding his response was Bermuda.

I told him I didn't have time for jokes. He said he was serious so my next step was to take him to the First Sergeant who took him in to see the Captain Whelan the company commander. He told the CO that he had chartered an Eastern Airlines plane to take him and friends to the wedding and that we could come too if we wanted to. Captain Whelan passed it up the ladder and Ed was for real and got his three-day pass. He was marrying a girl whose father was a member of the Government in Bermuda.

When Ed got back he came in the orderly room to apply for separate rations and permission to live off base. While I was filling out the papers I had to ask how much his rent was. He stated $500+ a month. I said, "Wait a minute" you only make $77.10 a month how can you afford that. He said he had some outside income. When asked how much, he stated $18,000+ per month from one trust and he said if that wasn't enough, he could get papers on more. I asked him what the heck he was doing in the Army. He told me that he wanted to go into the Diplomatic Corps and that one of the requirements was having served in the Regular Army.

Needless to say I had to consult with Captain Whelan. Then we found out that he was the Great-grandson of Jay Gould who built the Pennsylvania Railroad and tried to corner the Gold market with JP Morgan.

Also during this time Ed did a lot of socializing and sometimes had difficulty getting in on time. He would call me and ask me to put him on sick call, which I did with the understanding that if he got caught he was on his own. Well, he got caught and got an Article 15, which meant two hours of extra duty for 14 days. His new bride was a super gal. Ed had bought her a Bentley automobile as a wedding present and while he was doing his extra duty she would come to pick him up. The only bad thing about all of this was that I had to stay until he was done. His job was to take some cots out of an old building, sweep the floor and put them back. There were hundreds of cots so it would take the two weeks. Ed's wife would come to pick him up and would come to the orderly room to wait.

The class that Ed was attending was a 26-week class and he had been recycled a couple times for not doing well. He finally got recycled to another company where I knew the company clerk and he helped Ed a little.

Finally after almost a year Ed graduated and was sent to Korea. He was assigned to a small island with nothing to do during off duty time. He bought a Chris-craft boat and had it sent over there for the guys to use. He gave it to the unit he was assigned to but the company commander said he couldn't accept it legally so Ed suggested that he pick it up as "found on Post." That worked and the guys used the boat for a long time.

Being stationed at Ft Devens and newly married brought a lot of realization into our lives. I got a promotion to PFC, which meant a little more each month, but not much. Joy received what was called a Class Q allotment of $137 a month and I brought home about $100. We managed but we didn't live anything like high rollers.

The apartment being so small was like being in a cage. Luckily with Roy and Donna on the second floor we had some friends. We went to the movies once in a while and fishing out at the nearby lake quite often. We would walk there and back about two miles each way and when we did catch fish they ended up being a good meal.

The summer came and Joy became pregnant with our first child. We moved across the hall to a little bigger apartment and of course a little more money. Janice was born in April 1957 and that summer we decided that we should buy a trailer. We moved into a 22-foot travel trailer. A couple months later we sold it and bought a brand new big trailer that was 35-feet long. It was really something to be homeowners even if it was a trailer.

I had transferred to the Headquarters Company and we had some new friends. We took turns between five couples of cooking a big meal on Sundays for everyone. We did that for five or six months and really enjoyed those times. On one weekend when it was our turn to feed everyone I made 450 home made ravioli's thinking we would have some for the following week. There might have been enough left for one small meal. They were a big hit.

Being in Headquarters company afforded me the chance to get to know all of the people that were assigned to the Post Personnel.

During the past couple years I had been promoted in rank and my enlistment time in the military was coming to the end. I would either be getting out or would re-enlist. I had worked my way up in promotions to a SP-5 (E5). This was enough rank to have my family accompany me on overseas tours in areas that dependents were permitted.

Time to make a big decision – Stay In – Get Out
In my young life I had already accomplished much but still had not gotten to Africa to do the "real" hunting. With things considered as no objections from the wife, re-enlistment bonus, and some favors from friends I was assured that I could get assigned to the base at Kagnew Station.

At the time I first joined the Army I wanted to be a photographer but we only had one guarantee and I used it up with my selection of the ASA. However with the re-enlistment I had the chance to finally go to the Army Photo School at Fort Monmouth, NJ and still be assigned to Kagnew Station.

When it came time in June of 1958 for me to get out or re-enlist I had made enough friends to get the assignment to Asmara and in addition being able to go to Fort Monmouth for Combat Photography School prior to going overseas. I was to go to school, have a leave and then head for Asmara, Eritrea, Ethiopia. I made the "package deal" with the help of those friends and was off to photo school.

This was quite a deal for a kid that never had much. I told my buddies in Personnel that I wanted to go home after school and be charged for just a few days leave and wait for a Port Call. The way that worked was, if there wasn't a port call available immediately, you just stayed till you were notified and not charged for leave.

The help of my friends was my real first introduction to what could be accomplished by helping others in gaining preferences in duty. A young Sgt. Bilko was emerging in the form of me.

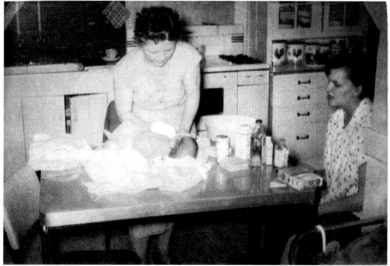
Mom cleaning Janice as Joy watches while waiting to go to Asmara

Chapter 6 – Heading Off to Africa

While I attended the photography courses, Joy and Janice stayed with my parents in Ohio. When I finished I went home. We had bought a little Ford Anglia that we were going to take overseas. I got home around Labor Day for my few days leave. While we were home the Steubenville newspaper came to the house and did a story about the young GI taking his wife and 18-month old daughter to the dark continent of Africa. It was really a nice story.

We waited and waited and finally in late October I thought I had better check in and see what was going on or if they forgot about me. I called my buddy and his response was he thought I might like to spend Christmas at home too. I said that Joy was pregnant and wouldn't be able to fly if we didn't get out soon. He arranged a port call for November for us. That was quite a long leave without being charged but for a couple days. *Politics – military style.*

We finally got the port call and headed for New York and to drop the car off at Brooklyn Army Terminal. We would spend a day and night at Fort Hamilton while I delivered the car. The little Ford Angelia ran pretty good until we got in the Holland Tunnel into New York. The traffic was bad and moving slow. The car vapor locked and quit right in the middle of the tunnel. I just knew it would cost hundreds of dollars to get pulled out. It was two lanes of traffic going into New York. One lane could get by me but the car would not start. In just a couple minutes this great big vehicle, the likes of which I had never seen, comes right up to us. It hooks on to our front bumper and over the loudspeaker they said to put the car in neutral. I did and we were off and out of the tunnel to a little side waiting space.

I waited about 20-30 minutes thinking someone would come and give me a bill and when I then tried to start the car, it started right up. I looked around and no one was in view so I gently drove off. No more problems getting to Fort Hamilton. We checked in the guesthouse and I delivered the car to the Brooklyn Army Terminal. It was so easy I was sure the car would not make it. I parked it out in a parking lot, went inside, and gave them a set of my orders and the keys and the man said it would get to Massaua in about six weeks. That is all there was to it. I went back to Fort Hamilton to get ready for the next day and the flight overseas.

People in the Military are from all types of backgrounds. We were two young kids that had never really been away from home till my joining the service. The three years in Massachusetts was still no real preparation for a trip half way around the world. The next day we were packed and taken buy bus for the flight to Paris which would be our first stop. The plane was a Lockheed Super Constellation, a graceful looking plane with distinctive tri-tail design. If you look at one of these planes you will understand why planes are referred to as "birds" because of the smooth lines of the plane.

Being what might be called "a couple of hicks" we had no idea how long of a flight we were in for or really what to expect. We knew the military would have people assigned to direct us where to go. We took off from what is now JFK airport in New York and headed up the East Coast. After what seemed to be enough time to have gotten to Paris we were told that we were stopping for fuel and the place was Gander, Newfoundland. It is really cold there in the end of November. We went inside the terminal, and killed time till they called for us to board the flight.

We boarded the flight and took off in a light snowstorm and headed East via Iceland and on to Shannon, Ireland where we again had to stop for fuel. Shannon had just a little wooden building for a terminal but we had a couple hours to kill. In those days I knew nothing about Irish Coffee, Irish Whiskey or their beers. We again boarded the plane and were off for Paris. The flying time from New York to Paris, including the stopovers had taken 26 hours of noise. The Super Constellation even though a beautiful plane in its day was extremely loud with its big radial engines.

Upon landing at d'Orly airport the military took us into town to a hotel that had been under lease by our Government for military personnel. We found out that we were going to be in Paris for four days. Right across the street there were two shops of which were a bakery and a wine store. One evening I bought a loaf of bread and a bottle of wine. We put the wine right outside the window and that was our pre-breakfast the next morning.

The hotel had a babysitting service and since it was overseen by the military we felt safe in leaving Janice there one evening while we "went out on the town." Another couple and we went to the Lido to see their famous stage production. The cover/minimum charge was the equivalent of $30 and so was a bottle of Champagne. The show was absolutely awesome. We figured since we had to pay the $30 any way we might as well enjoy the bubbly. We did get to go around and see some of the sights and eat at a real French Restaurant.

Then it was off to Frankfurt via Lufthansa Air Lines. It was really a fairly short flight of only a couple hours. At one point Janice got sick and puked over the entire area around us. Sour milk smells everywhere. It was less than a minute when the stewardess came to the rescue, grabbed Janice and the diaper bag had her back to the galley and all cleaned up. They gave us wet towels to clean ourselves and sprayed the cabin. In less than five minutes you would never have known there had been a problem.

We landed at Frankfurt's Rhein Main airport to make connections for our flight to Asmara. After several hours of waiting in the lobby, all of this with a pregnant wife and 18-month old child, we were off on the next leg of our journey. We left Frankfurt headed for Athens on a DC-6b of Ethiopian Airlines, and to spend the day and night there. On our way to Athens we found out that TWA was a partner in getting Ethiopian Airlines started and some of the pilots worked for TWA. The pilot we had was awesome. As we crossed over the Alps that night he pointed out little villages in the mountains and we could look right out the windows at some of the tall snow covered peaks.

We did walk around town but did not get to see any of the ruins of old Athens. We really did not feel safe walking around. Our next leg was to finally get on a plane that was going to take us to Asmara. Again it was an Ethiopian Airlines DC-6b, later found out that was all they flew on long trips and only had four of them. They had some DC-3's they flew around the country of Ethiopia. We had to make a fuel and passenger stop in

Cairo, Egypt and got to spend a couple hours in the airport where there were a couple historical displays.

Next stop Asmara, Eritrea, Ethiopia. We re-boarded the plane in Cairo and flew on to Asmara, which was as I remember about a six or eight hour flight. Keep in mind the planes of those days did not fly at the speeds of today's planes.

The total airtime from Frankfurt to Asmara, not including the day layover in Athens was about 25 hours. As we were making our approach into Asmara we could see some of the mud huts and houses the natives lived in. I knew we were really in Africa.

In 1936 the League of Nations gave Eritrea as part of Ethiopia, and Eritrea did not gain its independence back until 1993. This means the whole time we were there we were actually in Eritrea, Ethiopia.

Sign in front of Headquarters Company

The buildings such as barracks, mess hall and others were new and modern. They were built just as those new ones in the States. The base had a small amount of dependent housing and a swimming pool that all military and dependents could use.

Chapter 7 – Kagnew Station

Asmara, Eritrea, Ethiopia

We had finally arrived in Asmara this meant that I was really in Africa of which I had dreamed of since a little boy. The rest of the African dream could now be worked on since the impossible was no longer impossible.

Dreams can come true if you are willing to do what it takes to make them happen.

When we got to the door of the plane there was a distinct odor and best as I could describe it just smelled like spicy dirt. After being there a short while we didn't notice it any more because our senses got accustomed to it. We cleared the Ethiopian Customs and were met by a sponsor Bert Sachs.

We were taken to the Hamasien Hotel where we would stay for the allotted 60 days to draw the maximum per diem. I remember the total for the per diem we could collect was $1160 and to stay there for the 60 days would only cost less than $200. We could have a nice little profit to get settled into a house. The sixty-day time was so that your furniture and vehicle could arrive. The Suez Canal was closed and the ships had to go around South Africa and in to the Red Sea which was much longer.

The main gate of Kagnew Station in Asmara

After we checked in and got organized we were then taken to Bert and Barbara's house and a little tour of the town on the way. We had dinner and the next morning I was to check in with the Kagnew Station, Headquarters Company, and 4th USASA Field Station. Kagnew Station was located on a plateau almost 8,000 feet above sea level. Living at that altitude required getting what was called acclimatized. The weather on the mountain was ideal and the temperature ranged from 65 to 85 degrees. The rainy season was from the end of May till early September then no more.

Being a NCO it was proper for me to introduce myself to the company commander. I went into his office and there sat Captain Whelan, the same one that I had been his company clerk back at Fort Devens a couple years earlier. Both of us were surprised to see the other and then we reminisced about a few old times and especially about Ed Gould and some of the dinners we had with the Captain's family. This started a great relationship with the company First Sergeant, since he had listened as we talked. His being aware I knew the Captain, I guess, made him think I was all right.

Bert at that time was the NCOIC of the post photo lab and I would be working for him. We were both the same rank but he outranked me in time and I had no problems with that.

After attending the required introduction to Asmara courses and being told where we could eat, not eat and what water to use and a million other items, we were not so sure this would be an ideal place to be stationed. Some of the good things covered were things like how much to pay for a maid and houseboy and what to expect from them. We were told that we would be required to carry water for brushing teeth, cooking and all vegetables in a pre-soak solution and washing before eating or we could become deathly sick. The maids for the most part were aware of this but it was our job to be sure of compliance. The houses had anywhere from three to six barrels on the roof and the city pumped water for about two hours a day. This was to only take a bath, wash clothes and for the toilet and if you wanted to water flowers.

Bert and Barbara showed us around the base and the town pointing out where to shop and where not to go in the city.

The base had three clubs for the personnel, an officers club, enlisted men's club and the Top 5 club for the NCOs' of which I was. The clubs all served meals from about 6am till midnight and on weekends even later. The noon meal special which was usually a wild game meat meal complete with drink, salad, vegetables and dessert was a whopping $.10. Hamburgers were a nickel and other items very inexpensive also. Beer was $.20, mixed drinks a quarter, and you could buy a half-gallon of IW Harper whiskey for about $3.95.

As I look back at this there is no doubt many people drank too much. There were also slot machines that also took too much of some peoples income. In the club to pay your bill you had to use what was called "chits" which were like pieces of paper in values from a nickel to a dollar. If you were short of cash at the end of the month you could charge the "chit books" until payday. This was not uncommon because maybe gambling or buying something that came into the PX that you used your cash on.

I finally got settled into the post photo lab and met the other photographers, Joe Jackson was the same rank as Bert and me but I outranked him in time, Dick Spalding, Ron Schuster & Don Haith. Joe and I hit it off well immediately since he hunted all the time. I asked when he was going again and he said next weekend. I asked if there was room for me to go. Mind you, we would have been there only two weeks and still in the hotel. With his yes answer I had to get a license, find out about a weapon etc.

Going Hunting
I was to learn that you could go to the motor pool sign out a vehicle, from a jeep to a duce-and-a-half, with extra gas. Go to the mess hall and get food, go to the ice plant and get ice and if you didn't have a weapon you could go to the Armory and sign one out. Also we could go to any of the clubs and sign out up to ten cases of beer ($48 total value) for each four people going on the trip. We would exchange the meat from the animals we shot at $.10 a pound. It was not unusual to come back with a thousand pounds of meat. This kept noon meals cheap. Can it get any better than that?

They always took a camp boy that would cook for about four dollars in our money, which was ten dollars in their money. He was usually one of the barracks houseboy's or a waiter from one of the clubs. When they get to the hunting area they would also hire a guide for a couple dollars for the weekend.

I thought the hunting would be done in jungle surroundings so before we left the states I had bought a 30-30 Winchester rifle. I figured for up close that would be a good rifle. Not only was I totally wrong in the type of hunting but the weapons were so much cheaper at the PX since there were no taxes on them. I could have learned a lot and saved a lot had I waited but I didn't know the PX even carried weapons.

With all of the preparations out of the way the day finally came for the trip. Including me there would be six GI's on the hunting trip and we had to take an Eritrean policeman with us. We had a couple jeeps with trailers and a ¾ ton vehicle. The big 500-pound ice chests would be in the trailers and the ¾ ton vehicle. The plan was to leave right after work on Friday and come back Sunday afternoon. We took a few hours off early from work and got everything together and packed so we could be off the mountain and arrive in the hunting area before dark. This would prove to be about a four-hour ride.

We headed north out of Asmara and started down the mountain towards the town of Cheren. After a quick stop at the R&R center in Cheren we continued down the mountain to what was called "the flats." This was pretty close to sea level and the temperature was well over a hundred degrees, but dry. Shortly after leaving Cheren we ran out of paved road and now on a fairly nice wide gravel road. About 25 miles from Cheren we made a left turn in towards the base of the mountains and followed a dirt road to a village.

We visited with the village chief and picked up a guide. Joe mentioned that visiting with the chief, and hiring a guide of the chief's choice, was kind of a political guarantee we would not have any problems while hunting. This was one of the all time good lessons I learned. The Eritrean people are extremely loyal and wonderful people. By taking the time to visit with the chief and to hire a guide we made friends forever. We also took presents for the village chief of salt-tablets and malaria pills which we got from the post hospital.

My buddy Joe Jackson and Bill Golden on my first hunting trip

I was learning the value of being a photographer because we had "something to offer" we could get anything we needed. Everyone stationed in Asmara wanted pictures at one time or another. We never had problems getting gifts for the chief.

Since Eritrea had been given to Ethiopia in 1936 there was a lot of resentment by the Eritreans and there was a revolution going on. There was a band of revolutionaries that were called "Shifties" and later on became the Eritrean Liberation Front. They were really locals from all of the villages. If you were in good graces with the chief all was well for you.

We went a couple miles from the village near a dry riverbed and made camp. On the way into the camp we saw a couple Gazelles and I knew I had reached *African Heaven*. It was almost dark by the time we got camp made. The cook that had been hired in Asmara was Abe and I would eventually hire him on many more hunting trips.

Having really gotten into an African Hunting area was just awesome and unbelievable to me. I couldn't believe I was really going to hunt game. While Abe started fixing something for supper, everyone unpacked the cots, blankets and picked a spot of their own. *Again – Dreams do come true.*

As soon as we ate a little we were off to hunt. I was in the jeep with Joe and a guy from Personnel named Bill Golden. Being the "tenderfoot" hunter I thought it was necessary to try to figure out where we were by looking at the stars and then keeping an eye on which direction we were headed.

About a half-hour after we left camp we were riding through some of the brush alongside of the riverbed when we came upon a bunch of wart hogs. My first African game kill was a hog about 200 pounds.

I already knew enough about hunting that we had to gut and clean the animals where they dropped. If this isn't done the meat has a chance to spoil from any insides that might taint the meat. Also some of the animals have "scent glands" and if these are not removed they can give a horrible taste to the meat.

My first wart hog – (not real big but nice) and the native guide

By the time we cleaned the hog it was decided to take it back to camp. I was able to point the way fairly well, it kind of surprised Joe and Bill that I even had an idea of where we were. After dropping the hogs off we were back out hunting in the dark using the lights of the jeep and a spotlight to look for some gazelles. We stayed out all night and came in for some breakfast and a short nap.

It gets fairly cool on the desert at night even enough for a sleeping bag. We napped a bit and then it was up and out to get some gazelles. That afternoon everyone shot at least one, some more. One of the ways they were being hunted was with a shotgun with double O buck. It was common practice at that time to spot a gazelle and chase him with the jeep till you got close enough to shoot with the shotgun. I was to learn later on there were much better ways to hunt with a good high power rifle. After all, this was my first trip after being in Africa for two weeks.

We hunted all day and even ran into a flock of Guinea fowl. This turned into a lot of fun. When you got near a flock, if you drove slowly they would just run in front. When you were all set to shoot, if you sped up slightly they would fly for about 50 yards and you could shoot them with a number seven shot. We shot maybe 40-50 between us. The jeep was full so we headed back to camp for Abe to clean the fowl and put on ice.

After a good super of wild meat we headed back out to hunt during the night. We hunted all-night and about 3am the worst of the worst happened. We ran out of gas. Joe and Bill said they knew the way back to camp and would walk back and get some gas and have the other guys bring them back. They didn't take any weapons with them so I was left with the jeep and the weapons.

Scared to death

As the sun started coming up a fierce looking native walked up to the jeep. He was a member of the Kunama tribe and had one of the hatchets that looked like a tomahawk. The Kunama's wore their hair in braids with dried camel dung to keep them neat and keep the flies away.   My having had no hunting experience and being new to the country, I was just sure there was going to be trouble. I had not learned to speak Italian or any of the Tigrinya, the local language. Through sign language we communicated and I could tell he wanted some shotgun shells. There were several shells on the back floor of the jeep that were caked with blood. I figured that we wouldn't shoot them and I thought if I didn't give him some, my life might be in danger. I gave him a couple of the shells and he stood there scraping the blood off with his hatchet. Then he waived and headed off behind me.

By now it was really light out and when I looked in the direction he was headed I could see a big village a couple miles off. I was sure he was going to go get the whole village and come back and take me hostage.

When we had attended the introduction to Asmara we had been told in no uncertain terms to never let locals have a weapon. I decided I had better get moving and since it was flat I started pushing the jeep towards camp. I had pushed it a couple hundred yards when Joe, Bill and the rest of the guys came with the gas. I told them what happened and they rolled on the ground laughing. They understood my concern since it was my first trip and not having been in the country very long, only 2 weeks, but it was still so funny. As I would later learn I could have gone with the native to the village and had tea and would have been made to feel right at home.

It was Sunday morning and we had to get back to camp and pack up and head home. This had been quite an experience for me. I had so much fun, learned so much and met some good friends. We drove back to Kagnew Station and took the meat to the Top 5 club, which more than covered the ten cases of beer and the soft drinks we had taken. I had not shot my elephant on this first hunting trip, in fact there were no Elephants near this area. What had been accomplished was **chapter one** of real African hunting trips.

While on the hunting trip Joe talked to me about how little Bert really did around the photo lab and that he would sure like to see him gone so the lab would run efficiently. Bert did a lot of film processing for people at his house and quite often would take off during the day at lunch and maybe not even come back to work. It really wasn't too big of a problem since we always had plenty of skilled personnel to cover the assignments. I recognized this problem in the short two weeks I had been in the photo lab but with Bert not around it was usually quiet. After a couple more weeks and getting to know and work with the rest of the guys they all started complaining to me since I was "second in command."

70

I finally had about enough of the problems and talked to Bert but he could care less about the lab and was making more processing film than he did with his regular Army pay. The real problem was he was doing it almost exclusively with military chemicals and paper and equipment. One day Bert came in and took some chemicals from a drum we had and in the process spilled some of the powder on the floor. He didn't bother to clean it up and I saw this as the chance to make a good complaint.

Becoming NCOIC of the Photo Lab

I went into Captain Walsh's, the Post Signal Officer, office and my comment went "Captain Walsh, I don't mind Bert coming in and taking chemicals to use at home, but I really object to cleaning up his messes." Captain Walsh's response was "What do you mean" so I took him back into the darkroom and showed him the mess on the floor. It was only about a cup but it was right inside the door and you couldn't even get into the darkroom without walking in it. We only had about a six-foot by eight-foot darkroom at that time. The new area that was to be the darkrooms had not been designed yet. The military had only moved to this new base less than a year before. The base was known as the main post, while the old base across town was called Track "A", and the radio receiver site was called Tract "C".

Captain Walsh came unglued and on the spot placed me in charge of the Photo Lab. We took his car and went to Bert's house and Captain Walsh relieved him of duty and had him reassigned. I thought surely there would be a lot of repercussions from Bert & Barbara but Bert was reassigned to the receiver site and one day came up and thanked me. We remained good friends for years. Joe and the other guys in the photo lab thought that was the most ingenious way of handling the situation they had ever heard of.

Our clerk typist who was assigned to the photo lab was named Don Haith. He really wanted to be a photographer. I told Don that if he had all his paper work done he could play in the darkroom and read the manuals and if he could learn something I would teach him photography. I will say that Don read all of the Technical Manuals we had and watched over everyone's shoulders. He later got to go on assignments as a backup photographer. He was a great learner, because he wanted to do it. When he was returned to the states he got a job very easily at a big commercial photography studio in California. He didn't attend photo school but had his training right there with everyone's help.

Also in the lab was a secretary named Bruna Lorenzini. Her father was Italian and her mother Eritrean. Bruna was only 16 at the time and became a very special girl to the photo lab and post Signal Section. Bruna was just learning English and the slang was hard for her to pick up on. She would ask the guys in the photo lab what a phrase would mean and they would explain to her and sometimes if it was not nice, they simply would tell her she didn't need to know. Bruna was always so pleasant and helpful and later we would help her get promoted.

She brought a pound cake into work one day and it was out of this world. Her mother had made it with a liqueur called Zibib, which had a licorice flavor. I liked it so much that when she knew I was going hunting with some of the guys from the photo lab she would have her mother make one for us to take on the trip. The cake was always gone before we even got to the hunting area. Once in a while Bruna would ride her bicycle over to the house and play with the girls and they loved it.

Bruna Lorenzini

Christmas of 1958 was here and we would celebrate Christmas in the Hotel. Joy was in her 9th month expecting our second child. We celebrated New Years at the Top 5 club and by this time we had made some new friends in Harry (who ran the line crew in the Signal section right down the hall from me) and Edith Whispell and Harold (Smitty) (who worked at Post Finance) and Helen Smith. Then a few days after the New Year on the 5th of January it was time to go to the Kagnew Hospital and welcome Mary Elizabeth to the family.

This was our first house in Asmara – the Street was to the right

Soon thereafter we found a nice house with a big yard and all walled in with glass imbedded in cement on the top of walls to keep strangers out. In the city there were some people that like to steal and those in the city were called "Clifties." We hired a maid (Tabatu) and a houseboy (Willie). The house even had room for me to have a little darkroom to process some film for personnel at the base. The only way to get film processed was to send it back to the states and wait six to eight weeks or take it downtown where it was expensive. There was a photo shop downtown called Photo Vaghi. Franco Celeste that owned the shop became a good friend and always gave me a decent price on supplies. I think it was partly because I was in charge of the Photo Lab and we did purchase some supplies on the local market when needed.

Our little car also arrived in January of 59. Joe had a really wild truck, so he and I went to Massawa, the seaport, to pick up my car. I had not been down that side of the mountain and it was a different type of road than the one to Cheren. In one area of about 20 miles there were close to 20 switchbacks and being a little two-lane road, driving down through the clouds was a thrill a minute. The locals driving the big semi's with two trailers took most of the road. We got to Massawa, which was 15 air miles, but about 80 land miles and took a good two and half hours when really moving as fast as you could go. We got the car and started up the mountain. There was a place called the Halfway House, owned by Jesse Dobbins, a GI that got out of the service and married a local Italian lady. Coming back from Massawa it was located about 1500 feet above sea level at the foot of the mountains and the very first rise. By the time we got that far up the mountain the car started running worse.

The higher up the mountain the worse the car ran. We got to within 20 miles of Asmara and it just did not want to run. Joe's wild truck came to the rescue. We hooked a rope to the front axle and he pulled it the rest of the way up the mountain. The next morning I took the car and had the carburetor adjusted for the high altitude. I realized the car was either going to be good on top of the mountain or down at sea level but not both. We put that thing up for sale and sold it very quickly and bought an American-made car that would go up and down the mountain.

The guys in the photo lab started all working as a team and in addition to the duties of being the NCOIC I was assigned the task of designing the area to be our new laboratory.   The threat of a large war in the Congo and other parts of Africa were looming. With this in mind Captain Walsh said to think about making the new area capable of being a "Class A" photo lab. I did some studying on the different categories of labs and found that there was only seven "Class A" labs in the world. The main difference is in the equipment the lab is authorized to request. Of course when I looked at the manuals and called Joe in to lend a hand we went wild with the equipment. We needed to be a Class "A" lab to get all of the neat stuff. I wrote up the proposal and turned it in to Captain Walsh and he finalized it and sent it forward. Again, wished I had paid attention in English classes.

In the meantime we needed to get our new lab area completed. It was a room about 14-feet wide and 25-feet long. I made a floor plan with a layout where everything would go. In the corner of the big room I included a small room, six feet by six feet, for developing negatives and loading film holders. The rest of the large room would be for printing and processing the photographs. There would be enlargers and contact printers as well as a nice deep ten-foot long stainless steel sink.

Everything was to be construction from the local market and they scratched the stainless steel sinks. They said they could not do that but would make cement sinks. I suggested fiberglass, no deal it was going to be cement. I had my doubts about whether they would work but they promised they could seal them with a coating and there would be no problem. The cabinets were wood so they were not a problem.

The design was accepted and soon started to take shape. The day the sinks came in we realized how much they weighed. I was sure they would get dropped and broken or something. They were about an inch and half thick and very nice. The big long sink weighed close to a thousand pounds. We never had a problem with either of the sinks. We would be approved to become a Class "A" lab and could start ordering equipment. When the stuff started coming in the Post Supply begged us to slow down, as they had no place to store everything. We did have a lot of neat equipment to play with and eventually the supply started returning items through channels since the threat of war was not as bad as expected. (See "It's a Small World" at the end of the book).

Duke – the Guard Dog

We had a German Shepherd guard dog at the house named Duke. Duke would go to the fence and growl and scare off any natives that came to the gate to beg. There was one old man that collected newspaper and cardboard that would come by and ring the bell once. If he didn't get anything he would leave immediately. He was a pretty good old man and Duke tolerated him a little since he came several times a week. On more than one occasion I saw Duke run and jump at the fence like he was coming through it and the natives would run away. We never had any problems between having Willie to guard the house at night and Duke there also.

One of the things about Duke was that Janice could ride him, play with him, torment him and just about anything. If a native came to the gate Duke would sort of wiggle his way free from Janice and when a few feet away he would be totally different.

We had some friends that lived sort of behind us across the alley, Ed & Jo Brown and their three boys. For some reason Duke did not like Ed. We would have to hold Duke when they came to visit us. One evening we had done that but left the back door to the house open and Duke came in the back door and had Ed trapped in the corner. After that Ed didn't like visiting us and wanted us to visit them. Duke never even a second look at any of the other Americans there and our friends could go up to him and pet or wrestle with him without problems.

Janice climbing on the gate watching for Daddy to come home

Janice and Duke the guard dog

As we spent more time at Kagnew Station life was pretty good. We got a hardship area living allowance of $60 a month and a cost of living allowance of $60 a month, I passed the necessary test to receive Proficiency Pay (Pro Pay) of $80 a month and then I was processing film and making a little extra money.

Janice loved to sit on my motorcycle and play mechanic

Not long after we got to Kagnew, the PX received a shipment of floor model stereos, when items like that came in they were usually gone in a matter of days. We bought a really great Telefunken made in Germany. It was a real piece of furniture and it was $80.

The food in the commissary was sometimes a bargain. One time there were several ships that came into Massawa at about the same time with refrigerated items. The motor pool would bring the food to the base and it would go into storage buildings. There was so much this time that they had truckloads of butter. They asked the families to come and get it and take it home – free. I remember the base running out of toilet paper because the ship had not arrived and wasn't due for a couple weeks. The local toilet paper was really bad. An emergency request was sent back to the states and they flew a whole C130 full of toilet paper for the base.

Sometimes the meat was frozen and refrozen and really looked horrible but was supposed to be edible, we had our doubts. We certainly thought food was food. The local meet market downtown called Gola was technically off limits. An Italian ran it but a lot of the Americans bought from him anyhow. He was trying to get it approved by the Vet Department and had to put in big coolers, which he finally did then got approved. All beef was twenty cents a pound, no matter what the cut or ground meat, except filet which was forty cents a pound. Between the inexpensive beef and the wild meat food was relatively cheap.

As for milk, again there was an Italian named Grimaldi that had a dairy but it was not approved either. We were probably there a year before it was approved and you could buy the milk in the commissary. It was straight milk with none of the butterfat removed. Rich milk but it made good homemade ice cream.

One of the oddest things was making Kool-Aide for the kids. If you took a package of grape Kool-Aide and mixed it with the water, we carried from the approved water sources on the two bases, and put it in the refrigerator in an hour it would be clear. This was due to the fact that there was so much chlorine in the water to make it potable. We lived about two blocks from the old base called Tract A and would take our five-gallon water cans there about every other day and fill them up. We never had to carry them in the house because Willie always took care of that.

Willie would also keep my shoes shined, car washed and the garden planted and watered. The maid took care of the inside of the house including washing diapers and clothes, helping with the kids and washing the marble floor on her hands and knees at least twice a day and sometimes three times. She even washed under the beds. You could literally eat off the floor if you wanted to and all of this for $8 a month. Some of us got so attached to the maids and houseboy's that we would order material from Sears for new clothes and at one point we started giving them $10 a month. There was quite a stink about the people paying this higher price and people said it would ruin the help.

78

As part of the commissary, and off to the side, was a produce market. It handled locally grown produce, always fresh and very cheap. The bananas were from nearby plantations and ripened on the vine with really great flavor. I learned about papayas and really enjoyed them at ten-cents each. They were the size of footballs. As I mentioned earlier on all of the produce required soaking in a chlorine solution that came in packets and were free. You simply picked up what you wanted.

A couple gazelle I shot after my 30-30 arrived

Planning a Hunting Trip

In the military the individual units (Company's) receive a small amount of money each month from the Post Exchange (PX) service. The amount is based on how many personnel are assigned to the Company. This money is used to buy things like TV's, pool tables and furniture for day rooms. The money can be used on other things as the Company Commander sees fit. This money is placed in what is called "The Unit Fund" and really is like a bank account for that company.

I remember one week we were planning a hunting trip and wanted to take a ¾-ton vehicle to carry the big ice chest. I planned to take the ¾-ton vehicle that belonged to our Company's Unit Fund. I submitted the request, which was normal procedure and it was approved. However, the vehicle had been on another hunting trip, which got back two days before we were to leave. The First Sergeant called me and said the vehicle would not be available because it needed repair. I asked him what the problem was and he stated it needed new "shoes" meaning tires.

I inquired if there were any other problems and he said there wasn't. I told him I would come over and pick up the vehicle and get some new tires for it. I guess he thought I was made of money and would purchase tires for it. We could buy recapped tires very reasonable in Asmara.

What I had in mind was simply doing what I did and that was to pull into the Motor Pool, jack up the Unit Fund vehicle, jack up an Army ¾-ton and switch the tires. What was so funny was the Unit Fund vehicle was painted a very bright green and not the olive drab like the military vehicles.

While I was in the process of changing the tires the Motor Pool OIC came walking by and said, "Hi Rayl, what are you doing"? I simply replied that I was switching tires and he just looked and walked on by. I had cleared changing the tires with Sgt Grammer, who was the Sergeant in charge of the Motor Pool and also a member of the same Headquarters Company.

When I was all done and had the tires changed, I went by and told Grammer that he had a ¾-ton out in the lot that needed new tires, to which he replied he would take care of it immediately, we laughed. I then went back to the Company First Sergeant and said the vehicle now had brand new tires and I was going to take it on the hunting trip. He did not have a problem until I told him how I got the tires. I had to reassure him that all was cool and taken care of and there wouldn't be any trouble. As the NCOIC of the photo lab I had IOU's due me from a lot of people on base and we each scratched the other's back.

A nice gazelle taken near Cheren with the 30-30

Land Rover I flipped chasing a gazelle – we quit chasing and used high power, flat shooting rifles after that

Many weekends the families of those of us that hunted would accompany us as far as Cheren to stay at the R&R center. We would go on into the hunting area and come back on Sunday and have lunch then head home with the families.

The Cheren R&R center offered a quiet and relaxing place for the families to have a good time. Kids could run, play and chase the animals and always be safe.

Front entrance of the Cheren R&R Center

At the Cheren R&R center there were some tame gazelle and a baby greater Kudu for the kids to try to catch. There was also a nice swimming pool for the families to enjoy.

Mary Beth with the baby Greater Kudu at the Cheren R&R center (on our second tour in Asmara)

The assignment to Kagnew Station was passing quickly, with hunting a couple weekends a month, taking the family to the R & R center in Cheren to play while we went off and hunted. We always managed to squeeze a trip to Massawa to that R & R Center and even manage to camp on the beach under some covered shelters the Army put up. As I had mentioned before the lunch meals were so cheap that almost every woman met her husband for lunch at the clubs. Having a maid meant always having a babysitter so if the kids were playing they could stay home. Sometimes we might go back into the base after supper in the evening if a band was playing. We led an active life.

Haile Selassie

Being the NCOIC of the photo lab, I was responsible for scheduling photographers, including myself, for different affairs, ceremonies or visits by dignitaries. The Emperor of Ethiopia, Haile Selassie would visit the base at least once a year and sometimes twice. He had his medical work done at our hospital. When he would visit we would photograph almost every move he made and then on his departure present him with an album of eight by ten photographs, some of which were taken less than an hour before.

The Emperor of Ethiopia, Haile Selassie at Kagnew Station

We had some of the photographers as runners bringing film back for processing and taking more loaded film holders out in the field to the photographers. One evening Haile, accompanied by his wife and his son, was to present the graduation certificates and diplomas to a class of the local nurse academy and I scheduled just myself to do the photography. It was a very good ceremony and we learned more about the Emperor's work to bring the country into the Twentieth Century. What a lot of people did not and do not understand is the country was not too far out of the wilds of Africa. It takes generations to educate people to really see the difference schooling can make. You can't just start with everyone already educated. In those days we used 4x5 press cameras to take pictures with.

Haile Selassie at the Nurses Graduation

A Cool Army Captain

One day a Captain, that I did not recognize, came into the photo lab and asked who was in charge. I told him that I was and he asked if we had any coffee. I replied we did and how would he like his. He sat on the edge of my desk with his coffee and introduced himself as Captain Eurastus W. Roberts, the CO of a signal research unit. He asked if we liked to hunt. Of course that got a positive response. He said he knew that we were not allowed to give his unit any photo support but wanted to see what we could do. I said I had no problem giving him support; after all we were in the same Army. He replied he didn't want to get us in any trouble with the base commander but he really needed some photography for his headquarters.

We talked about clearances and I had the required clearance to be able to take the photos he wanted. I said I would do the job and just not log it into our work roster. Capt. Roberts said that if ever we needed a vehicle to go to town, go hunting or any weapons, or a vehicle for any purpose just to come to their compound, ring the buzzer and tell his first sergeant which one of the vehicles we were going to take. This created a great friendship between us and I took photographs whenever needed. We never needed a vehicle and quite often Captain Roberts would call and ask if I was mad at him since I had never come and taken a vehicle. I would tell him we had a good relationship with the motor pool and they would deliver a vehicle when we needed one. He laughed and said he could deliver also if we got in a bind getting one from my buddy in the motor pool.

Secret Hunting Area

One of the other guys had a secret hunting area and invited me to go with him to hunt. I had not heard of anyone hunting in that area but I was always ready to go anywhere. This private area of his was about a hundred miles south of Asmara past a town called Decamere and over the mountain to the west.

During WWII there had been an important military air base, even used by the US, right outside of Decamere. We would go right past it and the only thing left was the runway, now growing weeds.

We did not take a jeep on this hunting trip but rather a VW Microbus. The road was passable with little problem all the way into the village. The villagers would grow grain and during the harvest the huge dual-trailer trucks would come in to the village to haul the grain.

Again, as customary, we went right into the village and had tea with the chief. We made our camp right in the village area which was surrounded by thorn bushes to keep the animals out at night and the possibility of a hyena from grabbing a child. Needless to say all of the villages were happy when we shot the hyenas because they would also attack the calves from the village cow herd.

I was sworn to secrecy about the area from the guy that took me into it. This area would prove to be one of my favorite hunting areas especially on my second tour of duty. As time went by and I hunted more and more I learned of other great hunting areas in Eritrea. I learned where the different types of game was located and acquainted myself with the village chief's and felt safe wherever my desires took me.

Agordat & Tesseni

My first excursion beyond the area just west of Cheren was quite a trip. We packed up as usual with all the supplies from the mess hall, the ice, the gas from the motor pool and all of the vehicles ready to go. We departed shortly after lunch so we could make our destination before it was too late in the evening because the trip was a good six or seven hour drive.

The town of Agordat is about 75 miles west of Cheren and on a gravel road that ultimately leads to Tesseni and into Sudan. When we arrived at Agordat, a town of about three or four thousand, we slowed down and kind of toured the city. Agordat is a central shopping area for that part of Eritrea where natives brought their wares to sell, barter and buy.

We headed northwest out of Agordat and about seven or eight miles we came to a large river bed that sort of wound its way throughout the area. We would cross it and continue up the other side another ten miles or so and make camp not far from the edge of the riverbed.

While we were unpacking the vehicles, Abe already had a fire going and was preparing some food for us. The cots were placed in a circle around the campfire and we would park the jeeps on the outside of the circle. We quickly ate and all took off into the night and the river bed to look for some wart hogs.

The hours just after sundown always proved great for bagging a few of the big wart hogs. They would come out of the brush and down to the water holes the natives used for their cattle during the day. The natives would dig a well down into the riverbed and using a goatskin and rope they would lift water in the bag and put into large watering holes. Quite often these wells and watering holes were near the middle of the river bed. Some of the riverbeds were a half-mile or more wide.

We would drive with our lights out and just by the moonlight until we thought we heard or saw movement as we approached the water holes. When we were near we would stop and turn on the headlights and be ready to fire. Normally there were never any natives at the water hole since this time was strictly for wild animals and really not safe unless armed.

It was not unusual to see hyena, gazelle, pig or baboons feasting on the water. Never together but you never knew what you might see. The one thing you could predict was just at ten or fifteen minutes before and after sundown the game birds would descend on the water holes, have a quick drink and be gone. On some trips I would see as many as several hundred game birds from Francolin, Guinea fowl or wild turkeys.

We managed to bag a couple of good wart hogs which we promptly threw into the jeeps and went to the riverbed edge to clean them. We did not want to cause any problems near the water hole. After cleaning the pigs we headed back for camp to get a good nights rest. The camp boy and the guides took care of the game we had gotten during the day and evening.

Some wart hogs ready to cut up after hanging all night

Being my first trip in the area I really tried to pay attention as much as I could to the direction we left camp and what I could see of the hills and mountains by moonlight. We had not strayed too far from camp and easily found our way back. When we came across our tire tracks it was easy to follow them back to camp at night. There were a lot of things I was learning about this *"big game hunting in Africa"*.

As the sun came up in the morning it was time to eat a big breakfast of eggs, potatoes some back strap meat from the wart hogs, and good hot coffee all ready for us by Abe.

As we finished it was time to pile into the jeeps and be off for a day of hunting. It did not take long to find some gazelle and even a turkey. With those in the jeep we headed back to camp to drop them off for Abe to finish skinning and to hang for cooling. Grabbing another cup of coffee and we were off again.

To hunt the gazelle, turkey and guinea fowl we simply drove around the countryside looking for areas of vegetation and kept a sharp eye. There was always an abundance of game so it never took too long to find some. In the early morning and late evening the gazelle were up looking for food. During the heat of the day we would find them bedded down under thorn trees.

One morning of my hunting – 6 gazelle – 6 Turkeys & 10 Guinea fowl

Once we started using the high powered rifles instead of chasing the gazelles we knew the meat would be better since the animals were not put under stress of running. Quite often we could also get a couple from each group of gazelle's.

One of the things that blew my mind was allowing the wild meat to hang during a hot day. I had been so mystified by this practice on my first hunting trip that I visited the post Veterinarian to see if this method was for real. The Major explained to me that the wild animals living in such a heat needed time for the meat to cool down. If the meat was put on the ice right away it would spoil. He stated that it was important to gut the animal immediately, which we always did. It was important to remove the head and to prop the inside wide open so the meat could cool down evenly. He explained that the meat would need to hang all day and put it on ice the next morning. The carcass would have a glaze from the membrane layer right under the skin.

Gazelle hanging waiting to be skinned like one on left

Many years later I would learn that beer does not satisfy thirst but as a diuretic it is possible to dehydrate in the hot climate of Africa without some water. One rule we were to learn was it was alright to drink the cold beer while hunting but not the morning we were to head home. We sweated it out about as fast as we drank it.

With our base at an elevation of about 8,000 feet and the air much thinner it takes less alcohol to be intoxicated on the mountain than on the "flats". There had been an incident where a group returning from a hunting trip almost went over the side of the mountain. The group had been drinking beer and as they climbed in altitude the effects nearly caused their demise.

Today I would not drink beer on a hunting trip except after all hunting was done and maybe sitting around the campfire. It is not a good idea to mix alcohol and a deadly weapon, just as alcohol and driving. Many things have made us more aware of the hazards of consuming alcohol besides the fact of driving after drinking.

This was a jeep and trailer we passed on return trip. – Drinking and Altitude don't mix – The tree saved it from going over the edge.

We did a lot of hunting all over Eritrea from the north of Cheren, out to Agordat, Tesseni which were west of Cheren and in the Decamere area South of Asmara and in the Flats of the Massawa area. I pretty much knew all of the areas where there was good hunting and had made friends with the villages. It was imperative to be friends with the villages since there were usually some of the "Shifties" (Revolutionaries) in those villages. By taking salt tablets and malaria pills when we first went in we were assured of being safe.

As the NCOIC of the photo lab it did not take me long to learn what a valuable asset I had. Some of the cooks, other NCO's and influential people on the base always needed a portrait, some film developed or some extra copies of photos we took. Being willing to supply their needs with a nice understanding that "they owed me" I could pretty much get what I wanted. We always had coffee to brew, fresh pies or cakes and sometimes-even lunch served from the mess hall. All of the cooks naturally got portraits to send home.

As the summer of 1959 came we found out there would be another addition to the family shortly after the New Year. We spent our second Christmas in Asmara and decorated the house and even the trophy gazelles and warthog hanging over the mantle. Janice and Mary Beth got a bunch of toys and they were happy.

Massawa R&R Center

Kagnew Station had an R&R center in the seaport city of Massawa and located on the Red Sea. A large hotel was leased by the military and we could stay in the rooms for $2 a night and kids free. There was a great dining room and a swimming pool located in the rear which faced the Red Sea. The military had built some covered camping locations at "North Beach" about 5 miles up the coast. There was no charge to use these and you simply signed up. A couple of them were about thirty feet square and had picnic tables with them. The MP's patrolled the area and that kept the natives from stealing the wood.

An Aerial gazelle shot in the Massawa area

Quite often when we stayed at the camping area we would go out and find a gazelle for dinner or catch a mess of fish for a fish fry. Sometimes we would invite other GI's and families that were also camped to join us.

There were times in Massawa that we would try to catch sharks in a unique way. We would take a jeep with a winch on the front, and tie steel fishing leader about three or four feet long into the hook coupling on the winch cable. We would put a big shark hook on the end of the fishing leader. Then we'd hook and tie a gutted chicken or any animal parts to the hook and wade out as far as we could until we ran out of cable. We would then go back and take the jeep out of gear. If a shark took the bait we could see the jeep move if it was a big enough shark. We would simply start the jeep, wind the winch in and then shoot the shark with a pistol.

Hunting Baboons

Hunting baboons was always fun and the very best hunting was always near a banana plantation which there were quite a few in Eritrea.

Getting a jeep unstuck from the riverbed chasing baboons

One of the two very best places was between Agordat and Tesseni west of Cheren about six more hours of driving. It was a plantation owned by a "half-breed" Italian/Eritrean named Makalie. The baboons would destroy his crops and he was constantly chasing the herd as much as he could. He was always delighted when GI's came to his place to hunt the pests. Makalie lived in a grass hut however he did have a maid and a separate grass hut that served as his dining facilities. When we would visit for the "hunts" we would literally get tired of shooting. We knew of baboon herds that had completely destroyed plantations.

At the end of February 1960 it was time to make a visit to the hospital and see Laura come into the family. When she was born the doctors said there was a problem with her feet. She had been born with clubfeet and a severe case at that. We were told there was not much they could do for her in Asmara so we were going to be sent back to the states for her to receive treatment at Walter Reed Medical Center just outside of Washington, DC. We made plans to return to the states by having our furniture packed, closing the utilities, being debriefed and notifying our parents that we were coming back to the states.

Laura all prettied up – a couple months old before we left to come to the US

Laura and the maid just before leaving Asmara in 1960

Janice checking on Laura under netting & Mary Beth behind her –
Harry Whispell in cabaña on beach in Massawa weekend camping

Chapter 8 – Back to the States

Arlington Hall Station – Arlington, VA

The flight from Asmara to Frankfurt with just stops in Cairo and Athens and no layovers was about 25 hours from take off to landing. With two kids in diapers and one barely out of diapers it was a real adventure. When we landed in Frankfurt we were told there would be a flight in about eight hours and we spent that time messing around the lobby. We got on a flight to New York, again on the sleek Super Constellation with stops in Shannon and Gander as on the way over. This took us some 29 hours to make touchdown. We were some exhausted people but the girls handled it so fantastically it made the trip easier on us.

When we got back to the states we stayed at Uncle Bernard and Aunt Hazel's house. I went on to the Army Security Agency Headquarters at Arlington Hall Station in Arlington, VA to check in and see if I was going to be assigned there or possibly taken out of the agency for some other kind of assignment. At the time I reported for duty it was very clear that we had returned because of family medical problems and I would be granted time to take Laura to the Hospital. When I got there I was assigned to the photo lab and went to check it out. I walked into the lab and there was Bert Sachs and Dick Spalding that had been in Asmara. Dick was about ready to get out of the service. Bert was in charge of the Photo Lab. There were no hard feelings and we looked forward to working together.

I went and collected the family from Baltimore and we looked for a place to live. We just could not afford some of the nice apartments in Arlington but we did find a big house kind of off the beaten path but not far from Fort Myers and maybe four miles from Arlington Hall. It was going to be mandatory in my opinion that we live close in Arlington so that we could get Laura to Walter Reed.

Our first visit to Walter Reed Hospital with Laura was quite an experience because we would have to drive all the way through Washington, DC. The only thing that could have been worse was when they made all of her appointments for first thing every Monday morning. This meant driving through all of the rush hour traffic. At this time there was not a beltway around DC. We adjusted and learned to "go with the flow".

The doctors at Walter Reed almost became part of the family. They immediately started correcting Laura's feet, which at the time I really felt would never be straightened. Laura came home with a set of casts on her feet and they would be changed weekly for the next 18-months. Laura learned to crawl with casts on her feet that came above the knees; she was able to totally destroy the knees of the casts in a week or so.

Walter Reed Army Hospital

In the beginning the doctors would cut the casts off on Monday before putting the new casts on. After a while the doctors wanted her legs to get some air. These meant that Joy got up and put Laura in the bathtub and soak the casts off before we headed for Walter Reed. When it was time for Laura to learn to walk the doctors bent the casts at the knees to try to keep her from walking. She just learned to balance herself and soon was running around in her casts, so the doctors just made the casts with extra plaster to help them last for a full week.

The expense of living in Northern Virginia was difficult to sustain on the military budget. I decided I needed a part-time job and found a job, tending bar at the DC National airport. I was able to get the job because of one of the other guys in the photo lab, Dick Parsons, was already working there. I would work for the army from 7:30 am till 4:30 run home change clothes and be at the airport by 5:30 and closed the bar at midnight. By the time the bins were restocked and the place closed down it was usually 12:30 am. I would drive home and could make it in about 20 minutes at that time of night. By the time I took a bath, got in bed it was about 1:30 am. I would get up just before 7 am since it only took about 15-20 minutes to get to work for the Army. On the weekend I worked a double shift at least one day every other weekend.

After arriving back in the states finding a place to live and getting Laura scheduled for her appointments we went back to Steubenville on a short leave. I wanted to see my old High School buddy Dave. I found him working for Time Loan Company. I walked in and asked to speak to him, and was directed to his cubicle. When I asked how he was doing, he stated that he was doing great and he was the Assistant Manager. I told him it was great and he must be making a lot of money. His answer was "yes, $65 a week" to which I darn near fainted. I told him I was working part time at Washington National Airport tending bar and was making more than $125 in tips alone. He asked me if I could get him a job and I said just come to DC and I would get him on. Shortly after that Dave showed up and started working tending bar also. He worked there for five or six years and had a lot of fun.

A short time after we got into the big house, Dick Spalding had gotten out of the service and had taken a job as an Arlington County cop. He stayed in a room on the third floor until he found an apartment he could afford. Spalding would baby sit for us once in a while so Dick and Doris and Joy and myself could go bowling after we got off work at midnight on Saturday's. This was about our only form of entertainment since there was not much free time with all of the work.

Spalding, in his a job as a cop with Arlington County sometimes worked shift hours. One weekend Smitty and Helen, friends from Asmara, were going to come and spend the night with us. We told Spalding about this and kept him abreast of about the time Smitty and Helen were due, he also had known them in Asmara. He patrolled the area extensively and sort of laid in wait of them. Right as Smitty and Helen pulled up in front of the house Spalding pulled up behind them and turned on the patrol cars lights. He got out with his hat pulled down over his eyes, gave Smitty a hard time and told him he was going to have to arrest him. Then after not being able to hold it any longer he moved his hat up so Smitty could see who he was and gave Smitty a big hug. An hour or so later Spalding was off duty and came home to his room upstairs and we all sat and talked the night away.

At work in the photo lab things were progressing well. Color photography was just coming into its own. Bert and I decided we needed to add color prints to the photo lab. The only color printing in the military was by using the dye transfer system. We put in a request and had it quickly approved for the absolute minimum of equipment. The powers to be would not approve all that we asked for since they thought color processing was too technical for us. We got the necessary enlarger and processing equipment and did a little amount of testing and had the first color lab up and running. Within a week or two we thought we would give it a real dry run by photographing a big awards parade in color as well as black & white. That same Friday there was an award ceremony in the General's office, so we shot that in color also. On Monday morning we processed the film and delivered color prints. From that point on we ran the color processing at full maximum and quite often 16 hours a day by putting on a night crew.

We had a great relation with the Kodak Tech Rep and always had free materials to experiment with and he would give us any training we wanted. We got to practice on products that were not even released to the public. One of the things we played with was an inter-negative film, but using it to copy with. The results we produced were fantastic. We also made many trips to Kodak in Rochester for special training at government expense.

Bert had some connections with a studio in downtown Washington and took the knowledge we had gained about the color lab and convinced them he could create a color lab for them. He had asked me on a couple occasions to give him a hand when they got a big job in.   The studio was the only one at the time to do color weddings and color commercial photography in Washington. One of the commercial jobs was for the Smithsonian and involved a painting of the Pony Express Rider. It was copied and the first two prints produced, the bill, as I remember, was $1200. I helped Bert on this job and the Smithsonian quickly reordered several hundred prints at five dollars each. Being aware of the costs to produce I was wondering what I was doing in the Military with all of this kind of money to be made. I still had four years to go on my enlistment.

My parents came to Arlington one time to visit and see the kids. It was great to have them since now my father had a car and would not mind driving. When my parents came to the house and we sat down for dinner, my mother was sitting with her back to the windows and facing a wall. I had hung some of my trophies, such as gazelles and a wart hog on the wall. My mother saw the wart hog and screamed and said that I had to take the hog down or she wasn't going to eat. We all laughed and I complied.

Hunting in Virginia

During the fall of 1960 I was in charge of the Photo Lab at Arlington Hall Station and one of the guys that worked for me wanted to go deer hunting in the hills of Virginia. He had never gone hunting before and begged me to put together a trip so he could go. He had his shotgun sent from home and the plan was on for the trip.

The time came and we finally did get up in the hills and in good hunting area past Front Royal. Up at dawn and into the woods I picked a spot and told him to just sit by the tree and keep his eyes open. I explained that I was going over on the other side of the valley. I had not been over there more than 45 minutes when I thought I heard a shot from the area he was in. I waited a few more minutes and thought, Heck, I better go check on him. I got back to where he was and he was standing over this nice buck. He said that hunting deer was easy. He explained that the deer just walked past him about 25 feet to the right and he just shot it. He was so excited he did not know what to do. Of course he knew nothing about cleaning the deer so I performed that and we called it a day.

Doing the newspaper

Bert had gotten out of the Army and I had been put in charge of the photo lab. The Post Sergeant Major came into the photo lab one day and asked if we could do some unofficial – official photography at the NCO club. He wanted to start a newspaper for the club and wanted to have some photographs in it and some of it would require after hour's work that we really did not have to do.

Of course being the powerful position I knew that he would be a good person to have as an ally. I told him not to worry we would do whatever he wanted. Besides I had some young photographers that were not allowed in the club, except on official duty. The Sgt. Maj. said the photographer could have free drinks while he was there and that alone created a lot of interest.

After a couple months the Sgt. Maj. came in complaining that the Print Shop was so busy they couldn't get the paper out on time for all of the official printing. We asked what the problem was and were told the typesetting was the problem. Dick and I both had previous printing experience so we told the Sgt. Maj. to get us a IBM Typesetter and we would get the typesetting and give it to the Print Shop "camera ready." The print shop liked the idea. We scored points there and the Sgt. Maj. was ecstatic. We could do no wrong around the base; we did not stand inspections or parades, thanks to the Sgt. Major. My High School printing classes were a big help.

During the time at Arlington Hall Station the photo lab prepared the photography such as slides, lanternslides and photographic prints for the ASA War room. With the knowledge we were able to get from Kodak and by trial and error, lots of errors too, we were able to vastly improve the quality of the visuals. The fact that we did not just throw things together like had been done in the past, but really cared, did a lot to score points with decision making people. We did a job called "ASA Today that had 90K duplicate slides required for the sets to be sent out.

When briefings were given to people like the Chairman of the Joint Chief of Staff those responsible for the war room wanted a first class job and we gave it to them.

Me taking photo of ASA Gen Craig welcomes JCS to Arlington Hall

Photo I got of them coming up steps – Gen Craig loved it

I remember there was one visit of the Chairman of the Joint Chiefs of Staff which I was photographing a reception at the Officers Club. Electronic flash units had just been issued to the military but on the 4x5 cameras but they still required a synchronization cord from the lens to the flash. These cords were always giving us trouble and most times I had a couple extra. I was taking a picture of the head table with the Chairman of the Joint Chiefs of Staff, the ASA General, along with his staff when it was obvious I had taken a photograph but NO flash.

I must have had a disgusted look on my face as I turned the camera sideways to change the cord. The ASA general asked me what was wrong and without thinking I said, "If the Army would buy good equipment we wouldn't have these problems." I put another cord on and took another photograph of the table and had no further problems that evening. When I realized what I had said, I expected to be called on the carpet and maybe even some disciplinary action. Nothing was ever said and maybe delivering the color photographs the next work day helped, I don't know.

My Official Army Photographers ID Card

Inspector General inspection of Photo Lab
One of the other funny things that happened was when we had an Inspector General inspection in the photo lab. The IG inspection meant "everything" had to be perfect or it literally could cause you to get busted. I had all of the guys working for two days on the photo lab, everything dusted, and everything neat and tidy. We had a few drinks in the two evenings while getting the place ready for inspection. One of the things we had was Vodka and Collins mix. We got the idea of putting

102

cherries in the ice cubes to have with the drinks. We had a refrigerator in the Photo Lab for chemicals that needed to be kept cool and to make ice to cool down some of the chemicals. We would put the cubes in a plastic bag and put the bag into the big tanks to cool down things since temperature was critical on some processes.

What we had forgotten to do was to use all of the ice cubes we had cherries frozen in. Luckily as we were being inspected the Post Sgt Major was the one that opened the refrigerator. He looked in the freezer and asked what we did with the ice cubes. Without thinking I said to cool down the chemicals. I looked past him and into the freezer and saw all the stems sticking up and about died. He leaned over to me and his words were quietly "too cool the chemicals my ass". He promptly shut the refrigerator and went on about his business with a grin on his face. We passed the inspection with flying colors – and really we were good at what we did. He was always an ally and I always made a point to do anything he wanted, even what to him seemed impossible. He never forgot those that helped him and in later years he was a blessing for me.

Throughout the next year Laura received the very best of care. Her feet looked normal and we were told that she would need corrective shoes and would be required to sleep with shoes on that had a bar between them. We knew approximately when she was going to be released permanently so it was time for me to call in some of the favors I had done. I wanted to go back to Asmara since I never got to hunt my elephant.

Getting things ready to go back overseas was a real project. We had made some great friends and the kids all had playmates they would be leaving but they were up to the adventure. They would look forward to the move back overseas.

I would miss things at Arlington Hall also because I had made friends, learned a lot creating the color photo lab and the work I had done in the ASA War Room. I had worked hard and the quality of the briefings had been one of my great concerns. If you make the boss look good he won't forget you. With all of the different types of photo stuff involved and the different wattage of the bulbs, getting it to all look normal really took some professionalism. There were slide projectors, lantern slide projectors, movie projectors and overhead projectors. All had different size originals and different wattage of output light. We were proud of the part we contributed and documented everything for other photographers to be able to reproduce the results in the future. Major McDonald was in charge of the War Room and appreciated the hard work.

Janice, Mary Beth, & Joy holding Laura

Chapter 9 – Back to Asmara

The policy in the military was that if you had one "accompanied" tour then the next would be by yourself where dependents could not go. Ah! But being a photographer and having a fistful of IOU's it was not difficult to "pull off" going back to Asmara. There really wasn't an opening for my MOS at the time but there would be someone returning to the states in a couple months and they would also say they were trying to fill that vacancy early. They guys in personnel used the excuse of "since we did not complete the first tour but came back on medical emergency, it did not apply". They cut my orders and some of the officers I had looked out for and helped by raising no objections.

Again, it always pays to set your goals, do whatever is necessary, work hard and you can accomplish it.

Dreams can come true.

After experiencing the long wait on the port call that my buddies at Ft Devens had arranged for my first tour, I really wanted to get back to Asmara this time without too much delay.

We got everything ready for shipment and our household goods picked up. We had bought a bright red big Ford station wagon to take over this time. So we were off for New York again and to turn in the car at Brooklyn Army Terminal, spend a night at Ft Hamilton just as we did the first time.

Our trip over this time was on a Boeing 707 and only took us seven hours to get to Frankfurt. We made connections with the Ethiopian Airlines and headed for Athens, Cairo and Asmara with just short stops. We had been gone from Asmara a year and a half and they finished the construction of longer runways. We cleared customs and again headed for the Hamasien Hotel to spend the time drawing Per Diem. With our having been in Asmara before it was like "coming home." We went to the Top 5 club for meals and most all of the waiters were the still there. There were also several people that we knew before we left and it was easy to make new friends.

Arrive at Kagnew Station –
Asmara, Eritrea Second Tour

When I checked into the Headquarters Company and the photo lab I found that the lab had changed a lot since I left. There was not really the caring that I had in the lab. Sgt. Deemer was running the lab and he had many years in grade as the same rank as me. He had just gotten there so I could see there was not much chance of being NCOIC again.

While we were gone from Kagnew Station the hunting scene had changed drastically. Shortly after we had left the base closed the hunting because of the revolution fearing a GI would get killed. There were a few hunting trips allowed in certain areas but not too many. I thought this was the pits since that was why I wanted to come back so bad. It did not take long to find the guys interested in hunting and at least sport shooting.

We stayed in the hotel long enough to get our full Per Diem and found a house that was brand new after we were there about 45 days. We went ahead and rented it and took our time moving in. The house had a perfect setup for a darkroom in addition to maid's quarters. We wanted to find our beloved guard dog, Duke and I finally tracked him down with a family that was going back to the states in a couple months. They said we could have the dog back for sure. When we went to see him at the GI's house I know he recognized us, especially Janice that he had played so much with. We tracked down Willie again to be our houseboy but had a different maid than we had when we left the first time.

Rod & Gun Club

I helped get a Rod & Gun club started and met a couple guys that would be lifelong friends. Captain Barry Ross was in charge of Quartermaster and some of his responsibilities were ordering ammo for the base as well as gasoline and much more. Brian Britton was a cook in the mess hall and a SP5 also. Colonel Beimfohr was the Post Judge Advocate and really looked forward to hunting and was instrumental in helping get the club started. Since it was a Rod & Gun club we talked about buying all kinds of things that the PX did not carry or could not be bought on the local economy. When we had our first meeting I was selected to be the Club Treasurer. We all voted for small dues so that we would start small clubs store

106

and mark the items up 10% above all of the costs including freight.

I wrote to every company that I could find in the magazines and in a month the catalogs started coming in. I remember we had maybe a hundred dollars in the bank from dues and I had made an order for several hundred dollars worth of shell holders from a company named Herter's. They had given us credit and just shipped the items. When I mentioned it to the Colonel that I had ordered them he blew a gasket because we didn't have the money to pay for them. I said I would float the note but I was sure I was going to sell them. We had a meeting scheduled in a week or so and at the time of the meeting I already had those sold and had orders for more. I was vindicated and pretty much left alone to do all the ordering. It took about five or six weeks for items to come in so we always had multiple orders on the way from the same suppliers.

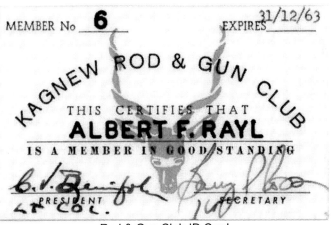

Rod & Gun Club ID Card

At the building we had acquired over on the old base (Tract A) we set up a place to reload bullets and had all of our supplies. Captain Ross (Barry) was in charge of ordering ammunition for the base and said he would see what he could do. We found out there were certain types of military ammo that we could use the powder from for our high powered rifles. One of the types of powder that was especially good was in 20mm cannon shells. Barry ordered a bunch of 20mm cannon shells. There wasn't even a 20mm cannon anywhere near Kagnew Station but we got the ammo and extracted the powder. Powder was always hard to get.

Sometimes we would get some of the Air Force to bring in powder for us. I sent an order one time to a company in Kansas for 25 pounds of powder and they sent it in the mail in a cardboard drum. I carried it in and showed it to the Colonel and he got excited. He said he didn't know there was an Air Force plane in. I said it came in the mail and I thought I was going to have to pick him up off the floor. I told him that I ordered it but didn't specify the shipping method, which should have been by sea. Anyhow, after he got his breath and said we were all going to jail, he wanted to know how much I had already sold because he wanted his share.

Rod and Gun Club patch I designed and had made for club

A trip to Aden

Being in the Photo Lab had so many "perks" and opportunities. One Thursday the MAAG (Military Assistance and Advisory Group) aircrew came to Kagnew Station from Addis. They were required to get "night certified" in their flying every 90 days. When that was due the crew would fly their plane from Asmara to Aden way down on the bottom of the Red Sea where it meets the Indian Ocean. The plane was a five passenger Beech aircraft. I indicated that I wanted to go with them and they were happy to oblige. We were scheduled to leave right after work on Friday and come back Saturday afternoon.

The pilot, an Army Captain, was from Fairmont, WV and that gave us something in common since many of my relatives were from that area as well as my being born nearby. He looked like he belonged in a commercial for the military. He was slim, had starched Khakis that fit perfectly and just looked the part. The co-pilot was a First Lieutenant. We took off just as the sun went down. We headed out towards the Red Sea and in only a few minutes it was dark.

At the time I had not learned about flying so some of what they said really didn't mean an awful lot to me. As we headed South down the middle of the Red Sea the Captain stated that there were no navigational signals to fly by so they would just fly South watching the lights on both sides of the Red Sea. This was literally flying by the "seat of your pants." He stated that when we got near Aden there would be a radio signal to home in on and find the airport. Now that I am also a pilot I understand the significance of their training.

Aden is located almost on the Equator and we arrived at almost midnight. The pilot wanted to make a couple "touch and goes" (landing and continuing to take-off again) and let the co-pilot make a couple also. After that was done we parked the plane and got a ride into town. Even though it was almost midnight it was so hot we immediately were wet with sweat. I mentioned that a beer would sure taste good and the Captain said that was where we were headed.

We went to a place he knew that was up on the outside top floor and about five stories up. We sat and had a couple beers that were Liter bottles and cold. After four or five apiece the barmaid came and said they were closing. The Captain ordered a bunch to go and we all picked up three or four apiece and the Captain a half dozen. He was drinking about one and a half to our one all evening long. We went to their room and sat and told stories and drank the rest of the beer. About 2:30 or 3 in the morning we all headed for bed. At 6 am the door was banging and I went and the Captain was standing there saying to get up and get moving it was time to eat and go shopping. He looked like he had never had anything to drink and was standing there in a nice starched uniform looking like a Recruitment Poster. The three of us that went on the flight were so hung over but we got up, showered and dressed. We had a quick breakfast and then went to the local markets and shopped. I bought some Oriental Brocade material for a dress that was very inexpensive and less than a dollar a yard. It would have sold in the states for more than ten dollars a yard.

When the shopping was done it was about noon and time to head to the airport. The sun had been burning for a good while now and it was really HOT. We got to the airport and opened the door to the plane and it was hot enough inside to cook a pizza in just a couple minutes. The heat was also bringing up the beer from the night before. The sweat was rolling down all of us and the Captain finally looked normal since his starched khakis were wet too.

We got in the plane and I immediately said to turn on the air-conditioning. There was no air-conditioning since the higher you went the cooler it became. We took off from Aden and it took a while to climb to just under 10,000 feet where it was cool. Had we flown back up the Red Sea and being daylight we could see everything on both sides. It was a pretty good flight but I was still having trouble with the beer. I asked for a barf bag and was told there wasn't any onboard. The next couple hours were really hard but as soon as we landed and got out of the plane I upchucked and finally felt normal again. It had been an experience. I thought I was a pretty fair beer drinker but the Captain was the supreme best.

Getting Promoted to E-6
After I had been at Kagnew station almost a year I knew there was no chance of getting promoted in the photo lab since the MOS was frozen, Sgt. Deemer would have gotten the promotion anyway because of seniority. I mentioned the lack of promotion to the Colonel, and he asked me what other experience I had, when I told him administration he said "come to work for me and I will get you promoted", so I did. It seemed that his staff NCO was getting ready to return to the states. In less than 60 days I was promoted to SP6 (E6). Being a hunting friend and a friend in the Rod & Gun Club always gave Colonel Beimfohr and me something to talk about.

Gearing up for a lot of Hunting
Col Beimfohr had gone on a hunting trip into Sudan during the fall of 1960 while I was back in the US. The one thing he did

not get was a lion or elephant. The more we talked the more we thought we should organize another trip into Sudan. As we promoted the trip throughout the R&G club, Captain Ross (Barry) was interested and said to count him in. CWO Howard Riley and CPO Freddie Ray committed to going to Sudan also. So this rounded out what we would need to mount a trip.

I had purchased a jeep from the salvage yard, as I had done on my first trip to Asmara. Barry and Howie (as we called Howard) had WWII jeeps. Freddie Ray had a fairly new commercial CJ-5 jeep. So the planning started in the spring of 1962 for a fall trip to Sudan. I had been back to Asmara less than six months and was already putting this big trip together.

When Barry was confident that I knew my way around the country we started going on short weekend excursions (to hunt) in areas that I knew. Of course the hunting was closed officially but that did not keep us from pushing the limits. There were a few legal trips that I also got involve in.

One of the most amusing was on a trip I was invited to go on with the Post Finance Officer, the Personnel Officer, the Post Sergeant Major and a couple others. We went on a legal weekend hunting trip to an area North of Cheren. This area was known for having a lot of greater Kudu as well as baboon, wart hogs and gazelle. I think one of the reasons I was invited was my knowledge of hunting areas and being able to help with natives and guides. This was quite a turn around from my very first hunting experience. I had learned how to play the politics of the villages and keep safe in the areas. After we arrived in camp on Friday evening we went out and looked for some baboons and probably shot 40 or 50 of them. When I was around 12-14 we used to go to the dump and shoot rats. Baboons are pests and just about the same as shooting rats but over in Eritrea, they can literally wipe out a banana plantation in a few days.

On Saturday morning everyone got up and had a good breakfast and went out to find some pigs or gazelle. We hunted till about 11am and came back to camp for some coffee, a snack and a little rest. Everyone else wanted to go hunt some more and I said I thought I would just hang around camp. One of the guides did not go with the rest of the group either and just stayed in camp. After they had been gone about a half hour I said to the guide "let's go" and we started walking towards the mountains which were about three fourths of a mile away. When we got to the base of the mountain I communicated to the guide that I wanted to find a Kudu. I knew about, as much of the area as he did but a second pair of eyes was always good. We started up the mountain carefully in a valley where we had two sides to look for the elusive Kudu. We had not gone maybe a half-mile working our way up the mountain when I saw a good bull Kudu. Naturally emotions got the best of me and with one shot he was dead.

We were in a valley and the shot made a lot of noise with its echo. We cleaned the Kudu and some other natives came and we gave them the meat, with the promise they would save some for the guide. We skinned the head and skull and hid it in a tree and headed back to camp. When we got back to camp a couple of the guys had already gotten back. One of them was a Captain that asked what I had been up to, and my response was just out checking the territory. His response was "my ass you shot a Kudu." I tried to play dumb and stupid and act like since you couldn't even get a permit to shoot one, "why would I shoot something like that." The rest of the guys got back soon and also had heard the shot up on the mountain, and their first words were "how big is it." Again I played dumb and the post Sergeant Major got me too finally 'fess up. I told him the horns and head were in a tree and he said, "Let's go get them" and we did. The rest of the weekend everyone was envious of my kill and there was not going to be a problem since they had all been known to shoot something they shouldn't shoot also.

When we departed camp on Sunday we stopped by the R&R center in Cheren. I don't know who it was that said something but soon the word was all around the center that someone shot a Kudu. The guy that ran the R&R center was going to go up the mountain for supplies for the R&R center in a jeep with a trailer and 500 pound ice chest. He said wait until he had been gone about half-hour and if anyone was to get stopped it would be him.

We left Cheren with our jeeps, trailers and with the Kudu horns and skin under the seat. We got to within ten miles of Kagnew Station when we rounded the corner and there was the jeep and the guy that ran the R&R center stopped by the Ethiopian Game department. He motioned us to go around him and not stop, then somewhat yelled "get to the base." We headed off on the road and after we had gone maybe a half a mile we could see the Game Department coming up after us. We drove as fast as we could and when we pulled into the main gate the Post Sergeant Major told the MP at the gate not to let them on the base. We went and dumped the Kudu horns and skin, and went to the Sgt. Maj.'s house and put the meat on the floor under his bed, tipped the ice chest up and rinsed it out with a hose and drove back to the main gate. This took no more than ten minutes. We played dumb and pretended when the MP called us back to the main gate we showed the Game department there was nothing in our 500-pound ice chest. They somewhat scratched their heads and knew we had outsmarted them but could do nothing about it. This was funnier than the Keystone Cops movies.

The post Sergeant Major took the meat over to the Top 5 club after retrieving from under his bed. His wife wondered what was going on, and when she found out she thought it was as hysterical as the rest of us. We laughed over it at the Top 5 club for many a day. There were many officers and enlisted that wanted to go hunting with me since I knew the good areas. There were only a few other people still left at the base that knew good hunting areas and how to work with the natives.

Chapter 10 – 26 Hours in the Red Sea

This was the Document concerning a Fishing trip prepared for the Military by Sp5 Albert F. Rayl, typed as it was with corrections in spelling or grammar.

On Saturday 5 May 62 PFC Donald M. Findlay and PFC Maxwell Duckett and myself, were at the boat dock in Massawa to take a boat for a weekend of fishing on Dissei Island. We loaded the boat while an Eritrean fixed a frozen shift lever. In the meantime I went to the rack behind the storage chest and got three life jackets. I called Duckett for a hand to carry them.

We got under way about 0900 and went across the bay to the South shore where we fished. Along the way we passed a school of fish just rolling over the top. I mentioned that if we were going to catch fish, now would be the time. Just then Duckett landed about a 14-inch Bonita. We trolled around the shore toward the point and just then something hit Duckett's line hard. I stopped the run of the fish by grabbing the line. Findlay took over the motor and I played the fish for Duckett. It was out almost a full reel. I landed him in about 20 min. It was a big Tuna probably 18 pounds. With no more big fish hitting we went on to the point. I had taken over the motor again after landing the fish.

We stayed about 300 yards from shore all the way to the point. We passed the point and proceeded to the island. The water was just as smooth as a tabletop and the motor was running fine. We came toward the North end of the Island so we could fish the length of it on the West Side. When we arrived we saw a large group of people swimming from a WWII landing craft about 100 yards from shore. We turned south, with Findlay driving and stayed in just about 15-25 feet of water. We started landing fish as fast as we could pull them in. After a while Duckett took the motor and we rounded the South end of the Island. The winds came up and I took over the controls and we put in at our destination, the second inlet.

I cleaned fish while Duckett and Findlay looked for a good campsite. They found a place up on shore about 100 yards. We went up with the necessary items for supper. We got to the island about 1300 or 1330 and it was now about 1430. I cooked eggs and bacon for Duckett and myself. Findlay fixed his the way he had wanted, with onions. Then we all lay down and slept for a while. Duckett got up and went to look around the island and he came back just before dark.

Our camp was over run by ants so we slept that night on the beach. At dawn, Sunday we started out in calm seas and when we rounded the Southern tip the wind came up so we put into shore. About 0845 we started out again. The sea had calmed a lot and we were headed toward the point on the main land. After about 45 min the motor started to run rough. Just then a big cabin cruiser came near. We had seen them earlier about 0830 while we were on the land and I had watched them stop while someone landed a fish. We signaled them to come near. We waived shirts at them and Duckett fired his pistol in the air. They were then about 50 yards away. I could see Sgt. Mohr and he waived for us to go toward the main land, the way we were going and nearly halfway there. They took off North through the waves, which had come up but were not too bad. The waves were a couple of feet, but not more than three feet. While the motor was running good the waves were no problem. In fact on a trip previous with Whispell and Britton we encountered five to six-foot waves and I brought it in with no trouble.

While the cabin cruiser was going away we put on the life jackets and poured the extra gas and water over the side to lighten the boat. As the cabin cruiser got out of sight the motor stopped and we had no control over the boat. The waves filled the boat and then the boat turned over at 0950. We all went over the side and we all clung to the bottom of the boat.

After a while we saw another small boat about a mile North with an outboard. The boat looked to be about the same size as ours but our efforts to get attention failed. We lost track of time, Duckett's watch stopped at about 1600. We were situated with me on the rear right, Findlay on the bow and Duckett on the rear left. I tried to ride the bow but they couldn't balance the boat. The person on the bow could sit and the others had to lie. Duckett seemed to have a hard time trying to keep his head out of the water, so he and Findlay changed positions. Sometime while adrift we tried to turn the boat over but we

116

couldn't get it high enough in the rear to clear the water. We did manage to take the oar from under the seat and I saw Duckett's gun and put it under the floorboards. Then we turned the boat bottom up and took up positions again. We unhooked the anchor and started to drift faster as we helped it along in a somewhat swimming position.

At dusk we were headed toward mainland and we continued kicking and swimming to push the boat toward shore. Several times we got close to shore that night since we could hear the waves on the beach. We could keep our bearing by the lights of Massawa. It was a dark night but when we got pretty close to shore we could see the outline of the mountain. We drifted south all night and by dawn Monday, 7 May we were about 1½ miles from shore, way south of the mountain. We tried all morning and couldn't get the boat closer than about 1 mile to shore.

As near as we could tell it was about 1100 and we left the boat and swam to shore about one mile. We all started to hold the oar and swim with one hand but could not make any progress so we all let go and went it on our own. Duckett reached shore North of Findlay and I hit shore about ½ mile South. I then walked to a tree where Findlay and Duckett were taking cover. As soon as I got under the tree the sun came out really bright. We lay on the life jackets because of the thorns.

After a while we started to get thirsty. Duckett said he would go and look for some water. After he had been gone for quite a while Findlay and I thought maybe he had found a village we knew was North of us and, because of the heat, was waiting for the sun to start to go down. Findlay had lost his shoes when the boat went over so I told him to walk along the water and I would track Duckett by following his footprints. He had rippled soled shoes that made tracks easy to see.

Findlay and I had put our life jackets over our heads to protect us from the sun. I also had Duckett's over my head because Findlay said it would be too much for him. Duckett had been wearing a police hat and I had a fatigue hat. We draped the life jackets over us and started out. We had gone about two miles; I had been keeping an eye on Findlay. He stopped under a big tree near the shore and waved and I walked to him. I had been about 75 yards from the beach. I laid down on the lifejackets with only my under pants on so that T-shirt and pants could dry out. Soon Duckett came. He said he never reached a village but he had gotten water from a woman and she mentioned that a village was not too far off. He also got water at an overnight camp of some natives. They still had their belongings there. The camp was about 100 yards from the tree. He came with the water and we strained it through Duckett's long sleeved shirt three times and drank some. We were waiting for it to get dark so we could start to walk back to Massawa.

Since I was the ranking enlisted person on the trip, the others were my responsibility. I knew the area we were in very well from having hunted in it many times. My thought and plan was to walk the shoreline till we reached what we called "the point" then get on the road. I knew exactly where the road was but it was hardly traveled and would be hot. I wanted to do the traveling at night while cool and take cover during the day. I figured we could make it close enough during the night to get to where there would be some traffic on the road.

We were going to walk the shoreline so we might see a search party by day. At about 1600 the plane came down the coast and we were spotted. After they circled us a few times it left, but we knew it had seen us so we knew to stay put. We remained there and about an hour and a half later we saw a big ship come toward us. They anchored and sent a dinghy in after us. I got dressed and put on my life jacket. We got to the ship (PC11) of the Ethiopian Navy and as soon as I climbed aboard I started to the bridge where the captain was standing. I took off my life jacket and laid it on a hatch near the engine room door. We talked for a minute and they took us to the galley for some food. We were given water, spaghetti, bread, meat and tea. They treated us like kings. Then we were shown to some bunks. We all stripped off our clothes that had gotten wet from the ride in the dinghy. I took the top bunk, Findlay the middle and Duckett the lower bunk.

We had gotten on the ship at approx. 1740 and arrived at the dock at approx. 2000. We were given tea, bread, butter and honey and told we would have transportation soon to the R&R center. We arrived there and were met by Lt. Col. Hackwood and Maj. Bridges. We were instructed to shower if we could

118

stand it then we were given a quick checkup by a local Italian doctor and told we were in surprisingly good shape but to check in to the hospital at Kagnew Station in the morning. After all of us showered we sat in the dining room bar and Findlay and I drank a lot of tomato juice with vodka. I don't remember what Duckett had but it was a soft drink. We came up the hill Tuesday and came to the hospital.

I might add that without life jackets we wouldn't have made it. The waves Sunday night got six to eight feet and we had a hard time holding on. During that night everyone kept each other awake by talking and yelling "Is Everyone Awake." I would also like to add that at no time did we panic. This too would have meant disaster. We were real scared the first few minutes before we realized what must be done. I have been told that the boat has been recovered but that the motor was not on it. I don't know how the motor could have come off because when we left Massawa I tied the motor to a tie down ring on the left rear. I tied it with a 3/8" anchor rope. All the time we were with the boat the motor stayed on. I even sat on the leg of the motor during the night and it was solid. However had it come loose the rope would have held it. The boat seemed to drift southeast toward shore when we left it. I doubt if the boat hit shore more than four or five miles from where we did.
ALBERT F. RAYL – RA 23497416 – SP5, Hq Co

My buddy Brian Britton was at the R&R center in Massawa and drove us up the mountain in my car. On the way up the mountain he said the military had told my wife there was no hope of finding us alive and she should prepare for the worse. Findlay and myself checked into the hospital as instructed. Duckett said he felt good and was going back to the company. We had not been in the hospital beds more than 30 minutes when all of our muscles tightened up so much we could hardly move. The nurse came and made us get up to go to the latrine.

About an hour after we were in the hospital, here comes Duckett. We asked him what was up and he said when he got back to the company the first sergeant told him there was 9000 pounds of mail and since he felt good he should "get on it." Right away he said he did not feel too good and headed for the hospital. Within 30 minutes of getting in bed he couldn't move. The nurses made us get up and move around and as we were moving we felt pretty good but as soon as we lay back down the muscles tightened up again. This went on for a couple days.

I had a blister across the center of my back about six by ten inches. The doctors didn't want to break it for fear of infection, but finally my being on my back broke it and with antibiotics I never had any trouble. We finally got out of the hospital and I was back at home. Findlay and Duckett lived in the Barracks. Findlay was assigned to the Photo Lab and Duckett was the lead mail clerk.

Another amusing thing about this venture at sea was the powers to be from the base had set up a command center in front of the CIAAO hotel which was the R&R center in Massawa. The plane that had seen us was a MAAG (Military Assistance and Advisory Group). We thought they notified the boat to come and get us. They had not but did notify the command center and they sent out a search party that promptly got lost for two days due to their inexperience of hunting and knowing the area.

Again it proves that with the help of the Lord and your own determination you can accomplish unimaginable goals. We were still alive.

A couple weeks later I went back out to the Island with Lee Ruebush but we used his own private motor that was a good one. While out on that trip Lee hooked a big grouper that went under some coral. The water was so clear we thought it was only four or five feet deep. Lee thought he would step out of the boat and poke the grouper with his spear gun. The plan was then as the grouper ran, for me to land it. Lee stepped over the side and it was about twenty feed deep. He came up coughing and gagging and asked for his flippers. He went down and when he poked the grouper I landed him with the hundred pound test line. It was about 30 to 35 pounds of good eating. Other than that the trip was uneventful, but Lee was insistent that I go back out to the Island or he said I might be so hurt as to never go near the water.

Chapter 11 – Hunting Trip to Sudan

Planning the Trip

We were getting more and more serious about our trip to Sudan and decided to have some formal meetings. Trying to now remember all of the details can be hard for someone getting older. Luckily I haven't gotten old yet and remember a lot about the trip. I even found the paper that I wrote from my notes when we got back. I kept a notebook on the trip and when we got back I typed them out and stuck them in my safety box. The trip was quite an experience. As I look back on it now had anything happened to us, no one would have ever found us. The area of Sudan we were in was truly unexplored by "whites". Some of the natives had never seen a white man.

We started planning the trip in May of 1962 and had meetings at my house most of the time. The meetings consisted of planning the parts needed for the vehicles, the food we would need, how much gas, how much salt for hides, and who would be responsible for what. I was appointed Treasurer for the trip. As I remember we had monthly meetings. Colonel Beimfohr had made a trip the year before and it had cost him around $1800. Being appointed Treasurer I was determined to make it cost less. The Colonel was on a previous trip where they had to buy everything.

During the first meeting at my house the Colonel immediately said we all needed to put up five or six hundred dollars each for needed supplies. I said there was a lot of time (about six months) before we would be going and no need to have the money just sitting. The Colonel was pretty adamant since he had been there before and he said it cost him $1800 for the trip. I suggested we postpone putting up any money for a couple months and I got Freddie Ray, Barry and Howard Riley to be of the same opinion, so we held off on putting in money.

With a good friend, Bryan Britton working in the Mess Hall I knew we could come up with a lot of the food. Later on Bryan also had the idea that if he took five gallons of gas a day, every day including weekends from the duce 'n-half that ran to the receiver site, no one would be the wiser. He brought it over to the house and we dumped it in some 55-gallon drums I had acquired. He also started bringing us some canned supplies and items that would keep.

As time went on from May thru the end of October I had accumulated a lot of food in my garage and some 350 gallons of gas but I had not said a word to anyone, not even one of my best friends Barry. The Colonel kept insisting at every meeting that we needed to put some money in the "kitty" and I did my best to play down the idea without saying anything about what I was accumulating. Finally it got to be such a heated thing that I broke down and said OK let's all kick in $125 and that should be enough. The Colonel came unglued and said we wouldn't even get out of the country with that little, he said we needed food, gas etc.

I made the comment that I had been accumulating some materials and we might not need as much as everyone thought. I asked everyone to follow me and we went to my garage, which had seven of the 55-gallon drums full of gas, footlockers and boxes of food and some cots and items I had scrounged. Upon seeing what I had accumulated he damn near wet his pants. I said I had things under control and as far as I knew the only thing we would have to buy would be the Wyler's Lemon-aid for the water to make it drinkable after using Clorox for purification. I made mention I had made arrangements for bread, eggs and perishables to be ready as needed. Other than that most everything on our shopping list was in the garage. When I showed everyone the food and other stuff the Colonel said, "We're all going to jail." I said don't worry, it's all right.

Barry, being the Quartermaster officer asked how I had come by the gas. When I explained we had gotten five gallons each day, every day he made the comment that they checked trip tickets and since it was every day they would have just thought the vehicle was using that much. He really felt kind of snookered on the whole deal.

We went back into the house and it was agreed that we would each put in only $125 since now there was not a lot we needed. So with five of us going we had a nest egg of $625. Pretty soon the doorbell rang and I scooped up the money and went and answered the gate. I came back with a handful of money

122

in Sudanese Pounds. Barry asked what had happened and I mentioned that I had arranged with Gus to exchange the money at a rate of three for one. That meant than now we had $1875 (US) worth of money in Sudanese pounds. The Colonel said "hell I have been trying to catch Gus for a year and a half." I said "well he was right here a few minutes ago" and we all laughed and had another beer.

We now had plenty of funds to make the trip to Sudan. Now the only obstacle was getting the final permission. Having the Post Judge Advocate on the trip would have a lot of influence with the Ethiopian and Sudanese governments that we were "good upstanding military citizens that would do no wrong."

We wanted to go into southern central Sudan and on the outskirts of a game reserve. It was far into Sudan that would take about five days of driving at a rate of 14 to 18 hours a day. It was an area near, but not the same, as the Colonel had gone the year before. One of the problems for us was that the time we wanted to go was at the end of the rainy season.

Sudan is divided into to racial territories. The northern half is called White Sudan and the bottom half is called Black Sudan. There was and is a very strong resentment of the south by the politicians of the north.

There are areas where the natives of Sudan had never seen a White person and we were going to go into some of these areas. Looking back at this trip if anything unfortunate had happened to us it is possible we would have never been found.

A Little Local Hunting while waiting to go to SUDAN
Some of us kept on doing our own hunting in a couple of my favorite and secret hunting areas. In particular there was no one left at Kagnew Station, other than one other friend that even knew the place existed, let along how to get to it. Barry and I use to sneak off and do a little hunting in the area past Decamere. It was easy to slip out of town that direction since most people thought of the good hunting north and west of Cheren or east towards the Massawa area. We could slip out of town and no one was the wiser. Coming back we just looked like guys that were out for a ride. Usually we just took one jeep but once in a while we took two jeeps.

My buddy Barry Ross with a Dik-Dik shot in my secret hunting area

I was careful who I took into that area and made them promise not to go, unless it was with me, or take anyone else into the area. I never had anyone fail to live up to their word.

I shot this small wart hog with my Ruger 357 magnum

On one hunting trip down in the area we were hunting at night, one of the farmers cows accidentally got killed while we were shooting at something else. My native friends sent me a message of what happened, since we had not known it

124

accidentally got killed. The very next weekend we went to Decamere and talked to the local chief of police and he started giving me a story about how many generations that cow would produce and how much it was worth. I told him I had been around many years and that the cow was worth $200 and that was all we had, take it or leave it. I don't know how much he got out of it, but he smiled shook hands and all was well. No one ever knew about the cow or that we had been hunting without permission.

My jeep and the gang that shot the cow at night

Back to the Sudan Trip

As time got closer we didn't get our permission to leave, but the Colonel stepped in using his position and got us on the way. These are the events as I wrote them some 40 years ago. We had two WWII jeeps, mine and Howard's, one M-38 Korean vintage of Barry's and one nearly new CJ5 jeep. It was the CJ5 that was a lot of trouble since parts were not interchangeable with the others. All of us arranged to get spare parts for our jeeps. The old WWII jeeps were easy to get parts for since I had friends in the motor pool that I held IOU's on and with Barry being the Quartermaster and also in charge of a vehicle repair facility he could also get parts.

Each of us equipped our vehicles with a dual gas tank. Normally on the WWII & Military jeeps the gas tank is under the driver's seat and we got fuel tanks for the passenger side, to go under the seat, and with a valve so we could easily switch tanks. Also we mounted gas can holders on the jeeps so we could each carry about 40-50 gallons per jeep.

We carried extra fuel pumps, starters, belts, and spark plugs, carburetors, hoses and other items. I also modified a WWII carbine holder to fit my 243 Winchester (with Scope) and mounted it just behind the fender and up the side along the windshield line. This meant I could just release it and have it ready to fire.

We had modified our jeeps so we had a tubular steel frame from behind the driver and passenger side and back to the back end. The top covered up to the windshield, but wasn't hooked to it. This way we could put the windshield down and still have a canvas top to keep us out of the sun. The sun in Africa is so bright because of no pollution and we had to be careful.   Freddie with his CJ5 had to order parts from Sears so his took some long-term planning. The problem we would later find out was there were several different fuel pumps for the year model he had.

We had made the arrangements for getting salt for drying the skins. We had 300 Kilo (660 pounds) which we bought for nearly nothing, since Eritrea dries salt from the Red Sea. Camel caravans have traveled from Eritrea to the Sahara for centuries and salt was once used as money.

Barry all packed and ready to head for my house to head out to Sudan

126

Our trip finally got to the point of "go – no go" and lots of calling the Sudan Consulate pleading with them to get our papers approved which had been submitted months earlier. All of us had scheduled leaves and done so much planning that we finally thought we needed to do something drastic. So with a call to the Consulate we said we were on our way to pick up the papers and kind of hung up before they could say anything. We figured if they saw us all packed and ready they would issue the visas that we needed and we could get on our way. There was so much work already in this venture we needed to go. So we packed the vehicles, and were planning heading off directly from their consulate. Our families followed us to the consulate. They would say goodbye from there when we left. It never entered our military minds that we could meet any kind of unforeseen problem that might keep us from ever coming home to our families.

Our jeeps packed and ready to go in front of the Sudanese Consulate
Our families came, on the right, to say good-bye if we did get to go.

The trip went something like this from the notes I had.

23 November 1962 – As required by the military we all had to sign out of our units for our 30-day leave around 4pm. We departed Kagnew Station and proceeded to the Sudan Consulate at 1700 hrs. After long pleading and promise to go only as far as Tesseni, Ethiopia (the border town) we got approval. At 1900 hrs we departed for Cheren, first stop. There were military regulations that stated we were not to be on a road "after dark", but since we had signed out at a time that would have let us get to our first stop by dark we felt like we could do it. Also we had the Post JA with us. We arrived at the Cheren R&R center at 2115 hrs, already dark. We were sure there would be no problem from the Shifties since they knew my vehicle and may remember Barry's. We ate, drank cold beer and went to bed. We had a native from Asmara with us named Fadoul. His job was to be cook and camp boy. He also spoke the Arabic language we needed and we had used him, along with Abe, on a lot of local trips.

24 November 1962. - Up at 0300 hrs and ate light breakfast that Dillinger (club steward) left for us since we could not con him into getting up and fixing a hot breakfast. We were on the road at 0330 for Tesseni via Agordat. Shortly after leaving Cheren the road turns into a gravel road but a decent road with lots of dust. It was decided to keep a quarter mile space between jeeps and each was to make sure there was a jeep behind them. That way if anyone had a problem, we would all stop. We made the drive to Agordat in 1-½ hrs while still dark. Driving when dark is the thing. Then we were on to Barentu, the next town of any size, after coffee on the road. Thermos is a must for a trip like this and we had filled it at the R&R center. We made Barentu at 0730 hrs. Vehicles were all running good so far.

Then off for Tesseni and the Ethiopian and Sudan Border. We made Tesseni at 1000 hrs, which had been 6-½ hours of hard driving. After talking with the Sudan Consulate in Asmara by phone we decided to call Kassala in the Sudan, just across the border, to see if approval is there. It was and we returned a call to Sudan Consulate and informed them. We got the clearance to go on to Kassala. We left Tesseni at 1300 hrs Tesseni time (1200 hrs) Kassala time. We stopped and made all check points with ease.

All of our jeeps at the Eritrean border crossing checkpoint into Sudan

We arrived at Kassala at 1350 hrs Kassala time. Sudan customs was still open and Immigration came to customs to clear us.

After waiting in the customs yard and filling out required papers we needed a cold Camel beer. Cleared everything at 1530 hrs and made social call on Commissioner of Police. Then we were off to find a cold Camel beer. Rayl and Ray bought swords and Rayl bought a knife. About 1700 hrs we started down the road for Gedaref. Made camp after 1-½ hrs drive since all of us were really getting tired from the stress and the hard driving. The road was in pretty good shape for a dirt road, no gravel here just a lot of dust. We ate bacon and eggs for supper and all in bed by 2100 hrs.

25 November 1962 – Up at 0530 hrs to hot coffee that Fadoul had ready for us. We ate bacon and eggs again for breakfast since the bread and eggs would not last too long without having a big ice chest. This was a luxury we could not afford so we had a few army insulated Mermite cans. We got up and were on the road at 0630 after loading vehicles. We headed southwest on toward Gedaref.

We stopped at Setete river police station as we had been instructed to do. We were told to stop at EVERY police station and they would give us permission to go forward. We were getting a little bit of a hard time by the police until I took out the Polaroid camera and made a couple B&W shots. We gave the

Police Chief a photo and it was a big success. I had brought a Polaroid camera from the photo lab and 80 rolls of film.

The Setete River at the police station was fairly deep but luckily there was a railroad bridge there and that is how vehicles crossed the river. We would use railroad bridges several more times on the trip.

Me and jeep coming across the railroad bridge

All through this trip the way we navigated was to go in the direction of camel paths. When we found a native we would ask them the correct direction to whatever town or village we were headed for. Some areas did not have even a camel path, especially after we had crossed a railroad bridge. The natives would point in a direction and we would faithfully drive that heading until we came to the next native. We found the directions were really very good, as long as we had Fadoul who spoke fluent Arabic and could translate for us.

We did take time to wash off some of the dust in the river. We continued on to Gedaref and made Gedaref at 1330 hrs. Got gas since this was the last gas heading south. We had to have enough gas to get back to this point on the return. We then checked with police, which took a long time since the police commissioner was playing tennis of all things. We needed some more Camel beer since we thought this might be the last of it. Being treasurer this was to come out of the kitty. It has been a Hot ride in all of the dust and of course no baths for a couple days.

Fadoul pumping gas into my gas drums

Finally got out of Gedaref at 1645 hrs and headed down the road. Went about one hour and made camp, too much beer. After eating bacon and eggs again the Colonel looked up into Barry's jeep and asked where his rifle was. When we went into the bar to get the beer Barry had his rifle with him and leaned it against the bar. Barry forgot his 8mm rifle in Gedaref and the decision was made that Barry had to go back and get his rifle, and bring more beer while at it. He had to pound on the door of the bar, since people have their homes in the back of their business. His rifle had not been touched; it was still in exactly the same spot. All of us were in bed by 2100 hrs after fixing a few of the bunks, which had broken. Barry arrives with beer and rifle in middle of the night.

26 November 1962 – Up at 0430 hrs and ate breakfast on the road (Spam sandwich) at 0600 hrs. We headed toward Mafaza. Arrived at Mafaza and Rayl took pictures with the Polaroid for some chain and material made into clothes "while-u-wait". Polaroid camera is worth its weight in gold. Everyone wanted a photo and the black & white film was ten seconds and done. I had to limit the photos for only the stuff we really wanted to trade for. On down the road for Howata, road is getting worse. Rayl had a flat. Made Howata at 1000 hrs, gassed up, had flat fixed and bought necessary water bags.

While driving on a camel and cattle path I came to a wide spot in the road and all of the sudden I was chest deep in dust. Instinctively I reached down into the jeep and got it into four-wheel drive, kept my foot on the gas and went maybe 15 feet and came up a slope and out of the fine dust like talcum powder.

During WWII there were many reports of paratroopers jumping in Egypt and landing in dust bowls that were gypsum holes and never being found. After I got up and out of the dust hole I had immediate thoughts of that. I could have driven deeper into oblivion and not been found. We were following each other about a half-mile apart at that point and I pulled over into some grass, thinking it was solid and motioned the rest of the guys around the dust hole. Once we got the guys around it I again got in the lead and the dust was flying from every part of my jeep. It is a wonder it didn't quit while in the dust pit but it was only a second or two and the momentum I am sure kept it going. My instincts of going for the four-wheel drive without even slowing down helped I'm sure. I did not remember the exact spot and on the return trip none of us hit it but we stayed on the edge of the path.

The area where I went into a dust pit

On for El Guisi (Dinder). Arrived at Dinder at 1400 hrs got cool Coke from a bucket of water with a burlap bag in the water to let evaporate and keep them cool. We decided since it would be impossible to make camp in hunting area would make a wet camp then on banks of river and go on next day. All of us took well-needed bath. Colonel saw seven foot snake on bank. Rayl had seen a four-foot mamba on road an hour earlier. Ate supper and crashed.

27 November 1962 – Up at 0530 hrs ate and on road by 0700 hrs for our fifth day of driving. We made Duraba via Abu Hashim at 1100 hrs and zeroed rifles on bank of river. Got game scouts and on to camp. Had to ford river one hour out of Duraba and with the rainy season just ending the river was higher than usual. We talked about what we had to do and had one jeep drop it trailer and go across to test it. It was decided that you had to get enough speed and stay in second gear and keep the gas peddle down.

Howard Riley's jeep got stuck right past the guides

Riley's jeep got stuck we had a hell of time getting it out. The first order was to unhook his trailer and while another jeep came by to pull it over to that jeep and hook it "on the fly" since it could not stop. It meant pushing and a lot of work. It also had all 660 pounds of salt in it that we did not want to get wet. We got it done with the help of everyone there. Next we had to dig out under the jeep and get water flowing under it to release a suction that had been created with the wet sand in the riverbed. Of course water had backed up into the exhaust and it would not start so we had to pull and push it out and use the winch that Freddie Ray had on his CJ5. Luckily the cable was long enough with some rope we had for him to reach the stuck jeep. Finally the jeep was out and one more hour to camp.

As we got closer to camp the grass was getting taller and the last several miles it was almost driving blind. There was a camel path that we followed. We came upon a camel caravan loaded with dried fish and the natives just took off in all different directions. We chased them down since our scouts told us the natives surely thought we were game control officers. We got everything cool with them and got them on the way again. They had been fishing on the game reserve all during the rainy season and this was the fish for the entire village for the next year.

When we arrived at about the right area where we decided to make camp we turned down the side towards the river. The nearer we got to the riverbed the grass was really getting taller, about seven feet tall. We drove around in circles to pack it down and cleared part of it. Cleared campsite and made camp at 1600 hrs Then we and had to plow from camp to the banks through more tall grass and make a water point. Camels ordered at Duraba to arrive tomorrow at 1000 hrs. The scouts told us that we would need a couple camels. It was only going to cost us a couple Sudanese pounds so we thought that in the interests of safety we would do it. Little did we know we would be hunting from the backs of the camels?

28 November 1962 – The area around our camp had such high grass we decided to go back to the river we had to cross and check out the area just around that. The grass there was only about three feet tall and we would be able to see something. We had taken two jeeps with Freddie and myself in one and Barry and Howard in the other. The Colonel had stayed in camp. The main thing he came on the trip for was to try to find a lion. He was not interested in some of the small game that we were. We had not gone too far when Freddie shot Tiang, Ross shot Tiang, and then I got a nice Tiang. A Tiang is a type of a Hartebeest.

134

Our campsite in Sudan – Riley's jeep

29 November 1962 – Barry and Howard rode the camels to hunt and Howard shot Reedbuck. Riding the camels meant they were up high enough to see over the grass and could see game down in the grass ahead of them. Freddie and I were riding together in his jeep when it really started missing bad and then didn't want to go. We decided the fuel pump was bad so we out in the middle of nowhere got the tools out and took off the old one. We could see immediately the new spare he had was not going to work. The spare fuel pump was one of the items that had two different ones for that year. The problem was that the fuel pump gasket around the sediment bowl was cracked. We decided to improvise a new gasket. We did not have a new gasket for the bowl or gasket material with us. Barry had some but it was in camp. After thinking what material we could use, I cut a gasket. I used my hunting knife and made a gasket from the leather tongue of my boot. It worked like a champ afterwards. It worked until we were about 150 miles from Asmara on our return home.

30 November 1962 – It was now our turn to take a ride on the camels so Freddie and I hunted on camel and each got a Waterbuck. We got nothing else for the day but having the camels was a blessing because we were at least able to hunt. When you ride a camel for eight or ten hours your rear-end sure hurts when you get off. But the old adage goes like "if you want to play – you gotta pay."

Barry and Howard went back across the river and Howard shot a Tiang. The Colonel hit a stump with Ray's jeep but not serious damage. Freddie and I went to Duraba to get more Camels since hunting from them was producing some game. We had vehicle trouble on way back and spent the night on the road. The problem was from driving the jeeps through the tall grass. The seeds from the grass got into the radiator and no air could cool the water so it got hot. We had to try to clean out the radiator and then get some water to refill the radiator.

1 December 1962 – Colonel, Freddie and I go out to get camp meat with 12 ga., 243 and 300 Weatherby and as luck would be saw about 50 Roan Antelope. Colonel had first shot and got a great 30-inch Roan. We had to try to figure how to get it back to camp. We were not far from camp and Barry and Howard came to help. An adult Roan can weigh five or six hundred pounds. We tied a rope around its feet and tried to pull it up using a jeep with the rope over a branch of a tree. We got it up a few feet and the branch broke. We had to drag the Roan with the jeep a few feet to get to a stronger branch. We pulled it up high enough to get it in the back of a jeep to transport back to camp. We didn't want to quarter it all out since we weren't too far from camp.

The Colonel with his Roan – Freddie on the far right

In the afternoon Freddie and I went out for Roan and I shot a nice one a couple miles from camp at 1500 hrs. I got out of the jeep and told Freddie to go on for 15 or 20 minutes in pursuit of his Roan and if you don't get one come back. Freddie was not back by 1730 hrs when a big grass fire came up on the horizon. I started back to camp on foot and had gone maybe 50 yards when I looked up and could already see vultures circling. I went back to my Roan and got heavy branches from some fallen trees and covered it so the vultures would have a hard time getting it. Having seen movies of big grass fires I knew I had to get out of the area. The grass all around the area was five to seven feet tall. I ran back towards camp, which was about 1-½ miles. As I got to the point of the edge of the area where we turned down into the camp I met Freddie coming in from the side near camp. He said the scout got him lost and after Ray threw the scout out we headed back to look for the Roan. By then it was getting dark and I was boiling mad.

The grass fire was burning in full force

The grass fire was all over the place and I was sure my Roan was cooked. I wanted to hurt the scout for getting Freddie lost. About that time we went back to camp and Ross and Riley show up and say, "You should have seen the fire we set." They had set it about 20-30 miles away and it burnt as fast as they could drive. The scouts had been telling us to set fire to the tall grass even though at this time of the year lighting would often set the grass on fire. It could only burn to the river then would burn itself out. With so much dry grass, it would go at such a high speed it would not even burn the trees unless they were dead. After burning the grass we could now see for miles and miles. Later on, during the trip we set several other areas on fire so the hunting would be easier.

2 December 1962 – I got up at 0500 hrs and headed out to look for my Roan. I found it in good shape. The really odd thing was it was in the center of a perfect square about fifty-feet on each side. In the afternoon the Colonel was in camp and the rest of us saw two lions. Freddie had gotten first shot rights and he got out of the jeep, put his 338 magnum in the fork of a tree, and missed at 80 yards, the war was on. I shot right after we knew Freddie had missed. I was using a 375-H&H magnum and could see the lion take a hit. The lion went down and we pulled up to it and Barry climbed on the hood and shot down and hit the lion with his 375 magnum. Then Howard hit it and it ran off into the swamp. It was hit three times and I'm sure the bullets went straight through. We tracked it until dark. When we returned to camp we told the Colonel what happened and planned the hunt and tracking for the next day. The Colonel was really upset about the lion especially since that was what he wanted most.

Tracking the lion in the swamp grass – quite an experience

3 December 1962 – Up early the next day and returned to lion tracks at 0600 hrs. Found buckets of blood where it had bedded down but we lost cat in the swamp. The area the lion was last seen was only a couple miles from camp and went into the swamp with grass that was about 10 or 11 feet tall. We had carried shotguns with double O Buck and since a lion can leap more than ten feet we decided if any of us got attacked the rest would put the barrel of the gun in the lion's ear and pull the trigger. That afternoon we saw 400 or 500 pound lion in riverbed. There was a Lioness on the bank we had not seen but Barry fell out of the back of the jeep almost on top of the lioness. The Lioness was gone immediately into thick cover.

That night Barry got stung by something in his sleeping bag and is sure he is going to die. His foot got red and hurt a lot. There were a lot of scorpions in the area and we had netting over our cots. We checked our sleeping bags each night. It was most likely a spider and that could have been serious too. We had carried one bottle of booze for emergencies and after a drink Barry calmed down. We had sleeping bags even though it was over a hundred degrees during the day it got cold at night.

4 December 1962 – The Colonel and I went back up to where we crossed the river in search of Tiang. My jeep got hot in the high grass and ran out of water. I sent scout to get water and he found some Bushmen with camels and got them to go to the river and get water. I saw a Tiang and missed him with the only shot I got off. After the Bushmen came with the water for the jeep we made a fire and had tea with the Bushmen. Then thought with the radiator problems it would be best to go back to camp.

On the way back, when we got to the area where we had to ford the river, we saw a Sudanese Game Control jeep. They had a camp set up alongside the path that we had made and right near our river crossing. They had been assigned to drive down from their headquarters and bring us our hunting license and to check that we were not in the game reserve. We stopped, had tea with them and made small talk with what little English they spoke and what little Arabic we spoke. We invited them to our camp so they would not think we were up to something illegal.

The funny thing was that night Barry got into his sleeping bag and there was a short piece of leather on the inside of the zipper. The zipper had pulls on the outside and inside. Barry pulled the zipper up and felt that leather on his leg and was sure he was being attacked again. He came up out of the bag, knocked his netting down as well as the Coleman lantern hanging in the tree above him. When we realized what it was we all rolled on the ground laughing till we hurt.

5 December 1962 – Everybody loafed in the morning expecting the Game Officer to come and visit. We thought it would be a good time to do a little maintenance on the jeeps. So we took the radiators from jeeps and took them to river. We poured water through the coils, from the backside, to get grass seeds out so the jeeps would cool properly. All of us were having trouble with overheating and we knew that a good cleaning would be the only thing to solve it. We used tiny pieces of wire to push any seeds out that the water did not remove. After reinstalling the radiators and filling them we were anxious to see the Game Officer. Barry was sent to his camp and he finally came after Barry fixed his Land Rover. It was good that Barry had gone since we wouldn't have seen him unless we went back that way to hunt Tiang or on our way home. All was well and I guess we made a good impression on them because they were going to head back to their headquarters. We never saw them again. The rest of the day was spent hunting. Freddie shot a Reedbuck and Howard finally got his Roan Antelope.

6 December 1962 – The Colonel rode a camel for 12 hours and was so sore he almost couldn't walk. I shot a good Reedbuck and on the way back to camp saw a cobra snake on the road into the campsite. During the entire trip we shot numerous gazelles, Dik-Dik and other game too numerous to mention. This trip was turning out to be all I had ever ***dreamed*** of way back there on the Golf Course when I was 5 or 6 years old.

Me with a couple Dik-Dik and a Reedbuck

We had cleared a little area to store the trailers holding the gas and the salt. After driving around the area to flatten the grass, we put the trophy skins on top and salted them heavily to dry them so they would not spoil. Right next to that area we had constructed a fire area for Fadoul to cook the meat from the skulls so they would be ready for mounting later. It didn't take long for the area to get filled up with skins. To dry completely it would take several days and sometimes a couple changes of salt. When they were stiff as a board we put them in a trailer for the trip home.

7 December 1962 – A day of hunting produced a good Roan for Freddie. One of the funniest things to happen was while hunting for that Roan. Freddie was driving and went between two trees that were just barely wide enough for the jeep, but not wide enough for the two spare tires mounted on the sides. The trees peeled the tires and their mount holders right off the CJ5 effortlessly. The bolts that held the mounts just came through the fenders and the wheels went flying.

One day we had three natives come into camp wanting to sell us three tiny day old wart hogs. They had the feet tied with reeds. I pulled out the Polaroid and took a picture of them holding the pigs and the three natives thought this was magic. They just had to have a picture. They wanted to give us the pigs for a picture but we said no and as I remember I took a picture for each of them for a few shillings. We didn't want them to take the photos as a gift or we would have to take a gift from them and who knows what we might have been given. It could have even been a new wife and I am quite sure our wives would not have been happy about that deal.

Natives with the baby wart hogs they wanted to sell

8 December 1962 – Barry, the Colonel and I went to get some Tiang. I got three, one of which was a good 22-inch bull, the Colonel and Barry each got two. The first one that I shot was a couple hundred yards and I was using the 375-H&H. I held over his back and when I shot I could see the round hit the ground in front of him. I was so mad that I grabbed my 243 and held at his shoulder and shot him right through the heart. Even though a Tiang is the size of a good horse the 243 Winchester was "the killer" from then on. The trajectory of the 375 was horrible and I would learn more on another trip.

Me with a Tiang

9 December 1962 – Not a lot happening but Freddie shot Reedbuck. All the time we were on the trip Fadoul cooked every meal; made sure we had plenty to eat and even washed some clothes for us. He tended to the boiling of the skulls of the trophy animals we would take home. What a wonderful person he was. I only wish we could share these memories now with him. He was "our everything" on that trip and a good friend as well. Fadoul was always up long before us and last going to sleep.

Fadoul washing our clothes in 55-gal drum cut in half

143

10 December 1962 – Last stand for Barry with Roan. While the scouts were directing us around the area we saw a huge porcupine. The scouts were out of the jeep before we came to a stop. They ran up to it with their hatchets and in one quick swing the head was off, they had it cut open immediately and were eating the liver warm and raw.

Me and a nice gazelle

Barry with his nice Tiang

11 December 1962 – One of the first orders of business was settling up with the camel drivers and scouts. We would drop the scouts off on the way out, at their village. They had several hundred pounds of jerky they had dried and we would carry it for them. The Camel drivers we owed some money to, but they were also interested in some of the 55-gallon drums we had. So instead of just giving them away which we should have, being the treasurer, I felt obligated to sell them which I did. It made them happy and gave us a few more dollars for beer.

Tying things up for the return trip now too neat

My jeep coming home in front wheel drive leaving the hunting area

I found, just before we left camp, that I had a broken rear axle in my jeep and couldn't pull a trailer. We left camp at 1000 hrs with me in front of the pack, crossed the ford in the river which had gone down about three feet, and drove to Dinder, Howata, Quala-En-Nahl.

About the time we were 30 or so miles from Gedaref it was decided that I, since I wasn't pulling a trailer, would take Fadoul and head on into Gedaref and the gas station and try to get them to stay open till everyone got there. It was getting dark and we were worried about getting gas that night and having to wait till late in the morning.   I came to a fork in the road and could see Gedaref off in the distance to (right) the Northeast. With a roll of toilet paper and weighting the toilet paper with rocks I made an arrow on the road to take and on the other road put toilet paper across the road as if it was blocked.

When the vehicles started coming into the gas station Barry was not in his sequence and we assumed he had gotten lost. We had all said early in the trip that if anything happens we would meet at the police station. What we did not know was there was someone at the gas station 24 hours a day and getting gas would be no problem. So we made camp in the front yard of the police station at 2300 hrs. It had been a very long and hard drive, for the day from the hunting area to Gedaref. Freddie and I looked for Barry till 0230 hrs and returned dead tired.   Barry claims he did not see the arrow, only the paper across the road and took that fork.

12 December 1962 – Barry showed up at 0600 hrs and we woke up hearing him thanking the truck driver for bringing him. When asked where his jeep was he said it was in a village with three trees and he had a native guarding it. It was the trailer that had all of our skins in it. Also in it was all but one of Ross' rifles. The natives would not steal in the Sudan. Freddie and Barry went for Barry's jeep and returned at 1300 hrs. The native guarding the jeep was a small boy about 9 years old and the rest of the village was milling around the jeep. When given his pay of a Sudanese pound, for watching the jeep he was like the king of the village.

Later on, we found a military junkyard and we got a rear axle for my jeep but couldn't get the broken axle out and needed an axle-puller for the axle, which they did not have. This meant that I would have to make the trip home in front wheel drive. The old World War II jeeps were some really tough vehicles. I made it all the way home, some rough road and 5 days in front wheel drive. We left Gedaref at 1700 hrs headed towards Kassala and the Sudan/Eritrean/Ethiopian border. We could only go as far as the Setete River where we camped for the night. We were exhausted and tomorrow would be another long day.

13 December 1962 – We broke camp at 0530 hrs and made our way on to Kassala – two hour drive. Cleared Kassala and on to Tesseni which was the Eritrean/Ethiopian side of the border. At 1630 hrs we left and about 10km out Freddie's jeep went out with fuel pump and no gas getting to the carburetor. We rigged it by putting military jerry gas can on firewall and hose into carburetor, gravity feed, and on to Cheren at 1900 hrs.

14 December 1962 – We made it into the R&R center in Cheren at 0300 hrs. After coffee and one hour of sleep we were on to Asmara to reunite with our families. Howard's Jeep couldn't pull the trailer the last 40km so I pulled it in front wheel drive. We arrived back in Asmara at 0730 hrs after what was an exciting and unforgettable trip.

We all had to do some rebuilding on our jeeps but all in all they had performed well. It was quite an experience looking back at those times. Had anything happened to us down in the hunting area we would have been lost in history because surely no one would have found us. We worked together as a group, had fun and cherished each other's hunting successes.

The memories and experiences of that trip are something that money couldn't buy. We had gone into an area with only a map showing the main villages of a country, and no roads. We went into areas that had never seen white people. The fun we had and the wonderful memories and friendship will never fade in our minds.

We accomplished things *"Beyond our Wildest Dreams."*

My Sudan hunting license

Chapter 12 – Kenya – A Real Safari

Planning another Hunting Trip

Before we went on the trip to Sudan the Colonel was talking about taking a real safari complete with White Hunter in Kenya. He had said if he didn't get a lion in the Sudan he would have to make the safari. He had already sent off for all of the literature selected the white hunter, Ian McDonald and he finally talked me into going along.

I had been processing film on the side at home for extra money, just like on my first trip. However this time I was making color prints from slides. My parents would send me the paper and chemicals once a month. I charged $2.00 each for wallet size prints from slides. With the chemicals and the paper that I received I could make 800 color wallet prints. This related into a nice income on the side and would finance the trip to Kenya for me. We decided to make the 30-day safari in early spring of 1963 and would take 35 days leave.

It would be another Christmas in Asmara and this year I was to play Santa for the children on the base. Since we didn't have a Sleigh for me to arrive in, I came by a Gherry Cart, which was a horse drawn cart used as taxis in Asmara. This was really a lot of fun and was done in a warehouse set up by the PX. The kids all got a little surprise and what fun for me to see all their "wide eyed" and happy expressions. Even my own kids did not recognize me. It was a day of hard work but so much fun to watch the kids enjoying themselves and telling me what they wanted for Christmas.

On the old base (tract A) of Kagnew station the Ham radio club had a MARS (Military Affiliated Radio Station) which we would call home via the radio hook up. Some times the connection was great and sometimes not too good, but the only charge involved was from the Ham operator in the states to the parent's home. We called several times and always enjoyed hearing the voices of loved ones. I remember one time when we called there was a big snow storm in Newfoundland and North and there was a ham operator there that would relay to the Continental US (CONUS) for us. He politely asked us to wait 45 minutes so he could relay phone calls for the guys in

Greenland at an airbase. Of course we didn't mind and he got us through to someone in New York and when I finally got my mother it sounded like she was in the next room. I thought that this was the ultimate technology, which it was at the time. The phone call was collect to our parents from wherever we could find a ham operator in the US. So from New York to home it was not much and great to hear each others voices. What a great service the Ham Operators did. It was midnight in Asmara and suppertime in Ohio.

Off to Kenya and a "Real African Safari"

The preparation for a "real safari" included loading the ammunition we were going to carry, since we knew that our hand-loaded ammunition performed great. We practiced on the range with the 458 Winchester Magnum we were going to use on the Elephant. The 458 Mag. belonged to the Colonel and there was no sense in carrying two so we would both use the same weapon. At the range we did pretty well with the open sights. When we zeroed the 458 in at the base rifle range we thought we had been whipped. The one thing that did surprise us was the recoil of the weapon. When shooting at a target the recoil always seems more than when you are hunting.

The next morning the Colonel asked how I was and I replied that my shoulder was bruised pretty badly. We had each shot a half a box, which was ten rounds. It took a week for the bruises to go away. We would be shooting the elephants at close range so there was not a scope on this rifle. The Colonel would also take his 300 Weatherby and a 375-H&H Mag. I was going to take my 243 Winchester, 300 Weatherby and a 375-H&H Mag. As the plans finalized for our safari we got bags packed and were ready to leave Kagnew Station.

February 12, 1963 – We got up early on Tuesday and signed out of Kagnew Station for our trip. We arrived in Nairobi at 1135 hrs and had no trouble getting through customs, especially with our weapons. Ian McDonald (Mac as we would call him) met us at the airport. He took us and checked us in at the New Stanley Hotel. This is the same hotel that Livingston & Stanley had stayed in many years ago. We had some lunch and then went to the Game Department to purchase our hunting License's and the game permits.

Mac then took us on a ride through the Royal Nairobi Game Park. I shot a lot of movies and took a lot of still photos with my 35mm camera. We could get very close to the animals in the park such as the baboons and zebra. I think Mac took us there to see if we really knew what any of the animals looked like. Of course we had been telling him of our trip to Sudan and about the local hunting so he wouldn't think we were beginners at hunting in Africa. In the evening we had a couple drinks in the "Thorn Tree Lounge" at the New Stanley Hotel. The lounge has so much history since most all of the big game safaris have started from there. Any of the movie stars spending time in Kenya stayed at the New Stanley and drank in the Thorn Tree.

Directly across the street from the New Stanley hotel was an F.W. Woolworth 5 & 10. This just blew us away so we had to check it out. As a kid I remembered getting some orange slices type of candy, which were sold in bulk. They had it here in Nairobi and I could not leave without a few.

Looking out our room at New Stanley Hotel – Woolworth on left

February 13 – We got up at 0630 hrs, toured the town and waited for breakfast. While at breakfast Mac was telling us about a Police Auction of Land Rovers. The Colonel and I thought we should buy a Land Rover, if we could get it cheap enough, and drive it home thinking it would be the ultimate ending to the trip. Mac then took us by to bid on the Land Rover on the way out of town to hunt.

We talked about getting a good Leopard by using an Impala tied in a tree. We would get to camp and start serious hunting the next day. Mac already had his people at the campsite and everything ready for us when we got there. The tent had a sleeping area with cots, a screened in area with a table and washbasin outside the door. This was going to be much better than the trip to Sudan. Mac had told us to put our dirty clothes on a chair each night, after our bath and they would be clean and pressed for us the next morning. This was really living, but of course we were paying for it.

Our home away from home in Kenya

We were served our meals in our tent on the table complete with a tablecloth. The cook had his kitchen about 25 yards away from the tent. He baked fresh bread or rolls for the meals and pies or cake for dessert. When I look back at it now it was like the old chuck wagon cooks did, but we were in the wilds of Africa.

February 14 – The Colonel got things started by shooting a Wildebeest (also known as Gnu), is an oxen looking animal. Shortly thereafter I shot a really nice Wildebeest and then an Impala. I used the 243 on both of them even though it is really too small for an animal the size of the Wildebeest. After seeing me hit the Impala, Mac made the comment I was "hell on wheels" with the 243. I had a 2.5 by 8 power scope on the 243 and it made long distance shooting pretty easy.

Me with a decent Impala

February 15 – This was the day of the sale for the Land Rover and Mac had a friend watching over the bid for us. If we were successful bidders, Mac's friend would check the vehicle out completely and have an estimate for making it "return trip ready." However, we would not know for a couple days if we were successful bidders on the Land Rover. The Colonel shot a Zebra to be used for Lion Bait and it took us about an hour and half to get it hung up in the tree.

Guides getting zebra hung for Lion bait

About 75 yards away we had to make a good blind for getting the lion. I shot a nice Thompson Gazelle, which aside from keeping head and skin, would be good eating. Thompson Gazelle ribs are outstanding when cooked over the fire. We saw where a Leopard had killed a baby Giraffe. We decided right then to get "old spots'. We built a blind to try to get the Leopard. Mac had said for me to use the 243 on the Leopard since he said I didn't miss with it. Technically you are not permitted to use anything less than 30 caliber but Mac said the 243 had so much power and came out after the law; he wanted me to use it. We went back to camp and took a bath, had supper and took a Malaria pill. Mac is quite a white hunter and has lots of stories.

February 16 – Up at 0600 hrs and ready to get going, but breakfast was needed to hold us till later in the day. I shot a nice Wart Hog, Hyena, and Impala with the 243. I shot a Wildebeest and Zebra with the 375-H&H. We went by and no sign of the Leopard on the bait, then to check the Lion bait and no action on that bait either.

An Impala that just wanted his photo taken – did not shoot him

February 17 – We were awake at 0500 hrs had breakfast and off to check the Leopard bait – no action yet. Later in the day I shot an Eland with the 243, with one shot. Some Eland's can weigh up to 1500 pounds. Quite large animals for the 243 but as part of the Antelope family they are thin-skinned.

Masai natives visiting our campsite from nearby village

February 18 – Monday morning and we got out of the sack at 0500 hrs and checked baits. I shot an Impala it was the third one. The Lion was finally on Colonel's Zebra bait and the Colonel is waiting in the blind to get it but today would not to be the day for success.

February 19 – We slept in until 0700 hrs and first off to check baits. The Colonel got an Impala with a nice rack. After a lot of riding and shooting smaller animals we got back, had supper and got to bed at 2230 hrs. Placed our clothes out for them to be washed as we did every night and returned before we got up the next morning. Nothing like the Sudan trip of wearing the same pants four or five days.

February 20 – Slept a little later since the Colonel was out early in the Lion blind and spent the morning with no success. I got a gazelle but nothing to brag about.

Me with a Dik-Dik shot with the 243

February 21 – I shot a Steinbuck and the Colonel got a Zebra. We were really looking for quality game.

February 22 – We got nothing today.

February 23 – I shot a Zebra and on the way home from the Colonel's lion bait and we ran over a Dik-Dik that darted into the headlights of Mac's Land Rover.

February 24 – We slept late and early in the morning I shot Grant's gazelle that was about 400 yards away. Mac could see exactly which one and told me to rest my 243 on his shoulder and shoot from there. I looked through the eight-power scope and saw a whole herd of gazelles. I asked Mac which one he was talking about and he gave me some landmarks and I finally got the right one in my sights. Sure enough, it was a really quality rack on him. I said I thought we should go towards him to be a little closer and was assured that I would not miss. Mac covered his ears since the noise would be right on him and I held the scope about a foot over the gazelle's back and fired. Mac was steady as a rock and he immediately said I hit it. Mac made the comment that the bullet got there before the sound so it did not scare the herd until it was too late. That was the longest shot I had ever made.

156

Me with a Masai woman met on the way back to camp one day

February 25 – Monday, Still no Lion for the Colonel but he did shoot a Grant's gazelle.

February 26 – Shot three Zebra's today. I got two with one shot with my 300 Weatherby using Nosler Bullet.

Shot this zebra through the neck and got one standing behind him

February 27 – We were successful bidders on the Land Rover and we went into Nairobi to check on condition. *Happy Birthday Laura* (this was on my notes too). We sure were getting excited about the deal we got on the Land Rover and the prospects of driving home across the Northern Frontier and up through Addis Ababa. Mac had left instructions with his friend to fix the vehicle to a condition that would be sellable, to get our money back, even if we didn't drive back to Asmara. The Land Rover was really in pretty good shape as we had thought when we first looked at it. The repairs were just about done and not costing too much and the mechanic was sure it would make it to Asmara.

After checking on the Rover I went back to the New Stanley hotel early and since I had a couple hours before heading back to the hunting area, I went exploring. I went a couple blocks to the right of the New Stanley and saw an Indian restaurant so I decided to have curry. This was the most fantastic curry I have ever eaten. The order came with a lot of condiments and I really ate too much, but it was good.

February 28 – The Colonel finally shot the Lion. The Lion measured more than nine feet from nose to tail, quite a nice one. The breath of the Lion was the most horrible case of halitosis I had ever smelled.

The Colonel with his Lion

The Masai natives were glad to see one less Lion. They, (Masai warriors), carry a long spear and are sometimes attacked by Lions. They put the end of the spear on the ground and when a lion attacks they crouch down holding the spear towards the lion and as the lion jumps they try to make him land on the spear. I shot a pretty good-sized hyena and a nice Impala.

March 1 – Hunted for my Leopard – he didn't show so I killed a new Impala for bait.

March 2 – Hunted for the darn Leopard – This would be the last chance for the Leopard and if we didn't get any shot tonight we were going to have to leave the area to hunt for Buffalo and Elephant.

March 3 – We moved our camp and met Bill & Margaret Maples with Northwestern University. They were doing a project on Baboons. Mac knew them and we stopped for some tea since we were headed right past their place. They made us right at home and gave us some snacks.

We went on the road to Mombasa for a while and stopped at what we would call a motel with restaurant. The famous JA Hunter who did big game control for the British and Kenya, and who wrote many books on hunting in Kenya owned the place. He had photos and permits all over the place and we enjoyed talking to him. He was about 80 years old at the time but sharp as a tack. He could remember details as if they were yesterday and it was quite a thrill.

March 4 – We were going into a lightly wooded area where there were reports of Elephant roaming. As we were driving, it was about a hundred yards in from the riverbank; I saw a great Waterbuck feeding ankle deep in the water. Mac said it had my name painted all over it and to bag it. I quietly got out of the Land Rover and walked up ahead until I could get a good shot. He was standing completely broadside to me. I had the 357-H&H with the scope, shooting slightly downhill so I let off a round. The Waterbuck took off to the right and came up the hill and past me at about 50 yards. I shot at him again running, not really expecting to hit him, but maybe. I was sure I had hit him good while he was standing in the water. He didn't even miss a step and just kept running up the hill.

We waited a couple minutes because I was so sure I had hit him with a well placed shot the first time. We walked up the hill about a couple hundred yards and he was standing under a tree and again head to my right and full broadside. I shot and he took off running again and in about fifty yards he just crumbled. We went over and there were three holes in him in a vertical line about two inches apart and all through the heart.

I could only say the second shot I made had to be pure luck since he was running, but with a scope on the other two shots, I hit where I aimed. After discussing it a while we decided the Nosler bullets were performing well but since they only open a small amount they went clear through without doing too much damage to the meat. He had just bled to death with the three shots. Running the way he did is very common for a heart shot.

We cruised a couple more miles in the area and we could see a herd of Elephant in the distance. Since the Colonel had first shots on a Lion, I had first shot on the Elephant. We got out of the vehicle, a good distance away, and walked quietly and carefully sort of, from tree to tree while Mac checked the herd. We got near a tree that was maybe three feet in diameter and a good Bull was about 25 to 30 feet away. We were now in amongst a herd of about 40 Elephants. Mac said the Bull was of good size and would make a nice trophy.

I wanted to do a headshot but Mac had told both of us that when it came time to get the Elephants that it would be better to try for a heart shot. Also we had practiced holding extra shells in between the fingers of our left hand so we could chamber with our right hand. The 458 only held three shots, so we had three more shells ready to go. Mac had instructed us to "shoot till the bloody rascal was on the ground". When I shot the elephant started moving to the right and I emptied the 458 and reloaded and emptied those three more shells, before it had taken ten steps. It was on the ground and dead. At the distance we were, it was like shooting a bus from the size of it.

Me on top of My Elephant and
Beyond my Wildest Dreams I did it

It took several hours to clean and get trophies from the Elephant. We saw many Rhino, Zebra, Giraffe, Baboons, Buffalo, a Leopard, and Hartebeest.

March 5 – This was a day we were going to find a Buffalo. We got up to a good breakfast and headed out. Hunting buffalo can mean hunting on the plains or in the thick brush. As luck would have it the only buffalo in this area were in the thick brush. Mac's favorite words were "let's creep craftily through the brush." We heard this even when we were on the plains and what he really meant was walk softly and quietly. After several hours of hunting and tracking we finally came upon a really nice bull. We more or less walked up on him and were standing face to face at about 25 to 30 feet. I raised the 375-H&H and held right it under his chin and about even with the top of his shoulders. I shot and he just disappeared.

I had used a Nosler partitioned bullet so it should have penetrated as deep as the power was. We carefully walked over to where he had been standing and there was a lot of blood. This was the final blow for the 375-H&H in my opinion. I was completely disappointed with it as a rifle compared to other weapons. Mac handed me his 470 double and said if we came on the Buffalo and he was still alive to shoot him with both barrels. We started tracking him through the real heavy brush with Mac leading the way, when all of the sudden the Buffalo ran right over Mac and as he passed a couple feet from me I shot in the back of the neck with both barrels of the 470. I don't even remember the recoil of that big gun because of the adrenaline being pumped. Mac got up and brushed himself off and we walked over to the buffalo, which was just a few feet from where I had shot him. It was so thick in the brush that we had to have the natives chop some of the brush away to be able to get a photograph. I could not get back far enough to get the whole buffalo in a picture. What an exciting day this had been.

Me with my Buffalo in the thicket where it fell – a huge Buffalo
We had to chop the brush to get enough light for photo

March 6 – Now it was time for the Colonel to bag his Elephant. We had help from natives but came up empty handed on anything worth shooting. We traveled quite a distance in Mac's Land Rover but we did manage to get the word out to a lot of natives that we were seeking a nice bull.

March 7 – We went out early with some leads from natives that sent word over night, on where some elephants might be. Elephants can cover many miles in a day just grazing and eating the several hundred pounds of grass, leaves and crops they might find. We managed to find a small herd in the afternoon and the Colonel got his Elephant. While Mac's guides were getting ready to cut the tusks out, and the feet off, there suddenly appeared about 15 natives out of nowhere.

162

They wanted the meat and we gave it to them. Right away they built a fire and got some sticks, sharpened a point on them and started cooking some of the meat over the fire. They brought us the first that was done and it was really quite tasty much the same texture as beef. The natives later cut a piece of meat from the hindquarter that was about three feet square and a foot thick. Now that was some steak. It must have weighed at least a hundred pounds. They soon cut it up and were drying it for jerky. They had sent one of their friends to their village and brought more help about the time we were leaving. Mac said that would help them through a couple months. Mac knew the villages everywhere we went and had a special relationship with the villagers. That was the reason they were always willing to help him.

March 8 – An early start in the morning with dampness and fog made for interesting hunting. As the sun comes up through the dense patches of fog your eyes can play tricks on you. As we were headed cross-country out to my left I thought I saw a Lesser Kudu. I told Mac to stop and as he came to a stop, I got out with that horrible 375-H&H, since we had intentions of hunting bigger game than a Kudu. I walked back a few yards and sure enough there was a nice Lesser Kudu standing in front of some brush about 75 yards away. He was standing broadside and just munching on his breakfast. I held tight on his heart and shot and with the recoil of the big gun I took my eyes off him for a split second. When I again looked at where he was supposed to be, there was no Kudu.

Me with a nice Lesser Kudu

I thought maybe I had dreamed seeing him since he did not run nor could I see him on the ground. I was sure I could not have missed at that close distance so I walked to where I last saw him. When I got to the spot in front of the brush I saw my beautiful Lesser Kudu under the brush. The power of the bullet had knocked him about three feet and under the brush. He never knew what hit him, he never moved.

We were off to an area where there might be some big buffalo. The hunt was on for another day of hunting Buffalo. I had purchased a permit to shoot more than one. Since the thrill of the bagging the first buffalo was subsiding, and we were in the area of big buffalo, why not try for another. We hunted the bigger part of the day and came up empty handed – none – but getting a nice Lesser Kudu topped off the last day of hunting.

We went back to Nairobi with the thoughts of getting an extension on our leaves and driving back to Asmara. We were told that the Government of Kenya had closed the Northern Frontier, which meant we could not drive back. We had to sell the Land Rover that we had purchased at the auction, I fixed for the journey. We didn't take too much of a beating in the sale as I remember we lost about $75 and that was pretty good.

We went by the famous Zimmerman Taxidermist's and told them what we wanted done with our trophies. It was to take about six to eight months for them to complete the orders and they would have them shipped to Asmara. The bill for the items I was having mounted and cured was going to be about $5,000, a lot for someone that made $267 a month. The film processing I did on the sideline was sure a big blessing.

We flew back to Asmara and were a hit, at the Rod and Gun club we told the stories of our "big game safari hunt." Our re-living the memories, with guys that were also hunters, was a lot of fun.

Had we been able to keep the Land Rover we purchased in Nairobi and been permitted to drive back to Asmara via the Northern Frontier of Kenya we would have had the "ultimate" experience anyone could have ever asked for.

The Kenyan Government closed the Frontier only a few days before we were to leave.   It was just not safe to attempt the drive because of "bandits" and "Mau-Mau" could have easily captured or killed us on the trek.

The roads would have been passable in the Land Rover and the true stories we could have told would be like something out of make believe. We had good intentions but it just wasn't meant for us to top off our "real Safari" with an adventure unequaled before. We both had a great trip to Kenya and were left with dreams of what it could have been like. Sometimes dreams cannot be accomplished through *"no" fault of your own*. We were ready to accomplish the dream but things like safety for your life and governments can squash that dream.

Chapter 13 – Sneaky Hunts

Over the next few months I continued to sneak out and down the back roads to hunting areas that I knew. Barry Ross had become a very good friend and always enjoyed sneaking out to hunt. His wife Carol and my wife Joy would go shopping together and the kids enjoyed each other's company. Barry liked to go to my secret area down by Decamere where the hunting was good and we could get back into town without being spotted.

Barry and his jeep in my secret hunting area near Decamere

Hunting the Kudu and Breaking the Table

One weekend Dick, a friend from the mess hall, and Bryan and myself decide to go get some Greater Kudu. It was in the same area that I had shot one before on a trip with the Post Sergeant Major and a bunch of officers. This time being very careful we took our cars into the area. We hunted all morning; Dick had a brand new 264 Winchester Magnum, which was the latest thing out and a very hot rifle. About noon we found three Kudu high on a hill. We were down about 150 yards and several hundred feet lower elevation. It was almost straight up and down. Dick fired and we could see the bullets from his rifle were hitting branches so I opened up with my 243 and dropped all three of them. We climbed the hill and tried to figure a way to get them back down without ruining the meat. It was decided that we had to clean and quarter them in order to have any luck at all getting them back to the car. We could carry the two front quarters at a time but only one of the hindquarters. This meant we had to make quite a few trips up and down the hill. We got the meat into the cars and headed back for Asmara, some 100 miles away. Since we did not have a permit to shoot these, we were worried about making it home without being caught. We started to carry the quarters into my house where we were going to finish butchering them. We put a couple hindquarters on the dinning room table, not realizing how heavy they were and the table lost its legs and collapsed leaving another mess to clean up. Luckily the house-girl kept the marble floors clean enough to eat from. We got the butchering done and all shared in the good meat.

Search & Rescue Team

Major Royal was the Post Provost Marshal and concerned about some of the military going hunting and getting hurt or even killed by the ELF (Eritrean Liberation Front (the Shifties)). The one thing he did not understand was anything about going hunting in Eritrea and how to socialize with the natives. Some of us that hunted a lot tried to relay, that it was necessary to visit the villages, make small talk, have tea, leave salt tablets and malaria pills and nothing would happen.

He thought he knew everything and decided to create a "search and rescue" team. There was a "Duck" on base that was a WWII amphibian vehicle. This was going to be a main vehicle for the team along with jeeps and ¾ ton vehicles. We heard they were going into an area west of Cheren on a practice trip. Having hunted extensively in the area and knowing the villages and natives we again emphasized the need to make the visit to the village. However with Major Royal he was going to do it "his" way.

They departed on the trip and the next night, while a lot of us were in the NCO club, we got a call from one of the MP's about the "trip from hell." It seems like the "search & rescue team" was attacked by the "Shifties" while making camp in a riverbed and they had their weapons taken. To make matters worse the "Shifties" drained the water from all of the vehicles, dumped the drinking water and made everyone in the group strip to their underwear. The "Shifties" took their weapons and clothes and disappeared into the night. The team had to find something to put water in to, go find a waterhole and fill the vehicles. They had radioed the Provost Marshal's office that they were headed back to the base in their underwear and would arrive in the morning.

Naturally, all of us that hunted were rolling on the floor laughing and wanting to get to the main gate to see the arrival of "our search and rescue team" in their new skive underwear. A large group of the base turned out for the arrival early the next morning complete with many hangovers from celebrating the "we told you so's."   There were no more search and rescue trips except to the R&R center in Massawa.

Leading up to Trouble
On one occasion I wanted to go down to the area below the "Half-way House" and hunt so Barry and my friend Brian Britton, from the mess hall and me headed out. We got to about the 13km mark on the Massawa road about 5pm. It was notorious for large baboon crossings. We came around one of the corners and saw hundreds of the creatures and there were a couple of Ethiopian cops motioning us to shoot them.

Needless to say we could not control ourselves and just had to shoot some of the baboons. After shooting maybe 50 or 75 rounds of ammunition we got back in the jeep and headed on down the road. We went about 2km and as we rounded a curve we could see across there was an MP car. Knowing that they surely had to hear all of the shooting, since it was like a small war, we turned the jeep around and headed back up the mountain at a top speed hoping the jeep wouldn't fall apart.

We knew that the communications in the mountains were really bad and the MP vehicle most likely could not call out and unless they could catch us we would be home free. We got to within a couple of kilometers of Asmara when coming towards us was an MP jeep. They motioned for us to stop which we did. The Sgt. in the jeep was a friend and he radioed to the other vehicle that there were "no guns" in our vehicle. He was going to let us go. Well the other vehicle had the post Provost Sgt. in it and he said to hold our vehicle. This created a problem since we had about seven or eight weapons. We did have a blanket to cover the weapons. When the Provost Sgt. came he made a report and we were pretty well caught. The next morning we had to go see the Provost Marshal and he wanted us to turn in our guns. We turned them in and Barry and I got a chewing out for "fraternization" of officers and enlisted. We naturally agreed with everything they said and walked out but under our breath we were saying where they could go. Our weapons were returned to us in 30 days; of course we had more at home, so that didn't slow things down. Barry and I heard about the "fraternization" on more than one occasion since they didn't even like our wives together.

Going back to Makalie's plantation

One area that I had not gone to on the second tour was back out to Makalie's banana plantation to hunt baboon. One of the main reasons was that it was "off limits" going to that area because of the civil war. However, adventurous me, I had to push the limits. I had been talking about the place for a long time to my buddy Bill Ramsey and the more I talked the more he wanted to go.

We sat out one Thursday afternoon and headed to Cheren and then to Agordat where we had a late supper and a couple beers. The next morning we got up early and headed on towards Tesseni. We pulled into the Barentu Police Station to get directions and the Police commander was in shock to see us. He wanted to know how we got there. When I told him we had just driven he did not believe us. He said the "Shifties" would have killed us. My belief was they recognized my jeep and gave us a clear pass.

Since it had been some 3 years since I had visited the plantation I was not quite sure how to get to it from the town. Anyhow after getting Bill and I to sign a release form, in case we were killed, the commander gave us directions for the last couple miles to Makalie's plantation.

We headed towards the plantation and when we pulled in you would have thought it was "old Home week". Makalie was so glad to see us and immediately had his maid put out the red and white checked tablecloth and start preparing some spaghetti for us. We talked and talked about old times and the baboons. Makalie said how sorry he was that GI's could not come to his plantation on a regular basis anymore. He told us about the pack of dogs he had trained to kill the baboons.

170

I told him we had brought some ammunition, salt tablets and malaria pills for his friends (the Shifties). The Shifties were really revolutionaries and really in the right trying to regain their country and independence back from Ethiopia.

That night Makalie told us he had to go out for a while, we knew to go visit the Shifties, and he was gone about an hour and half. When he got back he assured us that we would have a great day of baboon hunting the next day.

Saturday we had a great breakfast and headed out to shoot the baboons. Between Bill and me we shot several hundred rounds of ammo. I am sure the shots could be heard clear back in Barentu and was driving the cop's nutso. After reducing the baboon population considerably for Makalie we said goodbye and headed back east to get to Agordat before nightfall. We stopped by the police station and said our goodbye to them. They just looked at us in amazement and we told them we were headed back to Asmara. I am sure they felt we would never make it. We arrived back in Asmara and home on Sunday afternoon like we had just been to the Cheren R&R center for the weekend.

Easter in Asmara

The girls in new dresses Aunt Frances had sent for Easter
Mary Beth – Janice – Laura looking pretty as can be

Chapter 14 – The Special Court Martial

On or about the 2nd of August 1963, I went into the Colonel's office and asked him if he wanted to go hunting on the weekend for a big Greater Kudu since I knew he didn't have one. There were rumors of a Kudu with giant horns in the hills behind the "Halfway house." I thought it would be a good weekend to see if we could find and possibly bag this critter. The Colonel said he was busy and my response was he was sure going to cry if we came back with it since he would have "first shot."

With some plans already in the works to go with my buddy Bill, I finally relented and agreed that the other clerk in the JA's office could go. Harvard (Harv) had been begging for a couple months, since his arrival, for me to take him hunting. I had explained in great detail about keeping his mouth shut and not to say anything to anyone. There were post regulations that stated you could not be on the roads outside of Asmara during the hours of darkness and this would later be an important item.

The three of us took off in my jeep and we planned on staying with a native named "Jimmy" in a small village just east of the mountains behind the "Halfway house", in an area knows as Fil-Fil. We arrived at the village late, about sundown on Friday, and Jimmy was glad to see me again. We went out during the nighttime to get a gazelle for camp meat and for Jimmy's family. We traveled the fields and finally shot a gazelle. The gazelle was standing almost facing us and I shot him with my 243 through one shoulder. We went over to pick him up and the bullet had gone in the left shoulder and ended up right under the skin of the right hind leg. The bullet had caused so much damage that it was like picking up a water bag. The gazelle was totally destroyed for meat. I don't think there was an unbroken bone in its body. So we were off to get another which we did in just a short while.

We went back to the village and turned in for the night. We got up at the crack of dawn, ate some breakfast and headed off in the jeep to the base of the mountain. After parking the jeep, we loaded up some canteens of water and started up the mountain. The Greater Kudu are found high up on mountains and to bag one requires a lot of luck, climbing, walking and being quiet. Where we had made camp was already a couple thousand feet above sea level so that helped a little. We were zigzagging up the steep slopes and had not gone more than a thousand feet when Harv said he was exhausted. So Bill and I took his pack and weapon to lighten his load. Harv made the comment that he would never say anything about my weight ever again. He used to tell me I needed to go on a diet but said the way I was going up the mountain I was really in good shape. We hiked and climbed up and down the mountain all day Saturday without success of even seeing any Kudu, let alone the monster bull.

We went back to Jimmy's and had a good supper and went back out looking for some wart hogs and gazelle. We got Jimmy some more meat for his family to dry into jerky for the weeks ahead. Sunday morning we headed back to Asmara empty handed but with another tale to tell.

Monday morning we all went to work and shortly after we got in, the CID came into the office, which was not unusual since they quite often talked to the JA about legal advice. This time however, they said for Harv and me to go their office. We walked up the street to their office and they called Harv into the office. I knew right away that there must have been some leak about our weekend excursion. About 20 minutes later they called me in and showed me a statement that Harv had made about having hunted the past weekend. I proceeded to read it and noticed some things wrong with it. For one it stated that we were on the "roads during the hours of darkness", which we weren't since we were in the fields beside the road. The other thing was that Harv stated that we were in an area known as Zulu when in fact we were in Fil-Fil. The area known as Zulu was south of Massawa and we had not gone anywhere near Massawa. I threw the statement at the CID Sgt Vowell and told him "I will see you in court." That made him mad. Then as I opened the door to leave I saw Bill sitting there and I said "keep your mouth shut, read the statement, they don't have anything." This really made Sgt Vowell speechless he was so angry.

I went back to work knowing we were in big trouble. The word then came out via friends that the Post Commander wanted to make an example to stop the illegal hunting. I have never found out if the Colonel was the one that leaked the information or just who did. The events that followed were somewhat amusing.

Within a few days it was clear that there was going to be a court-martial over the hunting trip. Harv was going to be spared since he was going to be one of the star witnesses for the prosecution. I had a feeling that Jimmy may be called as a witness so I sent word for him to "get lost." Jimmy got on a camel and rode some 250 Kilometers to the North but the Ethiopian Army got him and brought him back. This was an example of how hard the Post Commander wanted to make an example out of me.

I had to try to find an officer that would consider being a Defense Counsel and it is not an easy task. This is especially difficult since most officers are career officers and if they were to win, the Post Commander would have given them a bad evaluation. I found the Special Services officer, Captain Voetsch that agreed to take the job. Many of the officers I had hunted with illegally were afraid of their careers. Captain Voetsch was cool about it and said he wasn't worried about his career and if something did happen he would just get out. He had never been a defense counsel before but took the task with great gusto.

While working in the Judge Advocate's office I had come across a one paragraph Army Regulation that stated if a serviceman was to be tried by Court-martial that could result in a penalty of confinement. Then the Chaplain must notify his next of kin. This was not done and the possibility of confinement was real so I thought, we might have a good claim to have the case dismissed for failure to follow Army Regulations.

The case was referred to Special Court-martial in mid September and it went to trial in October. As it turned out, the officers on the Court-martial board were instructed by the Post Commander to find me guilty "no matter what." The trial was somewhat hilarious, looking back on it. Prior to the weekend in question I had been a licensed hunter for going on trips that were authorized. However, my license had expired a couple weeks before. One of the witnesses, Sgt Davidson, the Provost Sgt was called to testify. Captain Voetsch knew that my license had expired so right off the bat he asked Sgt Davidson if I was in fact a Licensed Hunter. One of the charges against me was "being a licensed hunter but not having the required permit." Of course everyone knew how much I hunted and on lots of legal trips so he thought my license was still valid. Sgt Davidson stated emphatically that I was a "licensed hunter but did not request or have the special permit to shoot a gazelle." Captain Voetsch produced my hunting license that had expired a couple weeks before the alleged hunting trip and request the charge be dropped. The request was, "if I did not have a valid license, how could I be charged with being a licensed hunter but failing to have the required permit?"

Naturally, the court board denied the request and we proceeded.

One of the other charges was "being on the road during the hours of darkness." The prosecution called a number of witnesses including Harv and Bill. Since we had hunted in the fields and not been on any road, how could I have violated that particular regulation since in the Post Regulations the word road was in quotes and underlined. Again, our motion was denied.

The prosecution brought in Jimmy as a witness. He had been brought to the base really against his will but in fear of his life. Captain Voetsch brought these points out in court trying to prove that he was being forced to testify to almost anything in order to protect his life and moved that his testimony be dismissed. No such luck on this points either.

Captain Voetsch's hard work was in vain, but greatly appreciated by me, but to make a very long story shorter, I was found guilty. I was reduced in rank by one grade from E-6 to E-5.

The court had done what it had been instructed to do. Most all of the officers on the board saw me over the next week and said they were sorry they had to do it. I understood and held no hard feelings against any of them since I knew they were

176

put up to it. I had not been relieved of my job as Chief Clerk of the Post Judge Advocate Office and I had learned a few things about the legal side of the military. I proceeded to write an appeal that would accompany the Courts-martial record when it went for review to US Army Europe. I took each of the charges and thought I did a masterful job of showing why even if I was guilty of hunting, why I was NOT guilty as charged. The Assistant JA Captain Norcross reviewed my appeal, quietly on the side, for me and thought there was no way the conviction would be upheld. My appeal was attached and sent to Europe.

After the trial Captain Cheatham, the Post Dental Surgeon, stopped me one day and asked if I would come to work for him and get away from the people in Headquarters Company since he knew about the "put up job." I said I would be happy to be reassigned to work for him. Being in the medical corps Captain Cheatham was not worried about anything the Post Commander would do as far as evaluation. I transferred to the Hospital Company and went to work as a clerk for the Dental Clinic. Everyone there treated me great and we laughed many times about the court martial.

After I had been at the Dental Clinic a couple weeks Captain Cheatham called me in one day and asked how I would like to work evenings and that way I would be "out of sight – out of mind" for any of the people on the base. I thought that was a good idea so Captain Cheatham gave me a crash course on being a dental hygienist. He thought it would be good to schedule dependents in for evening appointments to offer dental cleanings since it was impossible to work them in during the day. I had been instructed in the use of the machine and was supervised for a couple days. Being a quick learner I took to the job easily. I was also instructed to check for cavities and how to do X-rays and if there were problems to schedule daytime appointments for dental work.

As the New Year 1964, came I got a call from a friend in the Personnel section. He stated that the court-martial had been thrown out and I should put my stripes back on. But he also told me to come by and get a copy of the order from USAEUR so I would have a copy. The reason he did this was because he knew my copy had been intercepted from the mail. He also

showed me the correspondence that stated "under no circumstances is subject enlisted man to be retried."
I got the copy and put my stripes back on and the next day walked around Post Headquarters during the daytime. I was asked by one of the officers, while in HQ why I had my stripes on. I calmly said, "The court-martial had been dismissed" where the review board "set aside all findings of guilty" and restored my rank and back pay. I was asked how I knew about it and I said I have this copy that came in the mail and see it has my name as a recipient. You should have seen his chin hit the floor since he had known my copy had been intercepted.

I then went to the NCO club for lunch and everyone there noticed my stripes back on and there was a lot of backslapping and congratulations. I thought my troubles were over. I was really enjoying working for Captain Cheatham and with the other guys in the hospital. My mind was already made up to get out of the service at the end of my enlistment in less than a year.

Laura, Mary Beth and Janice Xmas 1963 photo

Chapter 15 – Gondar Trip

One of the other officers in the Dental Clinic was a Captain Coogan. He was married and his wife Geri made for a neat couple. We became friends and fraternized some on the weekends. I mentioned it would be fun to take a trip to Gondar and see the beginning of the Blue Nile River at Lake Tana. The Nile River is the longest river in the world, stretching for 4,187 miles. Larry and Geri thought it would be a fun trip also and we made plans to go which would take us five or six days.

Our plans completed we headed out for Gondar. I had my jeep with the family and Larry and Geri were in their car. The road would be graveled but very passable. We would camp along the way and stop in the ancient city of Axum where the Queen of Sheba ruled back in Biblical times. When we got to Axum we were directed to where the Queen of Sheba's tomb was located and still lying on the ground were massive columns that once held her palace. We also got to look at some of the Crown Jewels of Ethiopia that were kept in Axum.

Mary Beth and Laura in the entrance to the Queen of Sheba's tomb

One of the most amusing things was while we were driving along on the graveled road and I thought I heard Mary Beth crying. I slowed down and looked back and asked what was wrong, thinking the girls were aggravating each other. Mary Beth responded she had something in her eye, and the other girls said she had been crying for a while. We got the dust from her eye and then asked her why she had not said something? Her response was she didn't want us to stop.

Some of the ruins around the Queen of Sheba's tomb –
Remember these things are over 2000 years old and still standing

We went on and got to Gondar and spent the night in a hotel. The next morning we went to Lake Tana, which just looked like a lake. We spent a couple hours taking photos and looking around and headed back towards Asmara, camping along the road at night. The second and last night on the return it was getting pretty dark so we found a likely spot, pitched camp, cooked supper and slept. The next morning we awoke to natives all around us. We had made camp a couple hundred yards from their village. We didn't see it the night before when picking a spot for camp. We had breakfast, chatted with the natives and headed for the last leg home.

Chapter 16 – Second Special Court Martial

In February 1964 the rumors of my being re-tried for the poaching incident became a reality. Even though it had been made clear, in no uncertain terms that I was not to be re-tried, the Post Commander still wanted to convict me. So this time I would be tried for violation of Ethiopian Regulations rather than Post Regulations. It was back to see if Captain Voetsch would still risk his career and "do it again." He quickly agreed to represent me a second time saying that even though I had been hunting he just didn't like the way they were doing things.

The second trial was almost a repeat of the first trial with some blunders made on the part of the prosecution. We tried to get the case dismissed because of the correspondence that stated I was not to be re-tried. Of course the Post Commander had his mind made up that I was to be made an example. The main difference this time was that all of the officers from the Dental Clinic appeared as character witnesses and stated that my job performance had been excellent. All four of the officers knew it could cause repercussions but they were true gentlemen as officers.

I appreciated very much their statements on my behalf. I was found guilty again but this time I was only fined $100 a month for two months and restricted to the base for 30 days. I kind of let the word out this time that if the court martial was not tossed on appeal I was going to write to Cyrus Vance (Secretary of Defense and second cousin). I would explain the whole deal, even though I was guilty. I was going to show that many of the officers also poached since I had taken them and had photographs yet I was being singled out.

I once again wrote an appeal. However in mid March my mother passed away and I was returned stateside unexpectedly with only 30 days left to complete the assignment in Asmara. I had been planning for over two years on getting out of the service anyhow. When we received the notice many of our friends including Captain's Ross and Coggan, their wives and other friends came to help us pack and we were on our way in just two days.

By the time I returned to the states and got settled I received the notice the court-martial was dismissed and all rights and privileges restored. The Post Commander was relieved of his command shortly thereafter. I don't know if it was solely for the reason of the Court-martial or what, but I did know it was a contributing factor.

My enlistment was due to be up in June but since I had more than 30 days to go I was reassigned back to Arlington Hall Station. I only took a short leave and reported to AHS. I was walking down the hall headed for Personnel when I heard someone shout "Rayl" and I looked up and saw Major McDonald coming out the office. He ran up and gave me a hug and asked how I was doing and why I was back at Arlington Hall.

I explained that my mother passed away and I had 45 days or so till I was going to be discharged but I was headed for Personnel to be reassigned. He grabbed my arm and we headed for Personnel while he was telling me that the War Room hadn't been the same since a little while after I left in 1961. He was the officer in charge of the ASA War Room. I thought when I was there in '60-'61 that we had documented everything to make the presentations look great.

We went into the Personnel office and Major McDonald went right to the OIC and said I needed to be reassigned back to the Photo Lab. Needless to say, it was done immediately since he worked directly for the head of the Army Security Agency. I reported in to the Post Signal Office and then directly to the Photo Lab. It only took a short time to get the quality of the presentations back to the previous levels I had set.

We bought a house trailer and it was parked in Alexandria but an easy drive to work. Knowing the expense of living in the DC area I went back to work tending bar at Washington National Airport.

Not long after returning we wanted to take Laura back to Walter Reed Hospital so the doctors could see how well she was doing. To our surprise the doctors said they would like to operate on her feet. They wanted to schedule the operation in June or July. This posed a problem since I was due to be

182

discharged in early June. After much talking and more details we were told that they would need eight weeks after the surgery to check on her. I explained that I had planned to leave the Army but since the cost of such an operation outside would be prohibitive it looked like I would have to re-enlist.

I talked things over with the Post Sergeant Major, that owed me from my first tour for the entire photo support, and he said, "why not extend for 90 days." My answer was they never let career people extend that it was either stay in or get out. His response was if you wait until the last minute before you re-enlist they couldn't get you out that day because of clearance debriefings etc. He told me that if I then indicated I would extend they would have no choice since it took three days to process you out at the base. He then said that he would be called and he would approve an extension.

We lined up the surgery and on the date I was to get discharged I went before the company commander for the re-enlistment oath and stated I wanted out and could not re-enlist. I did mention that I would extend for 90 days. The CO said it was impossible but his hands were tied and he would have to call the Post Headquarters. When he got the Post Sergeant Major on the phone he was told "no problem let him extend." The extension papers were quickly drawn up and the CO made the comment that I must have someone in my back pocket and how did I pull it off. I just acted dumb and signed the papers. I immediately went to the Sgt Major and thanked him for his help. He said it was the least he could do.

Laura had her operation and all went well. She got a clean bill of health from the doctors and they said for her to do her foot exercises until she was in her late teens and all would be fine. I had taken another part time job back at the photo studio; we had put the color lab in during my first visit to Arlington Hall. We started making plans for my getting out of the service in September.

One of the guys from the photo lab that was in Asmara with me had a father that worked for the Government. He was applying to an Intelligence Agency to go to work when he was discharged. That sounded good to me also and since I had the clearances I also applied as well as my buddy Parsons. All three of us got hired and just changed buildings when we were discharged.

Chapter 17 – Out of the Army

Going into Business for Myself

I was discharged from the Army in September 1964 and the following Monday I started my new job at Defense Intelligence Agency. We wanted to purchase a house rather than living in a trailer and in order to qualify financially I had to show proof of future income. I worked at the photo lab of the studio after getting off from my full time job. We applied for a loan to purchase a new house in Manassas. One day when I was at the part time job at the studio I answered the phone and it was the Credit Company calling for credit check and employment verification. I gave myself a glowing report. I said I was due for a raise etc and that I would be promoted to a higher more responsible job, I put it on thick and we were approved for the new house. Soon after moving in to the house I was able to quit that part time job.

When we did the actual moving into the new house I got my HS buddy Dave, that bartended, to help me. We started moving around midnight from Alexandria to Manassas. We loaded the U-Haul truck and headed for Manassas around 4 am. As we moved in, we tried not to make too much noise at that time of night, but we had a whole house full of furniture to move. About 6 am we were down to moving in things like my hunting trophies. We carried the elephant tusks, feet, stuffed heads and a complete four-foot tall mounted bird. We got done and enjoyed a few cold beers and crashed for a few hours.

Later in the day one of the neighbors came over to introduce her self. She said we ruined her breakfast. She told us that when she was cooking the breakfast she looked out the window. First she saw an elephant tusk go in the house, and then a buffalo head, other heads and she burnt the toast, ruined the bacon and made the eggs hard because she wanted to see what was next. We all had a good laugh about it and assured her they were all in and she wouldn't be ruining breakfast anymore.

My plan after getting out of the Army was to go into the photography business. The one thing I had was a lot of experience and what I lacked was money. I got on the night shift at AHS and this gave me time to work on finding a location to open a studio. I checked around and found a small location on Rt 234 in Manassas that would rent for $140 a month. At the time Manassas had a population of about 9,000, but the way housing was being built I knew it was going to boom.

I didn't want to create a business that would drain the finances from my real job so I went to a finance company in Arlington and borrowed $600 on a signature loan. I was going to lease the building, buy a little bit of supplies to build counters and fix it up and divide it for a studio. I talked to a company about film processing and the more that we talked I got them to put in some merchandise on consignment. So in about 15 days I had a little studio and somewhat of a camera shop. I took out some advertising in the local newspaper offering just about any kind of photography and overnight passport photos.

I was going to be able to offer overnight film processing in black and white and color by taking the film with me and dropping it off on the way to work and picking it up at 1am when I got off. If I had taken any passport photos during the day I processed and printed them when I got home at 2 am. Then I was up and at the shop at 9 am to start the day over. The business started to pick up and more and more customers.

Our very first studio in Manassas VA

The studio was 10 feet by 14 feet, way too small to do a bridal portrait but would work well for head and shoulder portraits. I didn't even have a good set of electronic flash units but had taken portraits in the army with photo flood lights, so I could do it here till I got enough income to buy the studio lights. I poured everything back into the business and didn't have to touch my income from my regular job.

One day a very pretty girl came in and asked about wedding photographs. She was going to have an outdoor wedding and we talked at length. She liked some of my ideas then she asked about a bridal portrait. I said we could do a really nice one at the front of the church. She insisted she wanted one for the newspaper for the wedding announcement. I knew if I was going to get the wedding I would have to do a bridal portrait. I consented and we scheduled the appointment. She ran out to the car and brought in some "11x14 proofs" from a bridal portrait that she had done at the most exclusive studio in DC. She proceeded to tell me the photographer told her she was too skinny, put on some weight and the dress would look better and many more comments. She was a very slim girl, but all brides are beautiful and she was in tears from what he had said and understandably so.

I didn't even have a background for a bridal portrait so I went into DC the next day and got a roll of background paper and hung it on the wall near the ceiling. The next day she came in for the sitting and the roll of paper fell and wrinkled both sides of the roll. I thought Oh Well!! I will have it airbrushed out of the final photograph. I set up and took some close up photographs, then moved back and did some a little farther away. Then I moved back as far as I could go and pretended to be taking full-length photos. I played with the gown etc. All I could get was a ¾ length pose.

When I showed her the color proofs the first thing she said was "how did I get the neat marks on the background". I didn't say anything about the roll of paper falling, and doing it, she loved it. Then she asked about the full-length photos and I said she had her eyes closed in each one. I knew there wasn't time to redo and if she didn't back out we could get some at the church. She picked one of the others, a close up and said it made her head larger and people could see more of her. So all worked, the wedding went great and they became a truly happy customer.

I could see the potential in photography all over the area of Northern Virginia. The towns of Leesburg and Vienna were growing at a pace that was unbelievable so I thought they would make a nice place for a studio, since there was none. I was doing a lot of business at the Manassas studio and formed a plan to open a new bigger studio in Manassas and open in Leesburg and Vienna.

Things were going well and I would quit my Government job and work on the expansion. I rented a place in Georgetown Shopping center and created a nice business with plenty of room for the camera shop, dressing room, sales room, 20 x 30-foot studio, lab and finishing area. Business kept improving and we were doing lots of weddings and portraits. I then opened studios in Leesburg and Vienna that had office and photographic areas but no lab.

I would work two days a week in each studio, Monday and Thursday in Leesburg, Tuesday and Friday in Vienna and Wednesday and Saturday in Manassas. We scheduled portraits at 15-minute intervals so I could photograph a lot of portraits in the two days and it gave the studio four days to sell the work. I would photograph weddings on Saturdays and Sundays and hired other people to help with the wedding photography. I found myself working all the time.

As I look back from today's perspective, I sure missed some important times with my children but I was trying to create a better life. The marriage to Joy had gone sour and it was time for a divorce.

Chapter 18 – Shillelagh Travel Club

As time went on my marriage fell apart and my heart was not in photography quite as much anymore. I had been in an automobile accident around Labor Day 1967 for which I would later receive a small settlement in 1969. I was in the darkroom processing film on a Sunday afternoon, in the summer of 1968 listening to the radio when I heard an advertisement for a travel club open house. I had been somewhat familiar with the club and had earlier hoped to do something like that as a family. When I heard the advertisement I simply washed my hands, left the photographs in the chemicals, went to the office, and took some cash. I went to Dulles Airport to learn more about this club and see the airplane that was owned by them as well.

The club was running a special to get new members and it included a trip to the Bahamas round trip for $29 if you joined today. The membership fee was $160 so I reached in my wallet and plunked down the $160 in cash. The response was "don't you have a check"? I said I thought they might not take a check so I brought the cash. They didn't have any receipts so I had them write a receipt on a napkin for me. This was the beginning of what was to be many great times. The travel club was called "The Emerald Shillelagh Chowder & Marching Society" or Shillelagh's for short.

The Shillelagh DC7b

The Bahamas trip was in August 1968 and we were to leave on a Friday evening at 6 pm. I didn't know anyone in the club and not much about the club, but I was ready to have some fun. We were going to stay at the Holiday Inn in Freeport for $7.50 a night with double occupancy. The club would match people up if needed. I had arrived at the airport in plenty of time and while standing and waiting to board the plane I looked at my watch which said almost 6 pm, the time we were to leave. There was a dapper gentleman standing next to me looking about as lost as I was. I asked him why we weren't boarding and he responded it was his first trip and he knew nothing. We introduced ourselves and had a friendship that lasted, with Hank Jones, for many, many years. We ended up sharing a room at the Holiday Inn for that trip. Finally about 6:15 the announcement came to board the plane, a DC7. We loaded up and as soon as the plane's wheels left the runway everyone started clapping, a tradition I was to learn.

When Hank and I got on the plane we sat in what had been the first class section on the old plane. When the plane took off everyone clapped – a tradition. Soon everyone was up and around and making introductions to each other. Shortly a stewardess came by, handed us a 16-ounce cup, asked what we wanted to drink, mixed drinks included. She would pour the booze till you said "when" then add the mix. Some of the drinks were powerful. After we had been in the air maybe 30 minutes one of the girls sitting across from us got up and went to the back of the plane. She soon came back with cheese and crackers that she had brought on board. We were offered some and we got to know Carolyn very well. She had a date on that trip that would later become her husband for a while. Carolyn was working for the Bureau of Standards at the time. She later retired and currently (in 2005) is the Executive Director of the Shillelaghs (more about her later on).

I decided that I really enjoyed getting away and having some fun. During the winter of 1968 the travel club made some ski trips to Stowe, Vermont and Quebec, Canada. These trips were very inexpensive, around $40 air and about the same for the hotel, lift tickets and ski rental. I had met a girl on the very first trip to the Bahamas named Charlotte and we dated and went on several trips.

As time went on and I lost interest in working so hard, I simply closed the Vienna and Leesburg Studios. 1969 saw some more trips with the Shillelagh's to Cozumel a couple times and to Jamaica.

Myself with a bunch of Shillelagh gals I took deep sea fishing in Cozumel

On one of the trips to Cozumel I had planned to have a fish fry on the beach. A group of us wanted to rent a boat and go deep sea fishing. It ended up that a bunch of the gals also wanted to go deep sea fishing and made an offer that if I took them in the morning I could have the boat to myself in the afternoon and they would pay for it. I though this was a good deal.

Another group would take a second boat and fish. As it ended up the girls had so much fun we spent the entire day fishing and I never got to wet a line. Late in the afternoon a really hard storm came up and we literally had to tie the girls across the boat. They didn't know it was as bad as it was, but my 26 hours in the Red Sea let me know for sure. We made it back with several hundred pounds of fish. When we got back they insisted that we go the next day (Saturday) and the fish fry would be that night. It ended up that again I did not get to fish but I got really sunburned as did Carolyn and Sandy. I was too sick to cook so I asked the hotel manager if I could rent one of his cooks. He responded with the question of how much fish we had and if there was enough for his other 9 guests. I assured him we had over 400 pounds of fish. He said he would not only furnish the cook but also furnish the beer for the beach party. The other guests were invited and all had a good time.

The Shillelagh's had a trip planned for Casablanca and the Canary Islands over Christmas of 1970. The price round trip was to be $252 and I couldn't pass up a deal like that. I also had other plans to go with it. Since I had received a small settlement for my 1967 auto accident I thought I would go over with the Shillelaghs and when they were ready to leave the Canary Islands I would go on my own trip.

While we were stationed in Asmara there were two trips made by people in Airstream trailers led by Wally Buyum. They would ship the trailers to Capetown and pull them to Cairo and some would even tour Europe. It was a nine-month to twelve-month tour. I thought it would be nice to buy a Land Rover in Cairo and drive to Capetown. I said goodbye to the club in the Canary Islands and bought a ticket to Cairo. I had to fly back to Casablanca and then to Algeria and on to Cairo. I got to Cairo on Dec 30th and visited the museum, toured the town and pyramids. I looked for the Land Rover and soon found out there were no four wheel drive vehicles to be had at any price because of the '67 war with Israel. I decided I would then just fly back to Asmara and see the place and head home.

I purchased a ticket at a TWA office for a trip from Cairo to Asmara and back to Washington, DC. This was New Years Eve 1969 and the plane to Asmara was to leave Cairo around midnight and get to Asmara in the early morning. I went to the airport, checked my baggage and waited. A little before midnight I was called to the Ethiopian Airlines counter and was told the flight had been changed because of the New Year scheduling. I was told I could get out the next morning but I would have to fly to Beirut and change planes. I asked what the increase price would be and they said none and the airline would take me to the hotel for a night's sleep and bring me back the next morning to catch the flight. I went back into Cairo and returned the next morning.

I boarded a Mideast Airlines plane for Beirut. We arrived in Beirut on the short flight and as we landed I saw planes on fire and smoking. I wondered what had happened. We went into the terminal and were told that the Israeli's had come in the night before, blocked the road, got all passengers off the planes and blew them up and left. Because of the schedule changes, all of the planes belonging to Mideast Airlines except the one I was on were back at their home base and Israel wanted them out of business. There were a few bullet holes in the windows and I was expecting at any moment to be in the midst of a war. There was about an hour wait for the flight to Asmara and at one point I looked out the window of the airport and saw an Ethiopian Boeing 720 jet sitting way down on the tarmac. I felt good since I was sure the plane was here and we would be leaving on time. Not long after that they announced the arrival of the Ethiopian flight to Asmara and a Boeing 707 pulled up. It was a half cargo plane and half passenger plane. The front of the plane opened up on the side and there were two Mercedes vehicles in the front. We boarded and had an uneventful flight to Asmara.

I cleared customs in Asmara and got a short stay visa since I was only staying about ten days. I caught a cab into the hotel, checked in and headed for the base. Being in civilian clothes and being an American I simply walked on to the base. I headed for the Post Signal office to see who was still there. Bruna was sitting at the desk and when I walked in she screamed. She stood up and was looking very pregnant, ran around the desk and gave me a welcome hug. She filled me in on the happenings of getting married, her mother and father passing and having a nice new home. She had always said she would only marry someone of the same mixture of race as herself. She had met a wonderful guy that fit the bill and was a good hard worker to boot.

I had no problems going anywhere on the base so I headed to the NCO club to get something to eat. Many of the waiters were the same ones that had been there when I was stationed there. It was like "old home week" with the waiters telling stories to the newer waiters. Suppertime was fast approaching and people would start coming in after work. There were a couple guys that were on a second tour that I knew when I was there. Then Lee and his wife Vera walked in and I couldn't believe it. He had been going between Asmara and Turkey for almost 15 years without going stateside and this was his third tour in Asmara. We had lots to talk about since Lee was a big hunter (legal and illegal) too. He said things were really bad and it wasn't safe to hardly go out of town anymore unless it was in a big convoy. I visited some of the other friends such as Franco that owned the photo store downtown and a few others. I had a nice dinner one evening with Bruna and then it was back to Washington, DC via Madrid for a couple days.

Chapter 19 – Closing the Studios

When I got back from my trip I decided to close the studio in Manassas and look for a job working for someone else. I had been living in Arlington for about a year by then and my roommate Dick, that I was in the service with, had a nighttime job at a printing shop for a guy named Barry. He would photograph the work to be printed on the offset printing presses and prepare them to burn the plates. The deal was he got paid for eight hours and if he got it done in two hours he still got paid for eight hours. The average was about four hours and with a couple times the full eight hours. The pay was great and the work was easy and could be done anytime after they closed as long as it was ready the next morning. Dick had found a nice girlfriend after his divorce from Doris and he did not want to work nights anymore. Since I knew all about what he was doing he recommended me for the job and I took over.

I worked at the print shop for about eight months and one day Barry the owner of the print shop called me and said he had a good friend Morie that owned a big film-processing laboratory and needed a plant manager. He said he could find someone for the print shop easier than his friend could find a plant manager. Barry asked me to visit with his friend and if we worked something out he thought I would be way ahead. Barry also said that if I didn't work something out I always had my job with him.

I went to visit Barry's friend at Colorfax Labs and really didn't want the job. To politely get out of taking the job when I was asked how much I needed I gave a figure that I was sure he wouldn't pay. To my surprise Morie hired me and the first payday actually gave me a thousand dollar a year raise.

I worked at Colorfax for quite a while when I was approached about going into partnership on a commercial lab with the studio owners of the color lab that Bert and myself had put in for their studio back in 1960.

The deal sounded good and we opened a lab in Gaithersburg, MD. We got into production and I was able to obtain a couple of Government contracts.

Shillelagh Trip Director

I continued making trips with the travel club. With the Shillelagh's, after you had visited a location several times and were familiar with the area you could request being appointed as a trip director, and the reward was a free trip.

I was selected to be the trip director on a camping trip to Jamaica. The camping trip was to be a lot of fun and part of the trip director's job was to help fill the trips. I called my friend Charlotte and reminded her of the trip and suggested she sign up. Her response was could she bring her roommate and I said, "sure bring him along." She made it clear that it was not a "he" but a gal. I said sure the more the merrier.

I scheduled a pre-trip get together to explain what was going to take place on this camping trip. We took tents, a generator and all the items necessary for camping. I was going to do the cooking along with some help. We left Dulles on Wednesday night late and got to Montego Bay at sunrise on Thursday. We were met with a Rum Punch party by the visitor bureau. We were off to our camping area at a board of director's, of the club, vacation place. We spent the day setting up tents etc. I had arranged for a bus to take us where wanted to go. We went to some of the nightclubs on Thursday night.

Got up early Friday morning, made breakfast for everyone, cleaned everything and repacked. As we were ready to board the bus for a train to the Appleton Rum distillery, one of the older members came out of the tent saying she wanted breakfast. I had to stop things and hurry to fix her some breakfast. I could not believe she slept through the noise of everyone waking up and asking where the "potty" was and the noise of breakfast. I had cooked bacon and eggs for all of the members with some help from a couple other members. We went on to the train ride, had a calypso band and rum-punch all daylong. We stopped at a village where people could order wild color shirts and pick them up on the way back. At noon we stopped or a sack-lunch at a picnic area then went on to the Appleton Rum distillery.

Saturday morning a good friend named Hank Furr, a lawyer, came over to the cooking area and got a big pot and a big spoon. He said he was going to make sure "that old broad" was up this day. He went right outside her tent and beat the pan with the spoon announcing it was time to get up. Then he went to some areas where people were already up and away from their tents and did the same, knowing it would not bother anyone. To be sure, she was out of her tent and on time for breakfast the rest of the trip. I took everyone to the Playboy Club at Ocho Rios and Dun's River Falls. I met Charlotte's friend, Sheila on the trip and we all had a lot of fun.

When I returned from that trip one of the girls Jane, which I had dated off and on for a year and a-half, expressed interest in getting back together. We did and she wanted to get married which we did. However this was poor judgment on both our parts and the marriage only lasted about five weeks. I later found out her interest was really to keep me from dating and being with someone else.

Charlotte invited me over to her house for dinner one evening along with her roommate and another friend. Her friend, Sheila and I really hit it off and started dating. I was selected to be a trip director on a trip to Freeport in the Bahamas. Sheila went and we then started seeing more of each other.

Me doing the cooking on the camping trip to Jamaica

Chapter 20 – Marriage to Sheila

I was still running the photo lab in Gaithersburg but starting to have serious partner problems. Sheila and I decided to get married and she really wanted to return to Texas where she was from. I thought that would be a good plan since I could always go into business in most any location. I made arrangements with the partners and was to have my share of the lab bought out. I later got beat out of my share.

We visited Sheila's mother during Thanksgiving and to scout out the area out for a studio. I visited the local camera shop and while chatting an older man entered. He got into the conversation and when he found I was interested in putting in a color lab he said I should go to Clovis, NM where he had opened a color lab. He stated that his wife had unexpectedly passed away and he simply walked out and locked the door and told the SBA it was theirs. He talked about the equipment, which got my interest and directed me to the SBA office in Albuquerque.

I returned and told Sheila about it and then called SBA. They were excited to have some interest. I had no idea where Clovis, NM was really located but I checked with Texas International Airline and they flew to Clovis so I made a reservation for the next day. I made arrangements with SBA to meet at the local bank that held the loan. When we got to Clovis, I still had not looked at a map to see just where in New Mexico it was located.

We arrived at the bank and explained that we were to meet the president and the representative from the SBA.   Immediately the bank employee offered coffee and soon we were directed in for our meeting. We went over to see the building location and equipment. I made an offer of about thirty-cents on the dollar value of the equipment and SBA took the offer. We were given the keys and spent a couple days working on the building. I placed an ad to run in the paper right after the first of the year saying we would be open on the 7th of January 1971. The president of the bank told us of a nice house available and we checked it out and bought it. It was a plan that was coming altogether. The town was a really friendly town of about 35,000 people and a large Air Force base nearby.

On New Years day we departed for Clovis bringing Leon, a friend and employee, with us. We arrived on the 3rd of January and quickly started cleaning the equipment to open on the 7th. We made the opening by working long hard hours. There were a lot of other changes I wanted to make in the building and we would start working on those changes. Sheila was pregnant and due in mid March but all of the hard work and moving caused her to deliver in February. We now had Karen in our lives but she had to stay in the hospital for several weeks.

Clovis Studio – Camera shop and Lab

Getting the photo lab and studio opened and working smoothly was a monumental task. Leon and I put in very long hours working on the equipment, cleaning, painting, and even a little remodeling of the shop. We did make our opening date of the 7th of January even while in the midst of all of our work. We started with a reasonable amount of business.

I advertised Senior Portraits, even though most seniors already had theirs from the beginning of the school year. However, I advertised Color and a special package of wallet photos at a price that would cause students to have a second senior portrait. My idea was to prepare things for the coming year and using the wallet portraits as advertising. There had been no color senior portraits in Clovis up to that time. My plan worked well and it ended up that I took almost half of the senior's portraits a second time, since their first one was black & white from one of the other studios.

Before we left the DC area I had been friends with the Kodak Tech Rep, Dick Kramer, and when he knew I was leaving his territory he said if I made a stink I could get the silk finish paper for my new lab. In Clovis when the new Tech Rep came to visit I mentioned that I wanted the new Kodak silk finish paper because it did not fingerprint. At the time Kodak had trouble producing enough of it and was trying to limit it to school photofinishers. He told me he couldn't give it to me that it was not available for standard finishers. I said I really wanted it and that I had been told if I made a stink I could get it. He realized I was not just off the turnip truck and so I got it. Having this paper helped me with promoting the new photo lab. It was more than a year before my competitors got the paper.

Chapter 21 – Learning to Fly

The lab started doing well and a customer, named Dave, came in that was a spray pilot. The more we talked about flying I discovered he was also a licensed instructor. Ahhhhh! I figured a way to get flying lessons. I proposed to Dave that we trade out film processing for flying lessons and he promptly agreed. ***Again "what you can dream – you can accomplish" it just took me 30 years but I never gave up.***

There was a small airport about 20 miles away in Portales, NM where we could rent an airplane reasonably so that is where the lessons started. Normally it takes about 12-14 hours to "solo" (first flight by you). After only eight hours and after making touch and go landings we pulled up on the taxiway and Dave got out and he said, "Go around by yourself." I felt somewhat confident and took off without any problem. I made the pattern to land and then all of the things that you are supposed to do were going through my head at jet speed. I made the landing in what was comically known as a "controlled crash", in other words not the perfect landing but safely and just a little rough. I felt like I was on top of the world since I had now accomplished the second of my lifelong dreams.
I HAD FLOWN A PLANE BY MYSELF.
Another Dream Accomplished

Now I was hooked on flying just like I thought I would be. I learned of a Piper Cherokee 140 plane at the Clovis airport that had quite a few hours on it but was still safe to fly and could be purchased for $2750. I would need to have at least 40 hours before being permitted to obtain my Private Pilots license. I did the math and figured at the rental price of $25 an hour for the plane I could actually come out ahead by purchasing the plane.

My first plane a Piper Cherokee 140

There was a town south of Clovis about hundred and twenty miles known as Roswell about the size of Clovis. It's where the spaceship was supposedly to have crashed in 1947. It was a town that had no overnight film processing and not much in the way of photography studios. I went down and rented a vacant gas station and decided to take in film processing and open a satellite studio similar to those I had in Virginia. Having the airplane would allow me to build up flying time and not have to make that lonely drive. The area from Clovis to Roswell was desolate and after leaving Portales there was only one small town population of about 800 in the hundred miles drive.

I continued to take flying lessons and I made the required "cross country" trips. After having done that Dave "signed me off" to fly back and forth from Clovis to Roswell even though I still had the student pilot license. I built up more than a hundred hours of flying quickly and had not taken the test since I was really very gun-shy of testing.

I sold the Roswell studio to a person living in Roswell and continued to do the processing and really then only had reason to use the plane for enjoyment and not as a business deduction. The number of hours on the plane was such that I would have to overhaul the motor so I decided to sell it. I made a phone call to the guy that operated the airport in Roswell. He was familiar with my plane and he sold a lot of planes plus he had a good rebuilding operation. I sold the plane over the phone to him for $200 less than I paid for it. He said that if I would bring the plane down he would fly me back. It was all a done deal on the next weekend.

The spring of 1972 came with a plan for me to go after a large film processing account. There was a company called Gibson's Discount with headquarters located in Texarkana. Gibson's had stores located all over northern Texas. I had the idea of a plane flying back and forth from Clovis to Texarkana. Picking film up along the way from the larger cities and one day process it in Texarkana and on the way back dropping off film and picking up more and then processing it in Clovis. That way we could offer overnight processing that was still something rare.

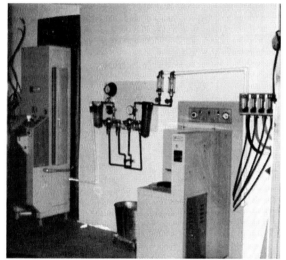

Film and paper processors in Texarkana

I visited with the people from Gibson's and they were very receptive and said as soon as I had the lab operating in Texarkana we would make a deal. I attended a photo trade show in Chicago and purchased the equipment for the new lab. I had been talked into a new type of processing equipment from a major manufacturer known as Pako. I had Pako equipment in Clovis and they were known for good equipment. It turned out the new equipment that I purchased just was not tested enough. We installed the equipment in Texarkana and were never able to get it to operate properly. I was running out of cash and could not try to change it for the older more reliable type. So Pako took the equipment back but would not give me any compensation for all of my lost time or money. My great idea of serving the "top of Texas" by plane had to be given up.

At the same time in the summer that I was closing the lab, Laura and Mary Beth were scheduled to visit us for several weeks of vacation. They arrived in Texarkana and made the trip back to Clovis with some items I had taken from that lab. When we returned to Clovis they announced they did not want to return to Manassas but wanted to stay with me. After much discussion with their mother, and her visit, Laura decided to return to Manassas. Mary Beth continued to stay with me. I had made it clear that Mary Beth's staying meant she would be living by my rules, and that she did very well, I am so proud of her.

The next summer Laura came to visit for the summer and I asked her about her foot exercises. She stated that "her mother didn't make her do them." I was furious to say the least and each day the next week I asked the same question and got the same answer. When Saturday arrived I asked her and when she said the same answer. I told her she had 30 minutes to pack and get to the airport. I said if she was going to be under my roof she must live by my rules and that I had made reservations for her to return to Manassas. I took her to the airport, told her I didn't want to see her and then called her mother to go pick her up at Washington National.

That was truly the hardest parenting I ever had to do, but it paid off big time since we are now as close as can be. It is sometimes very difficult to be a parent, but the next year I received a letter almost weekly saying that she would do her foot exercises if she could come back, and she did.

The Bloodhound

During the time we lived in Clovis, NM I had a good customer named Raymond Spradlin. My buddy Dave, that taught me to fly, worked as a spray pilot for Raymond's brother Wayne. I mentioned Raymond being such a good customer, and the fact that he always came in the shop in starched and neatly patched jeans. Raymond was a true cowboy and had a ranch outside of Clovis.

Raymond brought at least a roll of film a week to be processed and would always stand at the front door and chat for a few minutes each time he came in. The reason he stood at the front door was so he could occasionally open it to spit his tobacco juice clear to the middle of the street. On one particular roll of film I noticed a picture of him and John Wayne sitting on his front porch. Naturally, I had to ask him about his knowing "the Duke." When I inquired of his photo with John Wayne, Raymond acted as if it were nothing and said they purchased cows together. Raymond had met John Wayne while at a cattle auction and they became friends.

I mentioned to Dave about the photos of John Wayne and that is when Dave told me the story of the two brothers that went like this. Raymond and Wayne had been in the Spraying business and Raymond was the spray pilot and Wayne ran the office, ordered the chemicals and prepared the mixes for the loads. They had owned the business for many years updated their planes, bought new ones and were really making money and doing well. One day Raymond walked in to go to work and Wayne asked him what he was doing there. Raymond said they had some spray jobs scheduled. Wayne responded to him that there wasn't anything for him to do and in fact he no longer was a part of their business.

Over the preceding couple years Wayne had taken the money and put it into a private account in his name, purchased the new planes in his name, and when they had bought the new property, he also put that in his name. This left Raymond penniless and out of business.

Raymond started over and got into the ranching business, met and married his girlfriend. He put everything in his wife's name and ran the ranching business and was once again a millionaire.

On another roll of film there were six little cute bloodhound puppies. At the time being a fan of "Hee-Haw" and seeing the bloodhound on the show just lying there, I thought I need one of these pups. I asked Raymond about the pups and said I wanted to buy one because the one on Hee-Haw was my kind of dog. He told me first, I couldn't afford one of the pups and that second, and they were a first cousin to the dog on Hee-

Haw. Well that made me want one more and more and over the next couple weeks we talked about dogs every time he came in. I told him Mary Beth needed a dog and finally he relented to sell me one with conditions. The dogs were worth several hundreds of dollars but he would sell me one for the cost of the shots and registration, which would be $75, so far so good. He then stated that bloodhounds were nothing like the one the show. He said I had to promise to carry a two-by-four to get the dogs attention. He simply meant that the dogs had a mind of their own. We stuck the deal and when the pups were six weeks old he delivered one to us at the shop and when we took it home Mary Beth named him Mickey.

As Mickey grew and was not like the one on Hee-Haw but was a very loving dog. Mary Beth took the Mickey for a walk almost every evening and as Mickey grew he took Mary Beth for a walk or maybe a run. Mickey was big enough that he literally pulled her along.

Mary Beth and her dog Mickey in Clovis

Chapter 22 – Move to Amarillo

That year I thought of moving the lab from Clovis to Amarillo, TX a hundred and twenty miles east, and a town five times the size of Clovis with no overnight processing. I found a building at the old air base at a rental price that was very reasonable. I wanted to put in little film huts similar to a well-known chain called Fotomat. I was going to call mine Fotorama. I worked building the interior of the old warehouse and getting it ready to open.

We could rent a house on the old airbase very reasonable so we decided to sell the house in Clovis and move to Amarillo. I had my little huts built in Clovis and transported them to Amarillo and soon was doing a lot of film processing. With the new lab in Amarillo I had installed some new Kodak equipment, because of the changes in the processing. There were chemistry changes and new film types by Kodak. I moved the equipment from Clovis but kept the studio and had hired a young lady photographer to run the studio. She would ship the film to us by bus as well as the film from Roswell. We would process it overnight and return in the very early hours of the next day.

The Flying Bug Bit Again
One Sunday afternoon in September 1974 I got bitten by the flying bug and decided to go look at the new planes. The Cessna operator in Amarillo was open and I said to Sheila and the kids, let's go look at some planes. We were all in old clothes and didn't look like we could afford a plane. When we got down to the dealer I asked Mr Brown if he had any of the new 1975 Cessna 172's. He said they were allocated and he didn't have any. I asked what the changes were and he said they were minor just the cowling. I said did you have any of the '74 models. He answered yes they are out on the flight line. I asked what color, he replied Red. We went out to the flight line and there were a bunch of red planes. We went back in and said which ones?

He finally got up out of the chair and walked out and showed us. I asked him how much one of the new '75 models would be and he said he didn't know. I asked him to find out and call me the next day. Well, he didn't call and a couple days later I called him it seemed to be a bother so I said the heck with him. What Mr. Brown didn't know was I had already gotten approval for the purchase and finance from Cessna. I proceeded to call the guy in Roswell that I sold the Piper to and asked him if he had any of the new Cessna's. He said he didn't but could get one from the dealer in Albuquerque and the only problem would be he couldn't give me as good of price since that dealer would have to make some on it too. He called me back in less than 30 minutes and told me all of the pricing which was more than fair. We arranged for him to pick it up and bring it to me in Amarillo.

I went to the small airport and was waiting for the plane to be delivered. Mr. Brown came up and asked what I was doing and I replied waiting for my new plane from the dealer in Roswell. You could have knocked him over with a feather. Then two weeks later Cessna had a big show at Mr. Brown's and had all of their twin aircraft and I was invited to just come and see and meet the finance man that had approved my loan. We walked in and looked at the really high dollar planes talking to the guy from Cessna when Mr. Brown walked up. The Cessna loan officer turned to Mr. Brown and said "sell Al one of these and I will approve the loan right here." Mr. Brown almost died knowing he had been underestimating a real sale when we first visited. I felt so important for a long time.

My brand new Cessna 172 – N1597V

The new Cessna that I had was a real four-passenger plane and since I would want to take my family it was necessary to get my private pilot's license. I called Dave and we brushed up on things, I went and took the test and got my license. I was free then to come and go on my own. I used the plane to fly to Clovis and Roswell to check on the locations there and built up quite a number of hours. Almost half of my hours was night flying. It is very smooth flying when the hot sun goes down.

Going Blind one Sunday

About 1974 or 75 one of the scary things that happened was waking up one Sunday morning and being unable to see. When I woke up we were living at the airbase and I could barely make out the door to the bedroom. I thought I had something in my eyes but after rubbing them I realized I really couldn't see.

After being up for a couple hours I realized this was serious since the most useless thing would be a "blind photographer." I had the Sheila take me to the VA hospital and when we said what the problem was the answer was immediately "oh that is diabetes." They ran a glucose test and were amazed that all was well. They ran some other tests and told me to come back on Monday. I had not improved on Monday, but could see things about two to three inches away. I went back home and printed the negatives on the Kodak printer with my nose on the carrier right next to the film.

When we went back on Tuesday they said they were stumped and the only thing that might help would be a Dr Alpar but that he did not take any new customers. I said, "He will see me" because I processed all of his film. He is a very renowned eye specialist. I walked into his office late Tuesday and his receptionist said he would not see any new patients. I told her to go tell him that if he didn't see me he would not get any more film developed. She came back and said to have a seat and he would work me in. He gave me about a three-hour exam and checked for tumors and everything and said the prognosis had to be "a chemical imbalance in my system." At first thought he felt diabetes too since having that can cause a sudden loss of eyesight. He told me it was correctable and had I not been a photographer, as well as processing his film, he would have bet I had been blind for quite some time. We finished about 7:30 in the evening.

I happened to know an eyeglass shop that had moved to Amarillo from Clovis. In those days getting new glasses in less than a week was unheard of. Wednesday morning I was at their shop and they said they would have me glasses about 4 pm the same day. It pays to know people. I went back at 4 pm and got my glasses and to be able to see again was a blessing. After a trying four days and thoroughly exhausted from trying to work I went to bed and slept well. I got up Thursday morning and could see perfectly without the glasses and a couple months later even took a flight physical and passed with flying colors. Never did find out what the problem was but was glad to be able to see again.

My father was visiting my brother and sister in Tulsa so we flew up and brought him to Amarillo with us. It was about the only time I can ever remember my father saying he was proud of me, he did and I believe he really meant it. I had waited a lot of years to make him proud, wishing my mother were around to experience *my dream* with me. But I somehow know that each time I flew she was there with me.

As time went on the film processing business grew so big that we were working as much as 18 to 20 hours a day. I was really worried about our health and not having any time at all with the family. All of the work was not worth it if we couldn't have some family time. I had opened a camera store which was doing pretty good and I decided to sell the film drive-ins to a company from California and shut down the processing lab. Mary Beth was doing more than her share to help out and baby-sat Karen more than she should have been required to do. She was always there as part of the family and I have never really forgiven myself for not having the time to spend with her.

Meeting Greg "Pappy" Boyington
During 1976 one of my most favorite things to do was to watch Black Sheep Squadron on the TV. Even though sometimes I was working as much as eighteen hours a day, I squeezed in time to see my program.

The Confederate Air Force is composed of members that enjoy flying and working on "Old War birds." The Confederate Air Force (CAF) has a museum of old planes, some of which are not in flying condition, but many that are ready to take to the skies. There are also chapters of the group located all around the country. Some of the local air shows attract members of the group to bring their planes for display and some even take you for a ride. Every year, in the fall, there is an air show put on by the CAF at their home field. The CAF is now located in Midland, TX and was moved there to keep the gulf salt water from damaging the planes.

However in 1976 the CAF was located in Harlingen, TX and the annual air show had a special guest of Greg "Pappy" Boyington from the real Black Sheep Squadron. It was a thrill for me to get to see, meet and have Pappy sign one of his books for me. I flew my Cessna 172 from Amarillo to Harlingen with a stop along the way for gas. My buddy Dave went with me as well as Sheila.

On the way home we stopped for gas at a small airport and got a ride into town for supper. When we got back to the airport it was very late and closed up. All the sudden there were police and sheriff vehicles everywhere. We inquired what was wrong, thinking someone had landed with drugs or something. The officers told us that a small plane had crashed short of the end of the runway and the pilot walked to a house nearby to report the incident. The officers used their headlights down the runway for me to take off since the runway lights had been turned off and would not come back on. We made it home safely after midnight and the end of a long weekend.

Before WWII "Pappy" had been flying over China, India and Burma with General Chennault of the Flying Tigers when Pearl Harbor was attacked. I remembered about the famed Flying Tigers as I was growing up during the war and seeing their deeds and accomplishments in the Newsreels at the local theater.

The Flying Tigers flew P-40 planes with an open mouth and shark's teeth painted on the nose to make them look vicious, which they were. The Flying Tigers were an AVG (American Volunteer Group). Many of the members were guys fresh out of the military in 1940-1941 that wanted to make a lot of money. They were to be paid a handsome fee for each

Japanese plane shot down. General Chennault did not pay many of them because of the lack of funds.

When Pearl Harbor was attacked, Pappy flew from the base he was at and got his commission reinstated in the Marines as a fighter pilot. Pappy then took a group of drunks and misfits and turned them into the best squadron (VMF-214) in the South Pacific flying Corsairs. . He was a legend and of course the TV program made him even more of a hero. The F4-U Corsair was the first plane to exceed 400 mph in level flight and thus made it a great fighter aircraft. One thing I didn't know until recently was that Goodyear built over 4,000 of the Corsairs under contract.

Pappy Boyington in Harlingen, TX at CAF

"Pappy" spent a year and a half as a Japanese POW, was awarded the Congressional Medal of Honor, and was recognized as the Marine Corps top ace having shot down 28 enemy aircraft.

Since I was shutting down the lab I really had no need for the plane and traded the equity in it to a flying club for being able to fly their planes. This would save me the hanger rent; plane insurance and many other expenses and I could still fly. I would also not have to show any income from the sale of the plane.

My father had moved to Amarillo and I was looking forward to having him spend some time together. He would come over to the camera shop every morning and have coffee and many days have lunch with me as well.

I had an employee from the lab that I kept to work in the camera store that would free me up and give me some rest. We wanted to get out of the airbase housing and Mary Beth had expressed an interest in going to West Texas University for maybe a Veterinarian or something like working or running a Zoo. I saw some property and we bought 35 acres east of Amarillo.

Trying to Teach Life Experiences

As I look back on a lot of the things I did in raising all of my girls there are some things I might do different. Being a parent and trying to be a good parent is really very hard. It is much harder on the parent than on the child.

Some of my ideas in raising Mary Beth were revolutionary to me and some were good, maybe some not so good. There were some difficult times but the one thing I am very proud of is that *ALL OF THE GIRLS* turned out so well.

While we still lived in Clovis, Mary Beth wanted a stereo for her room. The way that I handled it was to tell her "Let's go get it, and you can work at the shop and do such and such and it is all yours to do whatever you want with." Not that I ever had a problem with Mary Beth not taking care of her items I just wanted to try to teach a value on a piece of merchandise. We went and bought it and Mary Beth fulfilled her part of the bargain, and then some. Later as I remember she wanted a TV and we did the same deal.

Then Mary Beth wanted a motorcycle. I added a few more stipulations in that she had to wear a helmet, jacket and ride it only in the alley that was protected by cement walls. I told her when she could ride the motorcycle well enough we would get her a license to take it on the street. She became proficient in handling the bike and then lost interest. It sat on the back porch for a good while. One day Mary Beth wanted a set of good roller skates and I told her to sell the motorcycle if she wasn't going to ride it. Her answer to me was "No one wants the motorcycle." A couple days later she had sold it and was able to purchase her roller skates. Mary Beth always held up her side of the bargain.

After we had moved to Amarillo and Mary Beth was in High School I had told her that I wanted her to enjoy school and not have to work. She did baby sit Karen quite a bit and was outstanding at that. We had an old Nash Rambler and I allowed her to drive it to school with me furnishing all expenses. Mary Beth was active in the Explorer Scouts and drove to the evening meetings.

One day Mary Beth comes home and said she had taken a job. I inquired about the job and where it was and what would she be doing. The job was at Grand Variety and would pay a whopping $1.25 an hour. I tried to explain to her she was worth a lot more than that because of what she had learned working in our store. After a long talk we came to an agreement where Mary Beth would now pay for the gas for the car, I would do the major maintenance and Insurance. She would also pay $5.00 a week rental on the car, save one-third of her income, and she would have to stay at the Grand Variety for at least six months before trying to find another job.

Every Saturday when Mary Beth would walk in the door, I would stick out my hand and say "Give me my $5." The first few months' things went well then as I stuck out my hand week after week. Then things went from unhappy to bad, then to worse. I'll admit I played it to the hilt.

Mary Beth changed jobs after six months and went to work for TG&Y and was paid almost three times as much. Our deal with the car remained the same. One Saturday she came in and stated she didn't think she should have to pay the car rental. I asked her how much she had saved, since she was supposed to be saving a third. I also knew she couldn't save that much. Things got just slightly heated and I asked Sheila to go get the bank book. What I had been doing was putting the $5 a week in a savings account and there was over $260 in the account and some money that had not been deposited.

Looking back today the jury is still out on whether it was a good idea on the car rental, but I am very proud that Mary Beth always held up her part of any deal we made. I think I should have told her sooner what I was doing but maybe I would have had a little trouble collecting her savings money. Years have proved she is none the worse for the stress I put her through and has used all of her working experience in landing a great job right out of High School where she is still employed. When Mary Beth graduated from Caprock High School in June 1977 she returned to Manassas with her mother and accepted a job with the Hecht Company in the DC area.

Mary Beth with Karen at her graduation

Chapter 23 – The Farm

Building the House

I decided to build a house myself so one Sunday I drew some plans on some butcher paper and on Monday I went out and started to dig the foundation. My dad came out and was being a "sidewalk superintendent." I got the forms up and dug the drain lines and water lines and my dad thought I was doing just fine. A friend of mine and me poured the cement slab and spent 12 hours of hard work getting it level and finished. It was midnight when we got it done. A couple days later we pulled the forms and started putting up the walls. The initial house was a Chalet A-Frame about 1500 sq ft on two stories. I later added about 700 sq ft of additional space to the main house with central heat and air. All of the construction would take about nine months to get at least livable. We moved into the house in the fall of 1977, unfinished but at least paid for and no rent.

The house that Al built before we added the addition in the back

I also built a large cement floored chicken coop. While I was building the chicken coop I decided to put a covered pen for the cows to get out of the weather. Quite often Karen would be with me during the day, during the summer or on Saturday's, as she loved to help out and to run around the farm. While working on the roof I was standing on top of a ladder working on the rafters that would hold the roof for the pen. The ladder was a standard home-style lightweight ladder. As I reached for something the ladder came out from under me and I fell six-feet to the ground, and flat on my back knocking the wind totally from me. Had I fallen a foot more to the left a stake would have gone through my head. Karen was about six at the time and happened to be right near me. Without a thought she headed for the house at a dead run to call her mother. I had Bill, a friend helping me and he heard me fall and came to see what the problem was. When I told him I was OK and nothing broken as far as I could tell, he ran for Karen. Karen as young as she was knew to go call her mother. Bill then let her call her mother but explained all was well and I would just be sore.

On Monday I headed downtown to make my next purchase of a real heavy-duty wooden ladder that was intended to stand on the top of and could support 300 pounds. I would use this ladder while building the photo lab and actually still have this ladder to this day. The ladder cost about three times what the regular type ladders cost but was so worth the investment.

I also built a large two-car garage complete with plumbing, an area to be used for canning and another area as a shop. I had planted over a hundred fruit trees and with a "Ditch-witch" machine I trenched all around the orchard and installed water outlets. I bought a new Ford diesel tractor to use for posthole digging, mowing and to move snow in the winter. I was becoming a real farmer.

We had a big unexpected surprise when we found out that Sheila was pregnant with our second child, she was due in May of 1978.   Lesley was born on a really rainy night complete with the city of Canyon, 15 miles south, getting more water than they needed and being flooded.

The Deal

I had expanded the camera store and so many of my old customers were begging me to get back in the processing business since quality was no longer available in Amarillo. In late 1976 a group that had put in a small film-processing lab folded because of the lack of experience. They only lasted about six months and it had been setting empty for almost a year when I came up with a complicated idea. One of my customers was interested in purchasing the camera store, so I put together a business plan to purchase the debunked lab for about ten-cents on the dollar. I could sell the camera store and by my financing half of it, purchase a lot to build a building on and get the financing to build the building. Each item was contingent on all of them being completed. I still had a lot of photo equipment in my building at the air base but at rent of $200 a month for 9,000 sq feet it was just as easy to keep it.

There was enough interest in the laboratory going back into business, which I calculated I would do just fine without having drive-in locations or having to do business for anyone else. I took my business plan to the bank and they approved it entirely. I sold the camera store and started getting the lab back in business at the location it was, until I could build the new building on the lot that I had selected.

I hired the architect and had the plans drawn based on my layout. The building would be a 6700 sq ft building to be built in two stages. The first would be the photo lab of 4,000 sq ft. I was going to be the general contractor for the building. I hired sub-contractors to do each part of the initial construction such as the cement work, the outside cement block work and the roof. I had a friend that was an electrician and since I knew what I wanted and how to do it, he would take out the permit. I was going to do the work, with him coming around to check my work and call for the inspections. The inside walls I could do since none were really support walls. I plumbed in the machines, having hired a plumbing company to do the rough-in plumbing up through the slab.

I had rehired Bob Pinchback who had worked for me out at the airbase, to work in the lab and help me with the inside construction. After we got the film processed we would immediately head for the new building to work on the inside. When we were about half done with the lab part of the building, I had someone wanting to lease the part of the building that I was planning to lease as a camera shop. I also had a small space of about 900 sq ft for a picture frame shop to go with the lab. We started construction on this and since there weren't any walls inside, except for bathrooms and one other small room in the Camera shop, I sub-contracted most all of the construction.

It took us about six months to have the new building open. We had some equipment already installed and we moved the rest over a weekend and were never out of business. We called the new photo lab Magicolour Labs. Business went well and we did all types of photography. We had the capability to produce over 20,000 color prints an hour. We offered in by 10am and out by 4pm color film processing.

One of the most profitable types of work we did was photographing high school reunions. We would photograph the reunion class either at the picnic, in the afternoon, or at the beginning of their banquet. We would deliver finished 8x10 color photographs before the party broke up. Laura came to visit one summer over the 4th of July weekend so I put her helping one night and between all of the locations we did over $8,000 on the one weekend. That was a real exception because of the number of reunions, but we would normally do a couple reunions a month from June to Sept.

Out on the Farm

Things out at the farm were fun since we were raising Jersey cows, pigs and chickens. The kids enjoyed feeding bottles to the calves and having space to run.

I ordered books and read everything there was about chickens. Before we got the chicken coop finished I ordered some day-old chickens, 500 of them. I penned off an area in the old warehouse at the airbase and we had fun for a few days. Chickens grow up so fast and as they grow they eat and eat a lot. When the chickens were about four weeks old there was one rooster that when Karen would get in with the chickens it would sneak up and peck her on the back of the leg. She would turn and point her finger and say, "you are going to be the first to lose your head." We thought it was really funny. I got the chicken coop finished and we moved them to the farm and as the chickens grew that one rooster kept it up. At about seven weeks when we were ready to butcher some of them, it was the first to lose its head.

I had watched my grandmother Hooton clean chickens but it was only one or two for a Sunday meal. I had a lot of chickens to do something with since they were getting so expensive to feed. I killed and cleaned a few but right away knew there had to be a better way. In the back of one of the books was information for a company that makes chicken pluckers. I

222

called, and not wanting to act stupid, said "can you tell me about your chicken pluckers." The response was "how many do you need to clean"? Again, not wanting to sound like I just fell off the turnip truck I told him "maybe a couple hundred twice a year." He said you need our Model 1A. I inquired about it and was told it would pluck a chicken in 30 seconds. I responded that nothing could pluck a chicken in 30 seconds to which he answered they had large machines that would do it in a second or two. I asked how much this machine was and the price was $169. I made him promise that I could pluck a chicken in one minute and I would buy it. He said he was sure after I got the hang of it I could do it in 20-30 seconds with no problem.

I then learned there were some other things about cleaning chickens, as he knew by then that I did just fall off the turnip truck. He gave me lots of information, included some other items I needed and in two days I had the plucker. It performed exactly as promised by following his instructions to the letter.

Then came the problem of cutting up the chickens for freezing. After some deliberation I came to an idea of removing the legs and wings and removing the breast carefully as to not hurt the insides. I then folded the chicken open and cut the bones around the neck area with tree pruning shears. Then I could remove the giblet items and throw the rest of the insides away by simply raking from the back. It got where I could clean a chicken in less than three minutes from plucking to packing.

With the farm fairly well completed and the raising of animals making it seem like a real farm, we learned a lot about the animals giving birth. We had some neighbors that lived up behind us that had very little money. They did have a Jersey cow that was about to give birth and were having some problems with the delivery. They could not afford to have the vet come and see what the problem was but on the other hand they did not want to lose the cow and calf. The vet knew their financial problems and when they called about the problems they were told there were two good experienced people near them.

The problem was diagnosed over the phone. The vet said if the cow did not give birth naturally in the next few hours the calf would have to be "pulled" as it was most likely already dead. The vet called me and told me what to do by reaching in and grabbing the feet and pull hard. If necessary to put a rope on the feet and pull the calf out with a truck while the cow was tied to the fence. I had read books on calving and felt comfortable so at midnight and with headlights I did as instructed and pulled the calf, which was dead. This was quite an experience for me. The worse thing was a couple weeks later the cow ate a small piece of barbed wire and it tore the stomach and died.

Along with raising the cows we had some pigs that were always fun. We had a big sow that was having her first litter in the cold of February. I had made some steel birthing pens for the sow and thought all would be well. The pen held the sow in the middle but allowed the baby piglets to go a little to the sides. The next morning there was only one of the eight piglets left as the sow had rolled on the others apparently while they were feeding. I did not want to see this one piglet meet the same fate so off to the house it went.

There is nothing more fun and hilarious than to see a baby pig in the house. We first placed it in a box on a blanket and took it out to feed. We fed it baby cereal from a mayonnaise jar lid by dipping our fingers in it and then into the piglets mouth. After a few days we started taking it outside every couple hours to house train it. About a couple weeks into this routine we gave the piglet run of the house during times we could watch. Soon it would go to the back door and stand wanting out. We would take it out, it would do its thing and come right back in. Karen and Lesley would give the piglet a bath regularly. The pig never had any odor to it and by April it weighed about 40 pounds. Quite a difference from the half-pound it weighed at birth. We raised it until it was time to butcher but we could not butcher the animal so we traded it off.

One humorous thing with raising pigs was, having to cut one of the big boar (male) pigs. I had actually waited longer than I should have because of the cold weather. The boar was weighing in about 220 pounds but was pretty tame and I could feed it from my hands. With my friend Bill we cornered the boar in the pen and grabbed him threw him down and did the surgery that was necessary. Had he not been "cut" the meat might have been too strong to eat. After that experience I could never get behind that pig again. No wonder either after him trusting me then my doing what I did.

By this time I was not flying my plane enough to make it profitable and sold it to a flying club. The deal was for them to pay it off and I would take out my equity in using their planes when I wanted. I would be able to fly and not have the expense of owning and maintaining a plane.

Flying back to the East Coast

Lesley was born in May of 1978 and Laura was graduating from High School in Manassas in June. I wanted to attend her graduation so I put a plan together to have Dave, the one that taught me to fly, go with me and we would see Barbara and Norman in Steubenville and fly on to Manassas to see Laura graduate. We would then fly to Asheville, NC to see Dave's dad and then to Atlanta and pick up my cousin Charlotte and bring her back to Texas for a visit.

We left Amarillo in a Cessna 210 that belonged to the flying club and headed for St Louis to refuel. Whenever Dave and I went anywhere he always ran the radio and I flew the plane. The plane was hot and we had a little trouble getting it re-started and were a little late getting off. I had called Barbara and given her an approximate time we would be there. We arrived in Steubenville about midnight with Barbara and Norman there to pick us up. We visited until the wee hours of the morning, but wanted to get an early start so we were up and on our way by 9am.

We left and headed for Manassas and after we crossed the mountains Dave called Dulles approach control. Even though we didn't file a flight plan we wanted them to know who we were and where we were going. Manassas airport sits on one of the busy approaches to Dulles airport. Dave said our plane number and then "do you think you can help a couple of country boys from Texas get to Manassas Municipal airport." You could hear the controller rolling on the floor. What this really meant was that we were not familiar with the area and to give advisories and us some radar vectors. Every once in a while we would get a new heading and finally the controller came and called our plane number and said "Manassas Municipal International Airport is one mile at 12 o'clock, do you think you can find it." This meant we were one mile from the end of the runway right out the windshield. He had put some humor into the trip for us. Of course the airport was not an "International" airport but it added to the fun.

Cousin Charlotte in the Cessna 210 I flew back east

We stayed and saw Laura graduate from school then we headed South and visited Dave's dad and on to Atlanta. We took Charlotte's daughters for a quick ride and then we left for Amarillo with a couple stops for refueling. I found out on the way that when Charlotte told Aunt Hazel that she was going to visit and I was flying her out her mom told her not to get in the plane with me. Of course when I was growing up no one would ever imagine me flying so it was understandable. Charlotte told her I had a license and she was coming. Once again this was all *"Beyond my Wildest Dreams."*

The First Flood
The summer of 1981 brought our first real problems when we had a week of hard rain and the area where the photo lab was located started flooding. I built the photo lab three feet higher that the original plans, because the alley wasn't already put in by the city. I didn't want them constructing it at the height of the surrounding lots that would have meant I might have water draining on my lot from the alley. When they did construct the alley they actually cut it down about two feet. My planning saved things this year since I only had about an inch of water in the lab which caused no problems other than being closed for six weeks while they drained the big lake that was the

collection for the drain off of the area. Some people really suffered a lot of damage because their buildings were lower than mine.

We all complained to the city and received their promises they would dig the lake 60 feet deeper, install new pumps and keep the lake drained. They did drain it, dig it and install new pumps but over the next year they did not keep it drained. It made a pretty lake but not a good storage lake. There was over 5,000 acres that drained into the lake. The water was pumped over a hill and to the Power Company and on to Lake Meredith. Without money coming in for six weeks it really put a cramp in the bills. When your business is closed in for that long of a time people tend to find new sources for their needs. It would take the better part of a year to get some of the customer's back.

Karen & Lesley feeding a Jersey calf born on the farm

The year of 1982 started out with some recovery from the previous flood and continued to improve. I had started selling artist canvas in the photo shop when a guy from Canyon, came around selling his wares. I had not looked up a retail price but I knew we had artists as customers and I could sell some if the price was right. The price that was quoted to me I knew was a great price and if I marked them up only a dollar I could sell some. I asked how many I had to buy to get the price and he said any amount. I ordered a dozen each of the four most popular sizes. Sheila came into the lab and saw them sitting in boxes up against the outside wall with a "special" price tag on them. She asked what I was going to do and I said we were going to sell artist canvas. She commented they would never sell to which my response was I would learn to paint. I sold those first 48 in about three days. I started ordering more and more.

Soon we were selling over 2000 canvasses a month and each time the guy came around for an order he had a different price. I complained and told him to settle on a price so I could advertise and make some money without changing prices weekly. Then in a few weeks he came in and said he was going to have to make R&S supply (a real art supply distributor) the sole distributor for the canvas and I would have to buy from them. I asked what the price was going to be and he said more than I was selling them for. I asked how big of an order they were going to place and it was very small. I said I was buying more than 2000 a month and I should be the distributor. He was unwavering and I said, "to hell with you, I will make them myself" and let it go at that.

I had found out where they were getting their supplies from casual conversation. I called the Woolsey Company in California about purchasing the equipment and made a trip to Woolsey to see what was involved and learn more about it. A week later the guy came around and asked if I was really serious and I told him I had just gotten off the phone and was going to make them myself. He responded "why don't you buy us out" and at a price for only what stock they had. I agreed and paid him the amount of $30,000 he had in equipment and supplies. I also agreed to hire his worker. I figured that if I was selling over 2000 a month at a dollar above cost I could make some money just buying him out. I planned to move the business in a week or two from Canyon to the building I had at the airbase. Then things went from bad to worse.

Second Flood

In August 1982 all things went to Pot. Sheila had been at her mothers in Texarkana for several weeks because her mother was not doing well. Sheila's mother passed away during the negotiation for the canvas business, so the funeral was planned for a Monday and I flew the girls down with my buddy Dave, because he was going to bring the plane back. The girls

228

and I were going to drive back after the funeral and Sheila would stay to clear the estate. We got back to Amarillo and on Thursday I had the girls at the photo lab with me. The space that had been rented as a camera shop was now our art and frame shop, since the renter moved to a different location.

It started raining in the afternoon and by 5 pm the rain was backing up into the streets because the lake was not emptied as it should have been. When we saw the water in the streets I started picking up as much stuff as I could and putting it up on tables to get anything lower than three feet up high on tables or shelves. The photo equipment was very heavy except for two color printers. I called my buddy Larry and he waded through water and made it to the building. I moved my car from in front of the store to a church lot a block away. Larry and I lifted as much heavy stuff up that we could. By this time the water was up in the driveway. I got the two lighter color printers up on cement blocks thinking the water wouldn't get that high. I had two color printers that weighed over 500 pounds each and were $80,000 new and we couldn't move them. One other color printer also was too heavy to try to lift.

The Photo Lab and Frame Shop during flood – I had built the building

We did everything we could and soon the water was coming in under the door so it was time to abandon ship. Larry and I each carried one of the girls across the water and got to the car that was only in a couple inches of water. We headed home totally exhausted. Karen and Lesley worked as hard as any grown-up. They had seen the flood the year before but this time it hit home with more certainty. We went home to the farm

229

and called Sheila telling her about the flood and there was no hurry now to get back as fast as she could. Her request to me was not to kill anyone before she got home; knowing that I was so upset at the city officials I really felt like doing most of them in for their lack of attentiveness.

The rainfall had been what was called a "100 year rainfall" and was about five inches in about six hours. With the lake full there was no where for the five thousand acres to drain except in the streets and businesses. I ended up with about three-feet of water in the building. It took the city more than eight weeks to get the area dry.

There was an offer from a dredging company from Houston that offered the city to pump the streets and lake dry in less than 48 hours. The deal was if they didn't do it there would be no cost to the city. If they accomplished it the city would buy the pump which was valued at around $350,000. The city refused thinking they knew everything about pumping water and they got a lot of aluminum irrigation pipe and ran it about ¾ mile up over the hill where it would flow into Lake Meredith. They put a 5000-gallon pump on the intake but only 500 gallons came out the other end. After a couple days and conferring with engineers they were told that the aluminum pipe creates a friction and you can run water through it but you can't pump water at high pressure through it. They then took a couple more days and changed it out with PVC and it started working. The pumps they had installed in the lake were not working because the electric housing for the controls got flooded and shorted out.

I had been into the building while it was flooded and ascertained the two lighter color printers were not physically wet but may have moisture problems. I recruited my buddy Larry again and another friend. I rented a tall Ryder truck that would not get wet in the lowest spots and I backed up to the building and the three of us carried the two machines and put them in the truck. There was mud and muck in the water and we just knew one of us would slip and fall which would ruin the machine. We took it real slow and got them both onto the truck. I took some photos and could do nothing but hope. We took the machines to the studio I had in Sunset Center and plugged them in and they did work and cycle.

I heard of someone in El Paso that was looking for some machines and called. He flew up and purchased one of the machines. He asked to see the Lab but we told him that we didn't allow anyone in or around the equipment. He bought the story, paid for the machine and arranged for it to be shipped to El Paso. We carefully took him back to the airport where he could not see that area of the city flooded. He was in the town maybe four hours total. The one machine that I had paid $32,000 for I think I got around $18,000 for it and considering it was used I came out all right.

They didn't use multiple pumps and it took about two weeks before the water was out of the photo lab. With all of the electronics in the photo equipment sitting under water for so long the equipment was worthless. A couple of the machines had motors up high that was out of the water so the motors were salvageable but the rest of the machine was junk. The enlargers were all right since they were up high on tables. There were other small items that could be salvaged but for the most part we put the equipment in dumpsters since it went down in the flood.

As soon as the water was off the floor of the building I was in trying to clean up and work on anything that I could. I was tearing Sheetrock out to kill mold and doing everything I could.

Meningitis

I had a wedding to photograph on the Saturday after we got into the building to start cleaning. There was a guy that I knew that wanted to learn how to photograph weddings and I told him I would take him. The wedding was in a town 60 miles east of Amarillo. We left early and on the way while I was driving I made the comment that the sun was bothering my eyes. We got to the town and by then I had a headache. I thought it was all the stress of the past week. We ate something from a fast food place and headed to the wedding.

By this time my head felt like it was going to explode. I sent him to the drug store to get some aspirin for me. He got back in ten or so minutes and I took three of them and the wedding started. I operated on automatic since my head hurt so much. We got to the reception and I photographed the cutting of the cake and set the camera and told my friend to stand about eight to ten feet away and take shots of the people at the reception. I was hurting so badly that he had to drive me home. We got to the farm and he dropped me off which was now about 11pm. I told Sheila that I did not feel good and went to bed.

About two o'clock in the morning I could not stand it anymore and woke Sheila and told her she had to take me to the hospital. We arrived where a doctor examined me and wanted to do a spinal tap. He dug on my back for about 15 minutes and then called in a neurosurgeon that did the spinal tap in about ten seconds. At the time the first doctor was digging on my back I hurt so much I really didn't care if I lived or died. The spinal tap was to confirm meningitis.
I was taken to intensive care where I stayed for four days. The only cure for the viral meningitis was to relieve the pain with the pressure between the brain and skull and in some cases cut a hole in the skull to relieve the pressure. The one thing that baffled everyone was my heart would stop periodically and then restart. I remember gasping for breath and that was what started the heart. The painkiller Demerol they could only give me every six hours so at the end of four hours they came in and made me take something else. I was so totally out of it I just remember them coming in and saying, "Take this." By late Wednesday they came in and moved me to a private room.

On Thursday afternoon the doctor came in and said because I did not have insurance he would let me go home if I promised to stay in bed for a couple weeks and do nothing. He stated that bed rest was now the only thing that I needed but if I didn't heed his instructions I would not have any energy for six months or more. I said I would go home and stay in bed. I could not fathom going home and not doing something that would cause me to not have energy since I had always been a workhorse. I went home, but on Saturday I went down to the lab to see what I could do to clean up. The following week I went to work as usual about 8am but by 5pm I was so exhausted I could hardly move. I toughed it out till 7pm and went home. It literally took me 18 months to have any real energy.

During the time the area was flooded I took the opportunity to move the canvas business from Canyon to the airbase. Of course now my location to sell them was under water. We heard of a frame and art shop out in a busy part of town that might be for sale. The lady Margaret, who owned it, would rather teach painting than have the art shop. She was also not really a custom framer so we negotiated and bought the shop. This gave us a retail location that was somewhat like what we had in the frame shop. We had managed to save a lot of our stock so that added to what Margaret had. We worked out a deal for Margaret to teach painting and we had the shop.

In the meantime I had my hands full with the canvas business and trying to get the photo lab cleaned up and organized so I could dispose of the equipment and sell the building. The equipment needed for producing photos in "One Hour" was coming on to the market and I did not want to invest in the new equipment. My decision was to salvage what I could and sell the building. Prior to the flood the building was worth about $250,000. The one lucky thing was when I made my business plan that I had taken to the bank, I proposed a ten-year commercial note on the building. The equipment that went down in the flood was over $450,000. This was more than ten years of hard work down the sewer in just a few short weeks. All in all I only owed about $80,000 on everything building and equipment. I managed to sell the two good printers and some small equipment plus the building for $127,000 so at least I didn't owe money. I had just lost all of my 10 years of very hard work.

Paper processing machines – "A State of the Art Lab"

I had filed suit against the city of Amarillo for 1.2 million but the lawyer who had taken the case on a contingency was not truthful and I have learned is the case with most lawyers. I am sure that the city had "gotten to him" and after two years he called and said he needed money for "expert witnesses." I argued that he had stated initially he would put the up-front money and take expenses out of the settlement. He said that was not the case and that he had an offer from the city to settle so we had to take the paltry amount. At least it did show that I was right and I was the only one that sued the city, some lost more than I did.

We had been told that because of the flood we would be able to write the equipment off as a loss. The worst thing was that when we filed taxes I ended up getting a bill from the IRS to pay back $9,000 in investment tax credits. Had I just simply hauled the equipment out and piled it on the farm I could have deducted the balance as depreciation. Things are not always fair.

One of 2 - $80,000.00 Color printer's lost in the flood along with more

Chapter 24 – Mail Order Business

I started working and getting things organized in the canvas business. I had airlines to run and production flow to organize and packing and storage areas. Since I had never made a canvas I needed to watch my new employee construct some and try my hand at it to see the best production methods. I have a knack for spotting easier ways to do a job. I timed each step in the production and put the time and costs on paper. I came up with an accurate price of the cost to produce the canvas. I was to later find out the previous owners did not do any kind of cost analysis. What they had simply done was to take the word of Woolsey and when they didn't have a little bit of profit they raised the price a few cents. That was the reason for the new price each time they came around.

I then had a brainstorm of creating a mail-order business with the artist canvas. With the knowledge about advertising, from the photo business seminars I had attended, I created an advertisement to go into a national magazine called "The Artist Magazine." At the time Sheila was handling all of the bookkeeping and the primary office work. I had done the research on the advertising costs and the lead-time needed which was 90 days. I made a camera-ready copy of the advertisement that I wanted placed and gave it to Sheila for including a check for three months of submission and sending to the magazine publisher.

When the 90 days had passed I commented the magazine should be about out, to which Sheila replied she had not sent the advertisement to the publisher since it was a stupid idea and no one would purchase canvas through mail order. My blood pressure that was already very high went through the roof and I blew my stack. I got on the phone and called the publisher and was told that if I could get the ad to them by overnight mail they would be able to get it in the issue that would hit the stands in two months. I sent the advertisement and had to wait another two months. I had used the first 90 days gearing up and learning the canvas production business. I also knew we would not be able to operate a mail order business using a tablet to take orders and using receipt pads to ship orders and keep track of customers.

During the time I had been building the house and the new photo lab I had little time. This went on for several years. Lesley having been born during this time meant we had little time to spend together. I made the best of every opportunity I could to spend time with both Karen and Lesley. Even though Lesley was an unexpected surprise she was about as cute as they come and developed into a real "daddy's girl" as was Karen.

In the evenings when I came home I would like to read the paper but this meant not having those few minutes to spend with the girls. I conquered this by having Lesley crawl up on my lap and we read the Wall Street Journal together and this provided some of the best times together. By the time she was about four and a half she could read most of the paper. When we came to a word she did not know or understand I would help her sound it out and explain it to her. This was some real "quality time" together. As I look back at this time I wish I had done something like this with all of my girls. It was easy teaching her to read and the time together was awesome.

Personal computers had just hit the market and Karen was learning about them in school so I decided a computer would solve our problem of tracking orders etc. I spent $2500 on an IBM PC-Jr with a couple of small programs. Karen and I learned about the computer and created a form for customers. The program was on a floppy disk, there was no hard drive on the machine, and only 256k of memory and the speed was 4.77mh. We did everything the computer was capable of doing but not all that we needed. We had to save all of our work on the 5-¼" floppies. Any dirt on a floppy meant it would not work so it meant backing up everything we did so if we lost one we would still have a copy.

When the magazine did hit the stands we received over 400 inquiries the first month. This was mind boggling since the advertisement was a one column by one-inch ad. I had prepared price lists to send to those that had written and we immediately started getting orders. Each month thereafter we received a couple hundred inquiries. It grew quickly especially when the customers started receiving their orders and telling their friends, the volume picked up.

As the orders increased the next three months it was apparent the little PC-Jr computer would not do the work needed, beside the fact that IBM was dumping them now for $700. It was time to upgrade the computer to what was called an "XT" computer that had just come out. This computer also cost $2500 but there was so much more capability with this, it was like the difference in walking and riding a horse as far as going somewhere. I also purchased a 15mb hard drive for the new computer at a price of $600. I added some memory that was $100 per megabyte. Now this was a real computer and you could save data right inside the computer. I thought there was no way I would ever fill up such a big hard drive. Also now there were things called "databases" available to use to write custom programs. Business programs were not available but at least now you could create your own, but you had to learn some programming. The computer business was truly changing very fast. The initial version of the database cost $50 and each upgrade to allow it to do more was an additional charge.

I started using the evenings to learn to write a business program. My friend Larry came out many evenings and we worked till midnight trying to create the program. I heard how useless this was to try to write a program. At this time in 1983 there was no such thing as Windows for the computer and it would be years before this was offered.

About this same time we were ordering the stretcher bars for the artist canvas from Woolsey in California and the shipping charges were out of sight. To get the best price on the bars and freight it meant placing a large order. I was quick to realize the stretcher bars were the most expensive part of the canvas so I started searching and tried to find someone closer that made stretcher bars. I located a company in Albuquerque that made stretcher bars for Grumbacher and then shipped them to Maine, a railroad car at a time. I went and visited with them to see if they would sell to me. The company was really in the wood molding business and making the stretcher bars was a sideline. There was a yard full of seconds that maybe had something imperfect on one side only so they agreed to sell me some of the seconds along with a stretcher bar machine if I took a large volume of the seconds.

I calculated things and decided I would take their deal. Having the seconds would allow me to stretch canvas while I got the wood factory set up to make my own stretcher bars. I would have to buy a big saw, a molding machine, dust collection system and locate a source for the truckloads of wood. I also decided I needed more room than the 9000 sq ft building, so I talked to the landlord of the buildings on the old air base and rented an old consolidated mess hall that was 29,000 sq ft. We moved in the spring and the building was supposed to have a working heating system.

I was also purchasing the canvas from Woolsey and thought I could buy direct from the mill. Living in an area where cotton is grown we saw ads on TV for "Cotton Incorporated" the organization of cotton producers. I picked up the phone and called them and when a guy answered the phone I gave my name and asked if he knew who manufactured cotton artist canvas. I know he didn't have time to research it but he gave me the names of two different companies and the phone numbers, which he probably got from his Rolodex. The call was less than three minutes and I then called both of the companies. One of the companies had the same exact canvas that I was using and it was a hundred dollars a roll cheaper. That was how much Woolsey was marking it up.

By making my own stretcher bars and buying the canvas direct I would cut my cost to produce by about 30%. By selling at the same price that I was, my profit would soar.

Next door to the frame shop downtown was a needlework shop that sent all of their customers to us for their framing. The woman, Betty, that owned the needlework shop would supposedly square and block the customer's needlework, and charge them for it, and send them to us to frame their masterpiece. Betty really had no clue of how to do an order correctly for the squaring and blocking so we ended up correcting her mistakes.

Sheila enjoyed the needlework aspect and the shop so we purchased the needlework shop from Betty and I opened the wall between the frame shop and the needlework shop. The frame and needlework shop started really doing well.

238

With the move into the mess hall at the airbase for the canvas business we did all of the framing except for assembly which Sheila would do at the downtown shop. The work Larry and I had put into the computer program was starting to pay off since the program was working great and I tweaked it often. I was signed up for trade shows in Dallas to show our canvas. I wanted to make contact with manufacturers of related art & frame items. I felt it would be a natural to add art supplies and ready-made frames to our catalog. At the trade show the booth next to me was an import/export company owned by an individual named Simon who was from San Jose.

I made some deals to handle art supplies and to be able to buy frames directly, that were made in Mexico. The price list for the canvas business was a one sheet folded in half, but now with the addition of the art supplies and frames I needed a more elaborate price list. Since I had named the mail order canvas business "Wild West Supply" I thought it would be neat to create a price list in the form of a newspaper. I called the price list "The Wild West Gazette" and wrote things such as shipping, payment, minimum orders and customer service in the form of stories. This was the point that I realized I wished I had paid more attention in English class in high school.

However, Sheila never let me forget that she was a college graduate and English major. I wrote the paper pretty "hokey" using things like the stagecoach (UPS) would pick up the orders daily and have it to your doorstep in a few days. I always had a news banner of some type and on one of the price lists I had a "Wanted" headline and then went into a story about wanting new customers. It was much cheaper to have the newspaper than having regular folded printing done. With the larger size of the newspaper it required fewer pages. There was a company that printed local newspapers for the small cities around Amarillo and I could buy the price list printed as a newspaper for pennies a copy.

When the first price lists started getting to the customers I got responses about how they loved the price list and the way it was written. I wrote the items pretty much as a person would talk. The grammar was not perfect and Sheila hated it, and she hated it more when the customers mentioned they liked the price list.

The winter was coming and the landlord fired up the boilers for the building and they wouldn't work. They assured me that everything else was fine but they couldn't afford to put a new boiler in the building. By this time we had so much equipment and work going on I couldn't think of anything but staying. I made the deal with the landlord that if I put a boiler in I could deduct it from the rent. I got a bank loan and arranged for a new boiler at $12,000 and it was installed and turned on the day after Thanksgiving. When it built up pressure it blew out the pipes under the building. Replacing all of the pipes and radiators would be cost prohibitive. We operated that winter having to shut down on the days too cold to work. Luckily it was one of the warmest winters the area had seen.

Business continued to grow and we were selling a good number of picture frames. Purchasing boxes for the canvas was not a problem since they are boxes that are specific for the size of canvas. However we allowed a customer to order up to six of any size frames in a box. This meant all kinds of sizes based on frames being packed. I knew we had to make our own boxes and I designed a little box-making machine on paper and took it to a machine shop.

I asked Mike, the machinist I knew how much to make it. He asked what it was and when I told him he responded that it wouldn't work. I told him it would and how much to build it for me. He said it would be $450, I OK'd the project and he had it in a week. I went down with a piece of cardboard and it scored the cardboard just right. Mike was so impressed he said now that he understood it he could see some things he could change.

I said I wanted to use it for a while and then we would get back together. We used it for about a month and I went back to see Mike. I had even had a couple more ideas and along with the changes he had, a new box maker was designed. I asked Mike how much it would cost and he said nothing, but maybe I could sell some, which I did sell a few. The new improved box maker would make a box any size in length and width up to 11 inches deep. We made a top and a bottom thus giving the frames good corner padding. We made the boxes so the frames fit securely and did not move inside the box. We had no damage unless UPS destroyed the box, which happened in about one in a thousand orders.

The summer of 1986 saw me getting ready for another trade show in Dallas. I decided to just take the computer and enter orders right on the spot rather than writing them in a pad and entering them when I got home. I set up the booth and also had my buddy Larry with me since he is also a natural born salesman. My booth neighbor Simon, from the year before, came by and said HI and asked about the computer. I explained that I brought it to enter orders. He was so fascinated that he spent about half of the show at my booth watching the computer do its work. His booth was farther down the aisle and he left his helper to run his booth. When the show was over and we started packing it Simon asked me how much I would sell him the program for. I had no idea but I conferred with Larry and said $2500. A few minutes later and feeling guilty for saying what I thought was a high price I said, "Since you live in San Jose that is the Silicone Village you could get it done cheaper." In fact the database I used was from San Jose.

A couple weeks later and back home I got a call from Simon asking if I would still sell the program for $2500. I said sure, and he said he knew I was good for my word and he wanted to purchase the program. He stated that he had checked around and the best price he could get out there was $13,000. Simon asked if I would come and put it on his new machine. I told him I could not leave the business but I would check with Larry and see what he would do. Larry was not real busy and he told me he would go for a hundred dollars a day and expenses. I got back to Simon and he agreed and sent a ticket for Larry. Larry went out and ended up spending about ten days modifying the program for specific things Simon wanted and he was wined and dined by Simon who was so thankful. While Larry was in San Jose he went by the company that wrote the database and showed them what we had done and commented we had it doing things they didn't know it would do.

Taking the Plotter to the Show

Also for the 1986 show in Dallas I had the genius idea of making an engineering plotter write on mat board. I thought this would revolutionize the picture framing industry and make me a lot of money. I had found a flatbed plotter that would handle a full size 32"x40" sheet of mat board. I thought it would be neat to draw pictures or to do lettering on a mat for things like little league teams etc. In those days we had Windows Draw and if you could create it on the screen the plotter could draw it on anything up to 5/8" thick.

I took it to the show and we literally stole the show with the plotter. Larry and I even gave a class presentation for the trades show on computers. We had people standing ten deep around the booth. We made 5x7 inch mats as cards for everyone. They would come up and give me their name and I would add it and the plotter printed a teddy bear, their name, and all of our business information. We didn't sell one of the plotters. I was devastated since I was so positive, I was going to sell a hundred. In those days an engineering plotter sold for over $10,000 and it printed on paper that rolled it back and forth. This flatbed one I could buy for $1400 and the retail price was $2495. I would later realize the average of the framer was late 40's or early 50's and they were just petrified of computers in those days.

When the fall and winter of 1986 came along we had a normal winter with a lot of cold and snow and then periods of nice warm weather. Being unable to do much of anything on the cold days, most of the help just took those days off, there were just a couple of us at work. I was having problems getting frames from Mexico that were undamaged by the time they got to us so I had to order large quantities and invariably the ones that got damaged were the ones we needed the most.

Mexican Mafia
One of the molding salesmen told me of a frame producer in Laredo that was having real problems. I called and talked to the lady that owned the factory and she was really having problems. She had been the office manager and bought the business from a man that owned it for several years. She thought she could just keep the same help and produce a lot of frames and make lots of money. The quality had gone down so much she was about to close. After a really nice talk I flew to Laredo and visited and saw the factory. I could see it was just about the same as the factories I had seen in Tijuana except smaller. We talked and came up with a plan for her to make

242

the frames with Stan, an employee – neighbor and friend) supervising the plant and me taking the entire output of the factory. We agreed it would be a three-way partnership. I would pay for the frames at the price I had been paying to the other factory and we would split the profits. Sounded easy but it didn't work out that way. Stan went to Laredo and got the equipment back to running well, I advanced a truckload of wood and he turned out a few nice frames after five weeks but we had anticipated it taking no longer than two weeks.

Over the next two weeks Stan produced a couple hundred frames that had great quality. He brought them home and spent a couple days with his family. When he went back the crap hit the fan. He arrived and was told to pack his stuff and get out of Laredo or he would be killed. After getting the factory to producing a quality frame the owner had a friend in the Mexican Mafia and it seemed she would rather have them as partners than us. Stan came back on Thursday. When I found out he had come home I called him and he said he didn't want to talk but would the next day.

When he came over the next morning and told me what had happened I said we had to go to the US Attorney's office and see what we could do. It seemed that when Stan had been home the weekend before he had gotten a call from someone in Amarillo that was a friend of the woman in Laredo. The person worked for the Border Patrol and wanted to meet with Stan. They met for a beer and he told Stan he should get out of Laredo, but he did not do the threatening, that was done when Stan got back to Laredo. This person was on the floor below the US Attorney's office and we told the office the entire story. I was set and determined to go get the truckload of wood that I had paid so much for. I thought by reporting it to the US Attorney's office things would be protected.

I had a friend with a semi that would drive down and back for $1500 to pick up the wood which was valued at about $9000. Not knowing what was going to happen, Stan and I headed down to Laredo with the semi behind us. We had weapons with us in the form of an AR-16, some shotguns and other high-powered weapons. The US Attorney's office said that since we were traveling it was legal to carry them and use them in self-defense.

When we got to Laredo early in the morning I rented a forklift and went to the factory. We were just down the street when they opened and the semi pulled up, the forklift started loading the lumber and within five minutes a lawyer showed up. He said not to touch the lumber. We told him we were taking it and after several hours we decided it might not be worth a life because the lawyer made it very clear we would never make it back to Amarillo alive if we proceeded.

We did keep the two bundles of wood we had loaded already and we headed the nearly 800 miles back to Amarillo. When we got back to Amarillo we went back to the US Attorney's office and made a complete report and as far as we know they never did anything. I gave them the card of the Lawyer that had stated he also worked for the Mafia.

Getting into Making Frames

At this point there was only one thing to do as far as frames and that was to make them myself. Having a lot of experience in the woodworking but not in finishing the frames it took a lot of practice, questions and research. It took several years before I finally perfected what I thought was the highest quality frame. We did produce frames that were acceptable but not of the quality that I was looking for.

We had wasted such valuable time trying to find a good supplier of frames we actually could not grow the business even though we had customers begging for our products. We could not face another winter in the cold factory so I decided to purchase a building in the small town of Panhandle, 15 miles east of Amarillo, where the kids went to school. I purchased a building that had been a tractor supply. I had an addition added to it that made it about 5000 sq ft. I rented another old building on Main Street for storage and shipping and rented another old building for several months for storage of miscellaneous stuff.

We tried to consolidate everything in one small town. The one benefit was that the buildings where people were going to be had heat in the winter. This downsizing and regrouping was really a survival mode because of the problems we had. What we really needed was a building of sufficient size and the finances to operate for a short period of time. Having started actually a couple weeks before the flood in 1982 we had been financially strapped. The idea and concept was a great one but some of the problems like the lack of heat and the Laredo fiasco took its toll.

Karen was now old enough to drive and involved in Band and other activities at the High School. Because of the financial conditions a decision was made to sell the house and farm and move into the city of Panhandle close to the school. We found a house about three blocks from the school and ten blocks from the factory. The girls had no idea of the financial problems and rightfully should not have been told.

Selling the Chicken Plucker etc

With our moving from the farm to the city I decided to sell some of the farm items we had. The local radio station had what they called "Tradio" (pronounced trade-e-o). People could call in during one hour in the morning and list items for sale and their phone number. I wanted to sell the chicken de-beaker that I used while raising chickens. The machine automatically cut off a third of the top beak of a chicken and by doing this they did not waste feed. When I called in the host of the program thought I was pulling his leg and I had to explain it to him. It sold in about five minutes for what I had paid for it.

About a month later I decided to sell the chicken plucker. When I called in the host said he had heard of everything now since a while back someone had called in selling a de-beaker. I said "yep that was me" and I told him how fast it sold. The plucker also sold in just a few minutes.

The marriage with Sheila was stressed and a couple months later Sheila insisted that I sell my Ivory so I put it on the program. The host said how unusual it was to try to sell Elephant Ivory and there had been a guy that sold a de-beaker and plucker so he knew now they had really advertised the limit. I said, "Yes it's me again" and he immediately asked if I had any other unusual items. I mentioned I had a lot of skins but was not ready to sell them. He made a big deal every once in a while about how people could sell anything from a chicken de-beaker, chicken plucker to Ivory to advertise the program.

Me with my Ivory tusks just before I sold them

One of the things that really hurt was before I sold the Ivory Tusks I wanted a photograph of Lesley with the Tusks. She flat-out refused. I could not force her but I pleaded and finally gave up. I had photographs of most of the other children with the tusks and it is not everyone's father that legally shot an elephant. It would have meant a lot to me to have that photo.

We got things organized and moving again but still in dire need of space. I found a company that makes Quonset hut buildings and I could purchase one almost 3000 sq ft for as I remember $4500. I had to put it together but they are easy to assemble. Being in Panhandle the property was not out of sight like in bigger cities. I bought a lot right down the street, had the necessary concrete footing poured and in two weeks we had the building up and secured. We were going to do the woodworking in the Quonset so the wiring was very easy. This freed up some valuable space in our main building and kept the dust level down. We were limited in the amount of production we could do but we were now producing the highest quality frame and could do it at a price that was actually cheaper than they could be produced in Mexico. I had automated so many of the steps to maintain quality control that it kept the costs to produce low. We could not produce more but we did have the best and it was making a small profit. The real key in the manufacturing is the production. If you produce twice as many then the cost to produce spreads the overhead and the actual cost is much less.

We were chugging along and trying to figure how to get everything located in a real manufacturing facility or we were going to do something else. I knew the idea was viable since we could sell everything we could make. The cost to build a building the size we needed was out of the question. Then adding some more equipment needed to produce the volume that would make the profit skyrocket was another factor. I also wanted to be in an area where I could have help that couldn't leave for real high paying jobs. Women could do a lot of the jobs in the factory and they could work during their children's school hours. With a few full time people during the very detailed, exacting and skilled jobs of operating the equipment we would have a perfect mix.

The state of Texas has what is known as Economic Development Corporations in most cities. They can use a part of the sales tax rebate to the city for bringing new businesses to town. In a few cases it can work really well and this depends on the members of the board. Part of the lure to bring business to a new town might be a low interest loan, construction of a building or building additions and maybe equipment or a combination of all and even tax deferment. The town of Panhandle was not large enough to do anything and it took a town of about 35,000 or more to be able to offer any kind of enticement.

My banker was also a friend and he knew what I was up against and alerted the city of Borger, 25 miles north of Panhandle, that we would make a good catch for their Economic Development. I was approached by the BEDC and prepared a business plan. I thought that at last we might be able to pull everything together. What we really needed was a building of at least 20,000 sq ft and approximately $75,000 working cash. In the business plan I had real facts and figures and growth. Our business plan was approved and the offers made to put us in a 10,000-sq ft building and within 90 days add an additional 10,000 sq ft to the existing building. We looked the building and lot over and there was even more space for expansion than we would need for the future. So I thought everything would be fine and if you couldn't trust a city when they put it on paper whom could you trust? I thought I had finally struck gold and now I would just have to mine it.

The plan was to move the heavy woodworking equipment into the new existing building and then when the addition was built it would contain the frame finishing, canvas stretching, office and packing and shipping.

We got the heavy woodworking equipment moved and installed in a period of less than two weeks working many long hours. Until the addition was done, we would assemble the raw frames and then haul them back to Panhandle to be finished, packed and shipped. I had an enclosed trailer that we used for shuffling the frames and canvas around Panhandle so I would just haul it back and forth. I had a woman named Irma that was my right hand in the factory and was capable of supervising any department's production. Irma ran the Panhandle operation with the ordering, finishing and packing. That way I could operate the heavy machines with a crew in Borger. This started out working just fine and the thoughts of having it all together and efficient made up for the temporary inconvenience.

Mike, Joy, Luke and me at the Borger factory

Chapter 25 – End of Marriage with Sheila

I came home on a Saturday evening in April 1994 after putting in a very hard day. It was the first real day of production in Borger. I opened the door to the house and found the house empty except for a bed, dresser and a couple dishes. Sheila and the girls had moved out. Not that it was totally unexpected but I thought things had been somewhat on the mend. This created more problems at a time when I didn't need any more. We had been having problems for years over money. We had made a lot of money but we never seemed to have enough to satisfy Sheila. A marriage of some 23 years was to end.

She was keeping the books and I look back now and wonder. To me it was just money not a material thing. On that day she left she had also gone to the bank and cashed a check for $9,000. I didn't know it until I got my bank statement a couple weeks later. I had removed her from the bank account for the frame factory a couple months earlier when she showed up one Friday and threw the checkbook at me and said I could keep my own books. When I started keeping the books it seemed like there was more and more in the account, so I wonder....

I called the bank and reminded them that I had removed her from the bank account and the response was they would press charges against her for return of the money. The reason she was able to cash the check was she went to a teller that she knew and they only checked the balance of the account and when there was sufficient funds they cashed the check. We had banked at the same bank for 20 years. I didn't want to create any more hate and discontent so I told the bank to forget it but be sure she could never cash another and to flag the account. I was so tired of the arguing and fighting.

When I did not see any action on the addition in about 60 days I started asking questions. The BEDC said they were still working on things and it would happen soon. Again at the 90-day point I questioned things again and was given the same answer. This went on for about eight months and I was trying to be as nice as I could under the circumstances. They finally told me they did not like the family that owned the building and they were going to buy some other property down the road.

A short time later the BEDC showed me another building they were going to purchase on a huge lot and they said they would build an addition there. I waited and waited and now we were a year and a half into the agreement and still unable to get into full production. I was doing all I could do to keep my head afloat. It was at this point when they had the steel for the new addition delivered to the site.

Sheila and I had divorced and I gave her the house, frame shop and the needlework shop free and clear, and I kept the frame factory and the bills. She started a campaign with the girl's which has resulted in no contact with the two girls to this day even at the end of 2008.

Karen and Lesley Grow Up

Partly because of the bitterness in the divorce with Sheila, some of the good times with Karen and Lesley are clouded in their minds, I am sure. It has been very difficult since the divorce and subsequent years not having contact with these two wonderful girls. I have followed their achievements and am very proud of them.

Things are not always as perceived and because children should never be made aware of financial conditions and I am sure they do not understand and cannot comprehend the years following the flood. I do not want to go into detail of the problems encountered after the flood, in trying to maintain a livelihood with our business. There was a lot of bitterness felt by the girls when we sold the farm and moved into town. This had to be done for financial reasons.

Karen

Some of the things I do want to take the time to mention are Karen's success in her education. Even though she had gone to school all of her years in the same little town, there were many "clicks", and Karen was just never a part of those. Karen always did her homework well, excelled in Band and was very active in the 4-H winning many prizes and achievements. Karen attended Panhandle schools and upon graduation from High School she was Valedictorian. This Honor also meant FREE tuition in any state college in Texas.

While attending High School Karen was looking at Austin College in Sherman. This is a private school and meant the tuition would not be free. She majored in Math and Biology and on Graduation Day was named Co-Valedictorian of the college. Sheila and I had divorced, but I attended the graduation, still as a proud parent.

Lesley

Lesley did not finish out her High School in Panhandle because of the divorce. Sheila had moved to Amarillo and was teaching at Palo Duro High School and that is where Lesley went and graduated. By the time she graduated, the divorce had been over and the bitterness her mother held was very apparent. I didn't even receive an invitation to see her graduate from High School.

Lesley also attended Austin College in Sherman. I always tried to get as much information as I could from the Internet, about both girls.

One of the things I though amusing was when I discovered Lesley had created a small website on the Austin College server. The site contained a link to Karen's website and had both of their email addresses on the sites.

At this time I was teaching at SMU in Plano and I knew they couldn't track me. I used each of the others email address to write the other and let them know I still loved them very much. I knew they would read an email coming from the others email address. I know they figured out what I did because they password protected their websites after that time, but my love for them was not diminished. Using the Internet I still "check-up" on the girls on a weekly or monthly basis.

As the time came for Lesley was to graduate I had not heard anything from her for more than four years. I received a letter from the Campus Police Department advising me not to try to attend Lesley's graduation or I would be arrested. The letter stated this was the wishes of "Lesley and her parents." I was devastated, as I'm sure they hoped I would be, but I still love my girls. Lesley has married and has two children.

I hope that some day these two girls will realize there have been way too many years gone by without settling any and all differences between myself and the two of them.

In the early summer of 2005 I tried to reach out to Karen via her husband but never received a reply. I was devastated, as I'm sure they hoped I would be, but I still love my girls.

Problems with the BEDC

With the steel sitting there for the new building I assumed it would be up in 30-45 days. We waited three more months when they finally started construction. I went to the BEDC and I found out they had not prepared all of the paperwork for a building permit and that was why the building was just sitting on the ground. Now it was June of 1995 and I went to one of the board meetings for the BEDC and explained how they had "wronged" me. I told them that I had just hung on and I needed an additional loan for $75,000 to get everything moved and to have money for payroll. I explained when we would finally get open; I would be hiring more people immediately and would have to train them, which was expensive, until they are producing. They denied my request.

I went to an attorney in Amarillo with all my facts and figures to see if we could file a suit against the Borger Economic Development Corp. He said I had a very good case worth potentially more than a million and he would take the case with a retainer of $5000, the rest would be on a contingency with no more money to be put out by me. When the suit was filed the BEDC immediately filed a counter-suit against me for the initial loan amount. This forced me to close the frame factory until the cases were heard.

After 18 months of waiting the case was referred to the Texas Attorney General. In early 1997 he ruled that the BEDC was a Government Entity and could not be sued. This meant I had lost everything except my frame shop that was not a part of the factory. I had previously opened a Custom Frame shop in a town called Pampa and had one of my employees running it. When I was forced to close the factory I took over the day to day operations.

Kagnew Reunion in DC

With the divorce behind me, and not feeling obligated to work as hard as I had been, I decided to attend the Kagnew Station Reunion in DC. I thought it would be a good chance to also spend some time with my girls and have them attend the reunion.

I was in contact with the guy in charge of the Reunion and he was mentioning some of the members that might attend. I said I wished that I could find Barry Ross my old hunting buddy from the Sudan trip and many other trips. He said "Do you want his phone number" and without hesitation I said sure. Shortly I was back in touch with Barry and mentioned the reunion, which he was not planning on attending. I told him I was going to come and stay with Janice and at least I would like to get together with him.

Barry had gone through a divorce from Carol, and had remarried a really neat gal named Jane. We made plans for Barry and me to meet 11 am at the Chesapeake Seafood House just outside of Fairfax on Saturday, the day of the banquet. The Chesapeake Seafood House was a really neat place to eat and the menu was set that when you purchased an entrée anything on the menu that price or below was available and "All you can eat." The most expensive item was Alaska King Crab Legs at $22.95.

Two old hunters after 30 years – Me and Barry

I arrived about five minutes early and Barry was already there. We had not seen each other for some 31 years. The restaurant opened at 11 and we were the first patrons. Barry immediately took a $10 bill from his wallet and put it on the table, telling the pretty 20 year old waitress that we hadn't seen each other for 30 years and we would let her know when we were ready for service. We started out with some coffee/tea and started to catch up on the years that had slipped by so fast. We signaled the waitress who was nearby and ordered some crab legs. We ate slowly and talked more and more and kept the crab legs coming. The next thing we knew it was 2:30, The waitress came over and said they were closing until the supper hour but, since we were already seated they would continue serving us. Barry noticed her standing nearby, but not being a nuisance, the entire time we had been there.

At three o'clock she came and said she was being reassigned to a different station for the dinner hour but she would be sure the new waitress took good care of us. Barry handed her the tip and asked her about the staying near us. She replied that she had never heard so many great stories in her life and she was fascinated with all that we had done. We continued to be served by the new waitress and then we looked at our watches and discovered it was past 6 pm and the banquet started at 7 pm.

We tipped the new waitress, looked around and didn't see our first waitress.   We figured her day was over and we headed for the door. The restaurant had a door out to a lobby and another to the outside. We got into the lobby when we thought a bomb had gone off behind us. We turned and the first waitress had run and pushed the door while on the run. She came over and said "You two aren't getting out of here without a hug", which we obliged. She said that we had really made her day and she enjoyed hearing our hunting tales. We had a great afternoon and had to run to get to the banquet on time.

I went back to Janice's, got dressed and headed for the banquet. Janice, Mary Beth, Laura and Mike met me at the banquet. We found a table for all of us plus Barry and Jane. There was a program and it included a little bit about Eritrea winning its Independence over Ethiopia and becoming a Sovereign Country in 1993. The Eritrean Ambassador to the

254

US was in attendance. He made a little speech and later Mary Beth and Laura went to him and introduced themselves to him. They explained having been born and the fact that they had to become Naturalized Citizens of the US because of having Eritrean/Ethiopian citizenship when born. He acknowledged the fact and Laura mentioned she hoped they didn't owe any taxes over there, which broke him up. We had a great time. The three girls brought with them little embroidered jackets we had purchased while in Asmara. They almost looked like doll clothes and made me realize many years had gone by since being in Africa.

Me, Laura, Mary Beth and Janice at the Reunion

Chapter 26 – Get Outta Dodge

Meet Mary

I kept the frame shop and started thinking of getting far away from the Panhandle of Texas. The Internet was in its infancy and with a lot of time on my hands I surfed a lot. In early 1997 I found a website for matching guys and gals and I posted my profile. Then I started writing to several girls from around the country. I met a couple of them but I received an email from someone in East Texas on July 26th '97. I answered in early August and we started corresponding which led to talking on the phone. The next step would be to meet each other and I explained it was going to be impossible for a month or so for me to get away.

I indicated that I would very much like to meet her and we could wait until I could get away for that long or she could come and visit me. *Mary* had never driven in a city explaining that her husband always did the driving and in fact she was terrified to drive in traffic. She had lost her husband of 28 years about 16 months before we started corresponding. Living 80 miles East of Dallas meant she would have to drive around Dallas to get to Pampa. Mary indicated she was up to the task. I sent her complete instruction and what to look for at each turn and how to get to Pampa. I had made the trip to Dallas many times and knew the road well.

Her friends at work insisted she purchase a cell phone before the trip and check in at half hour intervals. They had convinced her of all kinds of problems. Mary drove to Pampa and got out of the car in front of my shop about 7 pm and gave a little "Yeah! I did it sign for herself" not realizing I saw it. I thought it was cool and we immediately called her friends. At one point during her driving I had to call her work and give a report as to how far she was.

I had some wine in the refrigerator and we each had a glass. We went into my office and within a minute she knocked her glass of wine into my keyboard. She was so upset for having done it but I reassured her and took the keyboard, ran it under water and used a hair drier and cleaned it up. No real problems till the next week when a couple of the keys started sticking so I took it all apart, cleaned it, reassembled the keyboard and never had any more problems.

The first weekend Mary visited and we went to the play "Texas"

Going to School

The relationship grew and I was more and more convinced I needed to get away from the Panhandle. I had made up my mind to change careers in to the computer field since it was so lucrative and seemed to have no end of possibilities. I decided I would attend Southern Methodist University in Houston and attend the Microsoft Certified Systems Engineer course.

I made a deal with Irma who had worked for me in the factory, for over ten years, to take over the frame shop and I was headed south. At Thanksgiving time I moved to Grand Saline with Mary. Her children and some friends of mine from Pampa came to celebrate the holiday. Mary's son Scott was due to get out of the Army after seven years. Scott had no real plans so I suggested he might attend the same school since he was going to live with his sister and brother in law when he got out. He was a little familiar with computers but not much. I helped him pass the DOS and Windows test to be accepted. I had taken the test at the Dallas school even though I would go to Houston.

I remember calling Laura and telling her I was going to school and hearing her chuckle. She then said that I had always told the girls they could do anything they made their minds up to do, so she guessed I could do this at 61 years of age. I was scheduled to start the class in March of 1998. I found an apartment in Houston for the five months of school and got started. Mary was so supportive of the idea and had faith in me too that I could do it. I really never had that kind of support from anyone – not even my parents.

School began and we were told during the introduction that the course would be much harder and intense than any Master's course that SMU offered. I had not been in a classroom for some 43 years and my previous study habits were terrible at best. I knew what had to be done but I thought the 16 years of computers I had under my belt would make it easy for me. The course was to entail setting up giant networks including, around the world and learning powerful operating systems. Even though I had a network in my mail order business I thought I knew a lot. I soon found out how little I really did know. I got overwhelmed fast.

I went to class all day for about three weeks then we went from 8:30 am till 12:30pm. I had heard that a study group would help to learn the material but no one in the class wanted a study group. I went back to the apartment and studied every day, until almost midnight, except for chatting with Mary in the evening for 30 minutes on the computer. About every other weekend Mary would come to Houston and we would take Saturday evening off from studying. There were many times that I thought I had surely bit off more than I could chew, but I had to keep going. I knew I wasn't totally stupid and I could get the material.

Without the support of Mary I would have never accomplished completing the school since I might have said I didn't need to work that hard. Since I was not a quitter and with her support I gave it everything I could. There were certification tests to take at the end of each module. I waited almost six weeks to take the first test. I did not like tests but I knew I had to do it so I finally scheduled the test paying the required hundred dollars. I went in and took the test and for an allotted 90-minute time I was done and out in 17 minutes. I had studied so hard I pretty much knew the material inside out. I scored a 977 out of a possible 1000 missing only one correct answer. A passing score on the test was 637 so I really got a lot of confidence. Some of the others in the class had been telling me that I knew the material but I had not convinced myself.

However my delay in taking the test meant I was way behind in the testing. The next two modules were Microsoft NT Workstation and NT Server. I felt pretty good about Workstation but not about server so I got permission to re-sit an afternoon class that was starting. I went home and studied hard till late in the night. Soon our class was studying a harder module called TCP/IP. I understood this pretty well since it had a lot of math involved. A week after we finished the module I took the test and passed. I passed not with a real high score but midrange of the needed score and a perfect score. Score was not important since it was really pass or fail. The high score was good for egos and bragging.

I still didn't feel real comfortable with NT Server so I re-sat a night class. This meant I was in school in the morning, studied at the school till 6 pm and attended the night class till 10 pm. In time I finally felt comfortable and took the Workstation and Server tests and passed with flying colors. Each of the tests cost $100 to take and you could retake if you failed. It wasn't about the money; I just wanted the security of only taking a test once. Later it would be 20+ tests, all the first time, good ego.

Graduation time came and I had not achieved the MCSE certification but I would continue to study. Many students had not passed as many tests as I had. This was common with the classes since the course was so intense. At the time I graduated it was pretty easy to find a job in the field and the entry-level pay started at around 40k. While attending the school and being the oldest person to attend the program I got to know my instructors well. The stories of the possible pay for instructors were much higher than just going out and finding a job.

Having moved back to Grand Saline to be with Mary I drove into Dallas daily to spend time studying at the SMU Richardson Campus. While attending the school in Houston I attended meetings of the SMU alumni association for the Advanced

Computer Center. I was very impressed that members of previous classes still got together and helped each other find jobs. The association always invited Headhunters from placement agencies. At one meeting there were 40+ jobs offered to graduates that were looking.

One day while I was at the Richardson campus, I asked about the graduate's meeting for the Dallas campuses. I was told there wasn't one. I thought by starting an association it would be a good way to meet a lot of the recruiters and maybe even land a great job. While studying one day, a young girl named Michelle came in and I noticed she had the book on TCP/IP. I asked her how the class was going. She explained that she had graduated and was studying to take the test in a couple hours. Michelle mentioned that she had gone to school in Houston at SMU. She was in a night class and I had not seen her. I mentioned the graduate association and said there needed to be one in Dallas. After Michelle took the test she came back in the room and we talked a little more I congratulated her because she had passed the test and we decided that the two of us would start a Graduate Association.

The first Big certification I worked very hard to achieve MCSE NT-4, – more came later such as the Microsoft Certified Trainer (MCT), MCP+I, A+, N+, MCSE &, MCSA Win 2000 – a lot of hard work and study paid of for an old man.

Just Some Accomplishments

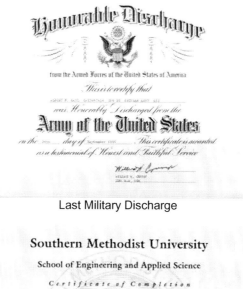

Last Military Discharge

Diploma from SMU Network Technology

Certificate for MCSE Windows 2000   Certificate for Microsoft Trainer Win2K

Chapter 27 – Teaching at Southern Methodist University

There was a class being held for "*Train the Trainer*" which was a pre-requisite for becoming an instructor. I signed up, paid the $500 (a discount price for SMU grads) even though I had not completed the Certification and knew I would not be able to instruct until I was certified. Also SMU's policy was that you were required to re-sit the course four times more before you were even permitted to teach a module.

Never in my wildest dreams could I imagine myself getting up in front of a group and trying to teach a subject. I never had the self-confidence that I could do something like teaching. I remembered teaching people to roller skate but there I did have the confidence because I was good. I thought, maybe it would be the same with this. I also taught my employees their jobs.

The instructor for the "Train the Trainer" course was Janice Thompson, the lead instructor for the Plano campus of SMU. She made a comment during the introductions that she was going to hire the best in the class. I had spent a lot of time preparing for the class and we were required to give a 15-20 minute instruction talk on any subject we wanted. Since I knew film and film processing I could talk at any length on this topic. I prepared with handouts, visuals and even a little test.

We got through the "Train the Trainer" class and were told that if we received a diploma then we would know we had passed. If we just received a letter we would know we did not pass.

The Dean of the Advanced Computer Education Center was located at the Plano campus. I wanted to clear the starting of the Graduate Association so on Monday morning I went to talk and get permission to start the association. I entered the lobby and the first person I saw was Janice Thompson. I told her why I was there and she asked me if I was ready to go to work. I said sure and knew I would have to start as a TA (Training Assistant) and go thru each of the courses four more times. Attending that many classes would take some time, I knew, but at least I would be gainfully employed. I also knew I would have to pass the remaining certification tests.

I got the go-ahead for the graduate association and headed back to let Mary in on the good news of the job. Mary was happy and proud which meant so much to me. I had never had a mate that stated she was proud.

I started to work and Janice scheduled me all the work I could handle which was from 8 am till 10 pm Mon-Thur and 8-5 on Sat. Even though the pay was not great, the overtime made up for it. I was not working on Friday and that was the day the Prep Classes were taught. There was an entrance test required on DOS and Windows to get into the program. If someone could not pass the test they could sign up and pay for the Prep Class.

After I had been working about a month Janice asked me if I would like to teach the Prep Class. Of course I knew I would still be doing it at TA pay but I jumped at it. I prepared a Power Point (which I had to teach myself quickly) presentation and was ready. The class would be for two Friday's with one being DOS (Disk Operation System) and the second part a week later on Windows. I took to this like a "duck in water." I enjoyed the teaching and thriving on the interest of the students. We were supposed to be done at 5 pm but many times I kept going and the security would ask me to shut it down at 6 pm. It didn't take long till the students started the full MCSE class after passing entrance tests.

With me working long hours and Mary changing jobs to a Title company in Dallas we decided to rent a small apartment in Dallas to cut the driving time. We would go back to Grand Saline on the weekends and take care of BJ, Mary's mother in law. BJ and I had a lot of things in common. We both liked News and Politics, but BJ was on the opposite side in politics. Our friendship grew every time we were together.

I had started teaching the Prep Class with an outline that I had been given, but kept adding what I thought were important and necessary things. Now I was working over 150 hours every two week pay period. The more information the students could learn in these two days would give them a lot of self-assuredness. I had some students that had never turned on a computer. I ran all of my ideas past Janice and she finally got to the point of saying I was doing such a good job I could make any changes I wanted. When new program classes started, quite often I was the TA and it was evident the students that had taken my Prep Classes were doing much better than those that did not.

Eventually I passed the other tests required to obtain my Microsoft Certified Systems Engineer (MCSE) certification. I completed the necessary work to also be a Microsoft Certified Trainer (MCT). I had gone through the entire course enough that Janice felt I was qualified to teach. I seemed to have a knack of interacting with the new students and getting them on the right track. I could get the students to form study groups and it helped their success tremendously. Since I had a good background in life and could almost be a father or grandfather image to some of the students, they trusted me and came to me with lots of questions. The new starting salary of $50 per hour was not too bad. A couple raises would come later.

During this time we finally got the Graduate Association off the ground with by laws and all the necessary paperwork. We scheduled a meeting and expected maybe 15-20 to show up and were hoping for 30-40. We had over 150 come to the meeting. It was a great success as I had encouraged all of my students to come. The name was "Graduate Association" was chosen so we would not get hounded by the Alumni Association from the main campus. I was elected president for the first year and we had meetings once a month.

Mary and I stayed in the little apartment about as long as we could stand it and found a duplex that was pretty nice. Mary's brother John had attended a school in MS to get his certification and I mentioned that the real money was in teaching. I encouraged him to come to Dallas and take the "Train the Trainer" class and maybe Janice would give him a job also. John took the class and did in fact get hired by Janice starting like I did as a TA. John came and stayed with Mary and me for about nine months.

By this time the curriculum for the school had changed and the CompTIA A+ certification was added. This involved learning to build a computer from scratch and to troubleshoot computers that had a problem. I took the test and passed it and Janice and I co-taught the first class. There were two tests required to get the certification, one for hardware and one for operating systems. The hardware part was really the only thing new since operating systems were taught later on in our MCSE program but we started them out in the second part of A+. Starting the program classes out with the A+ course really made for a nice complete computer education.

Many of the students that I had were finding the course extremely hard and contemplating dropping out. One of the things I had in my presentation was a phrase that I stole from Janice, but had somewhat been my sentiments, just not in a phrase. The phrase is *"Failure is Not an Option."*

I was able to relate to the students of how I felt when I was going through the course and assured them their minds could absorb much more than they thought. The dropout rate almost disappeared.

I realized the students needed a shoulder, a mentor, a friend, a confidant, as well as a teacher.

I also learned that an instructor could not just stand in front of a class and deliver the material. Caring about the students and helping the slower ones and keeping the class together was so important. Once the students got off on a good foot by passing a couple tests they were "good to go" on the rest of the program. At the end of each module of the program (about every 40 class-hours) the students were required to prepare an evaluation of the instructor, TA, School and program. I maintained one of the highest ratings of any instructor at SMU.

I looked back at classes I had in High School and realized one of the real problems today with teachers was they don't teach *"the WHY"* a student needs to learn and retain material. I gave a lot of thought to Karen going through High School. She was Valedictorian of her High School and Co-Valedictorian of her college. However, the High School would let her turn in papers with misspelled words as long as the theory was correct. We had many "moments" when I had her correct her spelling before submitting a paper. Another time was when I asked Karen how to figure the area of an Octagon. She stated there was a formula on the scientific calculator. I said it was just simple math and I could do it faster than she could on the computer. I did come up with the answer faster. The area of an octagon has four triangles cut from it which each make a rectangle or square. When these are subtracted from the total height time's width of the original as if they were still there, you have the area of an octagon. She didn't speak to me for three days.

Another example was when I had the frame factory, I had a High School DE Senior student that went to school in the morning and worked in the afternoons. I asked Mark one day to go up to the storeroom and get me three coils of wire 30 feet long. I asked him how he was going to do it; he responded he would measure them. I said "do you know how to figure the circumference of a circle" and he replied that the learned it in the ninth grade. I said "if you learned it you would know it and to go back to your ninth grade teacher tomorrow and find out how to figure it or you do not have a job."

Mark came in the next day all grumpy. I asked him if he now knew how to figure the circumference. He said he did and I told him now all he had to do with the coils of wire was to measure the diameter and count the strands and he would know how much wire was in the coil. It was as if I had hit him upside the head with a bat. He now had a reason to learn the formula. I am sure he remembers it to this day.

I continued to teach the Prep Classes in addition to my regular classes. I had a young girl named Julie in one of my Prep Classes that was a Dallas Policewoman. She wanted to change careers and the computer business was a lot safer. Julie had no experience but paid attention and seemed to enjoy the Prep Classes. I thought she would be in the next class to start but she wasn't.

A couple months went by and she came to a new class starting. I was glad to see her and she chose an empty seat between two guys that had some experience (she didn't know it at the time). As the class started and got a week into studying I would ask a question and Julie would raise her hand to answer. When no one else volunteered I would let her answer. Some of the material was very technical which surprised me that she knew the answer.

The two guys on each side would look at her in surprise. I finally asked her in front of the class how she knew the answers since she had said she had no previous experience. Her answer was "remember in Prep Class when you told us how much studying was required for each class hour"? I answered that I sure did, to which she said she was just doing what I had told her to do. She sailed through the program with her good study habits. She later worked towards being an instructor.

Teaching the Train the Trainer Class

While I was working for Janice at SMU in Plano I never missed an opportunity to sit in and help her when she taught the "Train the Trainer" classes. Each time when I asked if I could come and help out in the class, essentially be her TA, Janice would answer that she couldn't pay me. I would always answer "I didn't ask to be paid." The class was usually a two-day class of 16 hours and sometimes would go longer. The classes were held every other month or quarterly and limited in the number of people that could attend. SMU was known as the "Premier" place to attend the course. Even though I did not get paid each time I was in the class helping her, I learned more and more about teaching. I suppose I was in the class five or six times when she let me help teach a section of the book. I knew that sometime I would be able to teach the class and it would be a fantastic thing to have on a resume.

A class had been scheduled, and I had already told Janice I wanted to be there, when the day before the class she became sick. The school was going to have to cancel the class, which meant refunding about Eight Thousand dollars. Janice relayed to the Dean that there would be no problem if I taught the class. She had the confidence in me, along with my having been assisting her on so many classes; I was selected to teach the class. Some of the students in this class were students, whom I had taught, early on in their new careers.

I could now put on my resume that I had taught the "Train the Trainer" class for a registered and certified University along with being paid for it. This was but another accomplishment I would *"Never in My Wildest Dreams"* thought I could achieve.

Student Success Stories

One of my favorite success stories actually involved two people Jackie and Chauncy. Both of these special people were black and Jackie was a beautiful young lady and Chauncy a cool guy. Neither of them had any prior experience in computers nor had Chauncy even turned a machine on. Chauncy's wife was a dietician at a hospital and I don't remember what Jackie's husband did. About the second day of class I told the two of them they should be partners through the program and study together. They studied after class and on the evenings by phone. Both were determined to conquer the course and get good paying jobs.

With all of the hard studying and my prompting the taking of tests as soon as you were comfortable with the knowledge Chauncy took his first test of Network Essentials a few days before the end of the module and didn't pass. He had read ahead and finished the book but was not really ready to take the test. A few days later he re-took it and didn't pass. To most students they would have given up but not Chauncy. He studied and studied and the last day of class in that module he took it again and passed. At this point he was down $300 for one test. Chauncy had helped Jackie and she took the test and passed it.

They continued to study together and about three weeks before the program was completed Chauncy got his MCSE and a few days later so did Jackie. A week before graduation Jackie went to an interview for a job and the next morning we had to pull her from the ceiling, she was floating so high. She had been hired on right out of school for $54,000 to start. Jackie just had personality coming from every part of her body.

They were to graduate on Feb 17th and we had a Graduate Association meeting early in February and Chauncy thought Mary was the neatest (of course I do too). He was complaining to Mary that he had spent $1800 taking the six tests required for his certification and he only had $25 more he could put on his charge card. His wife was getting worried about the family since she had carried the brunt of things while he was in school. Mary assured Chauncy he would have a job by Valentines Day and things would be good. He got a job at good starting pay just before Valentines Day and thought Mary was the best.

A very special student started when Janice and I co-taught the first A+ class. Right in the middle of the front row was a very pretty 31 year-old blonde with long hair named Suzi. After about three days into class Janice and I went to lunch and almost at the same time we mentioned that Suzi would be another Stephanie.

Stephanie had been an instructor that I had worked with for about the first six months first as a TA. She was an awesome instructor and it got to the point were Stephanie and I became the Windows 95 Guru's since the class setup that was furnished to the school had some problems. The two of us got it to work the way it should. Other instructors had tried to teach it just told the students the parts of the MOC (Microsoft Official Curriculum) didn't work rather than trying to fix it. I had kind of adopted Stephanie as a daughter since she was about the same age as my daughter Janice.

Suzi of course was only worried about completing the course and the thought of becoming an instructor had not even entered her mind. Suzi was the single mother of five kids, three of her own and two foster children. She had just gone through a nasty divorce and since she had spent her life raising children did not have any work experience. A neighbor that lived across the street from her had told her about the school and that he was going to attend so they were both in the class. Suzi's husband was a network engineer for Southwestern Bell.

Suzi studied very hard and was doing well in school considering she had to help the kids with homework, do the housework and other Mom things. She studied till she couldn't stay awake. Her personality was very likeable and as time went on she adopted Janice as a surrogate Mom and me as Dad. Janice and I both pushed her all the way through the program and didn't cut her any slack. Suzi had not completed all of her tests by graduation but was determined to take the final two tests she needed. Suzi needed a job and Janice had some office work she needed to do so Suzi got a job helping do some Power Point and paper work for Janice. She was getting about four hours of work a day and really needed some more so she asked Janice if she could TA some for additional time. Janice told her to pass one of the two tests she needed and she would let her TA.

A week later Suzi came in with her test completion paper so Janice assigned Suzi to TA for me. Suzi TA'd for me for a couple months and on a couple occasions helped me in the Prep Class when I had a full class. After seeing the fun I had teaching the Prep Class Suzi wanted to teach also. She went to Janice and asked what she would have to do to be an instructor. The first thing out of Janice's mouth was "you still have one test to complete - pass that and we will talk." A couple weeks later Suzi came in a new MCSE with that last test passed.

Suzi then had to attend the "Train the Trainer" class and complete the paperwork to be an MCT. I then trained Suzi to teach the Prep Class and she started TA'ing some of the regular subjects as I had to do. We co-taught a few of the Prep Classes, then I sat and watched her for a class and Janice turned her loose to teach the Prep Class. It was very gratifying to see her come into class knowing nothing and a year and a half later teaching the Prep Class.

The problems of 9-11 put a damper on the entire Information Technology training.

Another student I will never forget was Alfred Delshad. He started school in August of 2001 and sat right at the very front of the class. Alfred was from the Middle East but had been in this country a good while and had no problem with the language. The problem he had was his lack of computer experience but I assured him he was not the first to tackle the program without experience. We got through the first module without any real problems but as we continued more and more Alfred seemed to be having problems. I had teamed him up with a good study group and I thought he would do all right. I tried to spend some time with him on breaks and give him some support so that he could handle the information.

On September 11th just before class started the first plane hit the first tower. With all the action I started class but then as news was coming in I took the entire class to the lobby where the school had three TV's. When we saw the second plane hit the tower and started getting information I was not sure how the rest of the day would go but I ushered everyone back to class and tried to make the class go by. On the breaks it took a little longer to get everyone back to class but we got through it. Alfred was so visibly shaken that he had tears in his eyes. I think he felt the class might shun him but being a likeable person, there was never a problem.

Alfred struggled with the material and one day came to me and said he was going to drop out. He said he just could not get all of the information even with studying until the wee hours of the morning. I asked, pleaded, and begged him to try it a little longer since the amount of money he would be refunded wouldn't change for another month. He finally agreed to stick it out a little longer. I assured him, as I did other students, that at some point a light bulb would come on and all of this material would start to make sense. A couple weeks later the light bulb came on for Alfred and he came in and thanked me for not letting him drop out. A friendship had been generated that I will never forget. Alfred then started calling me his "big brother" which is a big compliment. I became know as "Al 1" and Alfred as "Al 2".

We are still in touch with each other and even though Alfred is not in the computer business he still considers it time well spent. Alfred gained a tremendous amount of self-confidence by attending the course.

Alfred is now engaged and I look forward to his marriage and having been a part of his life.

Chapter 28 – The Move to the Houston area

In July of 2001, Mary and I decided we could handle a move from Dallas to the Houston area.

In January Mary's daughter, Lisa, and her husband Brett had finally received the blessing of a little boy after ten years of trying to have a baby. Mary and her children had grown up without the fun of grandparents and knowing cousins. She was determined that her children's children would know their grandparents. Mary wanted to be near her grandson to enjoy the early life. Her profession being very short of good employees, she thought she could easily get a job.

I went to the campus in Houston about a transfer with SMU and was told there would be no problem since the lead instructor had been my instructor. Also I knew everyone and they were aware of the job I was doing at Plano. I was committed to classes until the first of October at Plano and Janice really did not want me to leave but she understood. We looked for a house and finally settled on one. Mary moved to Pasadena in August staying with Lisa. The first week of September I brought a truck of furniture to the new house. The next week I brought the rest of the furniture except for a couch that made into a bed which I would stay on until I was to leave the first of October. Little did we know about what was to happen with 9-11.

I finished the classes I had in Plano and moved to Pasadena on October 3, 2001 and was scheduled to start a class on October 16th. Already in less than a month we could start seeing the toll being taken within the IT field. Compaq was cutting personnel by 4,000 and the Enron problems would add 5,000 more cuts in the IT field just in Houston alone.

I started the October class in the Houston campus where I had gone to school. I again was teaching the beginners and trying to get them off on the right foot. Things were going well and one afternoon I got a call from Peter, the lead instructor and the one that I had in school. He asked if I could fill in that night for an instructor that was sick. I asked what chapters they were on in the manual and it was going to be an easy evening since the chapters I needed to cover to keep on tract would be small. The subject was one that I knew inside and out and the students had been in school for two months already. I quickly put together a 20-question test. I walked into the class, did not introduce myself because "fill-in" instructors had a reputation for being bad. I handed out the test and told the students they would have 30 minutes to complete it. A few stragglers came in and by 6:15 pm all were present.

At 6:40 I said time is up, introduced myself and announced we would go over the test. I proceeded to go over each question as to why the correct answer was correct and why the wrong answers were wrong. Some of the wrong questions were just slightly wrong but still wrong. The students had not done well on my quickie test that covered some material from everything they had studied so far in the program. By the time we completed going over the test the time was 7:45 pm. We normally took a break at 7 pm for the students to grab a little to eat since most night students had full time jobs. I headed to the break room to get a cup of coffee and noticed a lot of jabbering amongst the students.

One of the students stopped me and said "Al you taught us more in one hour than we learned since we have been here." When I started after the break the class was almost mesmerized and was ready to believe anything I said. We ended up staying until close to 11 pm, an hour longer than we were supposed to.

The next morning before noon I got a phone call from Tom, the head of the Houston Campus saying *"Al what the hell did you do last night?"* I thought I was in big trouble and responded that I had simply taught the class, that I had given a test so I would have a better feel where they were. I was told that the class had sent 22 emails either wanting to recycle into the class I had just started or for me to take over the class. Tom asked me how long I thought it would take to get them up to speed. The class was a 40 hour class and they were two-thirds the way through it. I told Tom I honestly thought it would take 32 more hours. Tom indicated to me to take over the class but this was going to change their graduation date and everything. I said I would do the best with them I could. He then told me that some of the emails stated that if I didn't take over the class they wanted their money back.

Because of picking up the class we had to further change their schedule by one more day since Mary and I had planned a trip to Ireland over Thanksgiving. The schedule with the other class was not affected but with the second class I was not going to be back for the first day after the Thanksgiving break.

I finished the module with them and got them up to speed. Their next instructor was to be Peter who would really dazzle them, so all was well. There were three of them that did recycle backwards into the class that I just started and stayed until the next scheduled module after my instructions. The class that I filled in and then took over ended up graduating and I attended their graduation. I had made it a point to attend the graduation of any class that I was involved in teaching. The students appreciated this and since the graduation was really a big day I was treated as family to most of the students. Many friendships were made during the time.

The enrollment in the program all over the country had become almost non-existent after the spring of 2002.

Westwood College

With the collapse of the Information Technology business and the scarcity of teaching opportunities I was referred to a possible position at the Houston Campus of Westwood College. Westwood has college locations throughout the United States. In the fall of 2002 I interviewed for the job and at the end of the interview I was asked about my college education. I was informed that since the college was only offering accreditation courses and not certification courses I needed at least a BS and most of their campuses preferred a Masters.

Mamie, the Director of Education said she wanted to hire me and would try to get all of my business experience and my certifications to qualify for an exemption to allow me to teach the computer courses. She was not successful in obtaining an exemption. Mamie told me she was impressed by my experience and attitude and would like to have me serve on the

Program Academic Board for the college in the computer education division.

The purpose of the Board is to monitor the courses offered, the quality of instruction and make recommendations. Many of the board members are asked to speak to some of the classes. I was asked to speak before two classes in 2005. Because of the feedback response I have been requested to address more classes in January of 2006. Being a member of the board has been interesting and I feel fruitful as well as good for my Ego.

Currently I am the longest serving member of the Board and enjoy making a contribution to the college. Westwood College cares very much about their students and that satisfies a big part of my concern. Some of their programs have over a 95% placement upon graduation.

I do enjoy very much being asked to speak to their new classes and have done this virtually every semester. I am still a board member as 2008 closes.

Chapter 29 – Fun Times

On my birthdays Mary has always tried to do something very special and unlike anyone else has ever cared or tried to do. The first birthday we were together we went to a Bed & Breakfast in Jefferson, TX and on a steamboat on the lake nearby. A wonderful thoughtful time we shared with two good friends of ours.

A trip to the Bahamas with the Shillelagh's was a birthday present to remember always because it gave me a chance to see members I had not seen in many years.

My fun times would not be complete without mentioning FiFi. So enter FiFi the French Hottie, which is a character that Mary has dreamed up to, provide me a fun time on my birthdays. Mary usually works very hard getting the house cleaned up and then I am either sent out of the house or told not to come back till a certain time or banished to my room. Mary has done things like fixing Hors'dourves and sprinkling rose petals on the bedroom floor, filling the bedroom up with 67 balloons and always a bath by FiFi. In 2004 I was escorted blindfolded by Lisa (FiFi's assistant) to a spa where we enjoyed a bath and massage then home to Hors'dourves prepared and placed on our kitchen bar by the assistant. The effort that Mary has put forth to make my birthdays memorable has done just that and I will be forever grateful. How lucky I have been to meet her and win her heart.

FiFi has always been welcome on the Ireland and other trips of the Shillelagh's and afforded many laughs from this French speaking Hottie.

Las Vegas Kagnew Station Reunion

The spring of 2003 found us planning to go to Las Vegas in July for a reunion of personnel and families of those stationed at Kagnew Station. I had not attended a reunion in eight years and thought since it was in Vegas we should go. I talked Jim to bring his girlfriend Sheila and joining us for the weekend.

Mary and I flew into Las Vegas on Friday and stayed at the hotel where the reunion was being held. After checking in and getting settled in our room we visited the get acquainted suite for Kagnew Station. I had not met Rick that is the webmaster for our Internet site, and was looking forward to meeting him. The main function was to be held on Saturday evening and after making the appearance we met up with Jim and Sheila.

We decided to go to "downtown" Vegas where the Golden Nugget is located. We were walking down the street and were "hustled" to see a show for the cost of a drink. We all were getting tired of walking so we thought "what the heck." It was to be a musical impersonator type show and turned out to be a fantastic show featuring Robbie Howard. Robbie and two other performers played and sang songs just as the original recording artists. If you sat there with your eyes closed you would have thought Elvis, The Platters and many others were in front of you performing, a great show for $5.

The evening saw us in amazement of the unbelievable light show overhead in the promenade downtown. I will never go to Vegas again without seeing this light show. I had been to Vegas many times but never had I gone downtown. This is now a "must see."

Saturday evening the banquet for Kagnewites saw about 150 in attendance. My old friend Lee was there with his wife Vera and doing well for his age. They stay busy and I am sure that is what keeps them young. There were quite a few others in attendance that had been stationed the same time as I was. This was pretty much a double fun weekend for me by spending some quality time with Jim as well as some of the people I was in the military with. The fun always ends too soon but we look forward to visiting Vegas again with Jim and Sheila.

Grown-ups Can Dream Too

It really does not matter how old you are, you can certainly have dreams. I have been a member of the Shillelagh's and done quite a bit of traveling with the club in the late 60's & 70's. All of that came to a halt with moving to Texas and being in business for myself. With all of the problems of business I had to keep chugging on to keep the businesses afloat and try to raise my family.

So once again it was time to **dream** of the days when the children would be grown, and on their own, and maybe it would be in the cards to travel. Over the years of hard working and little playtime the Cruise Ship industry had grown and grown. I dreamed of the day that I might be able to enjoy a cruise trip before I was too old and feeble.

After the divorce from Sheila and subsequent meeting of Mary we talked of things we would like to do. Mary had been a dreamer also and for her taking a cruise was just about as impossible as my learning to fly. Since dreams do come true when you want to put forth the effort I started doing some research. With my teaching at SMU and Mary having a better job in the Dallas area they allowed the financial where-with-all to try to make a dream come true. We thought of starting a saving fund for enjoying life.

With the advent of the Internet and, all of the websites, offering just about anything for sale I found a website called "Egghead." This website offered just about anything you could imagine for auction. I bought some computer equipment from this website and had no problems so I started looking at the Travel link they offered.

In May of 2000 I saw a cruise on Carnival's Paradise (non-smoking ship) for seven days. I watched someone purchase it and the next day there was another cruise on the same ship. I asked Mary if she would like to go on a cruise and to come to the computer, pretty much as the bidding was about to close. I bid on the cruise and was the lucky bidder in getting the cruise for both Mary and myself for seven days for $750.

I called some friends, Bob & Linda and told them about the cruise and sure enough one came up the next day and they were the lucky bidders on it. The cruise was for September and at Labor Day and was to go on the Eastern Caribbean to Nassau, San Juan and St Thomas from the port of Miami. I was able to find some cheap airfares and then we waited in anticipation. We were sure we would be somewhere in stowage or some not real great room but we didn't care.

To our surprise we arrived at the appointed time for the cruise and had a fantastic room that included a bottle of Champagne and Swiss Chocolates from the travel agency. The trip was great and on the last night again we had Champagne courtesy the travel agency. The food on the cruise was nothing short of extraordinary and plentiful. It was nice to have *a dream come true*. We did our thing, Bob and Linda were able to do theirs and we met again at supper. The shows were fantastic and we didn't miss anything on board. Needless to say, we were hooked.

Mary and I on the Paradise – our first cruise

While we were on the cruise the four of us talked about a road trip. It would be on the Eastern Shore from DC to Norfolk, Williamsburg and back to DC to visit the Smithsonian. We would fly to DC and rent a car and take a week for the trip. We scheduled this for Easter week of 2001. Being familiar with the Virginia area I would do the driving. We decided to stay in Vienna, VA as the base when we got back to the DC area. We could catch the subway to DC and not have to worry about finding someplace to park.

I wasn't going to get anywhere near DC without seeing my good friend Carolyn, who was now the Executive Director of the Shillelagh's. Staying in Vienna meant we would be right down the street since the club is located there. We met for dinner and caught up on lost time. Carolyn mentioned how much she loved the trips to Ireland and that the club was going to spend

Thanksgiving in Ireland. She started recruiting us for the trip. Little did we know how the world would change between Easter and Thanksgiving?

We got back to Texas and decided that we needed to see Ireland so we had Carolyn book us on the trip. It was going to work good since we would not have to lose too many days of work because of the trip scheduling. We also did not know we would be moving and the world would be turned upside down.

As I had mentioned earlier during this time we had moved to Houston and were able to clear the time for the vacation with our new jobs.

Ireland – First trip

Mary and I had scheduled the trip with the Shillelaghs in April of 2001 totally unaware of the earth shattering changes that were to take place. We would fly from Houston to Baltimore and visit Cousin Lois for a couple days before leaving. Lois and Mac took us to the bus terminal on I-95 to meet the Shillelagh's that was bussing us to NY. We were supposed to depart from Baltimore but Aer Lingus had cancelled the flights from Baltimore after 9-11. It had been quite a while since I had been with the Shillelagh's and Mary had heard all kinds of tales of fun and frolic. I knew this was "her kind of group" nothing could have been truer. We were waiting in the terminal when the bus arrived and some of the members of the club came into the terminal for coffee.

It had been so long since I had been on a trip with the club so I looked over the trip list and noticed Joy and Steve Huffines. Joy had been the trip director on all of the ski trips back in my early days before she and Steve got married. They were to board in Baltimore also since they lived in nearby Annapolis area. My good friend Carolyn was the trip director for the trip so I knew all was going to be well. When the bus started reloading we went out and found a seat. Joy and Steve boarded and it was "old home week" since I hadn't seen them in many years. Those years had been good to them and they only aged slightly. Joy also had her son on the trip that I had not seen since he was a small child.

Carolyn was in the back of the bus making us a Bloody Mary to start the trip. It was going to be just like the old times I remembered. Carolyn had brought snacks and some adult beverages to consume on the trip to New York. She introduced Joy/Steve and Mary/me and the fact that Joy and I had been trip directors. The four-hour trip to New York seemed very short with getting to know everyone on the bus and getting up to date with Joy and Steve. Joy had a daughter, Susan that was studying in Ireland at Trinity University to get her Ph.D. in Theology. I had known Susan since she was about eight or nine years. Now she was all grown up and a beautiful lady that had been an Attorney, a Prosecutor, in New York and then decided to be a musical missionary and subsequently go after her Ph.D. We would get to see her in Ireland and she would travel with us.

When we got to New York we saw the Statue of Liberty and the void where the Twin Towers had stood from just across the river. We got to JFK airport at the time we should because for the overseas flight we needed to check in at least three hours early. A week earlier there was an Airbus 320, leaving JFK when the tail broke off and caused it to crash. We were flying on an Airbus 320 but different airline and in the short week they had made some changes in the climb-out and turning allowed in the plane so I felt safe.

The flight over to Ireland departed about 8 pm and with a five-hour time difference and the five-hour flight we arrived in Shannon a little after 6 am. Carolyn had told us if we could nap just a little on the plane and stay up until a normal bedtime the night we arrived we would not have the jet lag. Mary arrived with a bad headache but I was fine having spent a lot of the flight talking to club members.

There were some other Shillelaghs that were going to fly from different areas of the country to Boston and on to Shannon and meet us in the morning about the same time that we arrived. All in all there would be about 40 members of the club on this trip to Ireland. Our tours guide and bus driver, Dave Spillane, met us as we came through customs. He is the same bus driver the club uses on all of the Ireland trips and hails from Killarney. We would learn why as the trip continued. He was such a delight to be with.

282

There was a club member that was coming on the Boston leg that I knew. It was Alice Frankel, who with her husband had owned Colorfax Labs that I worked for in 1969. When we got to Ireland and got on the bus she was already aboard. I recognized her and said Hi she looked at me and as soon as I mentioned my name she was excited and remembered my work. We always had a monthly meeting with dinner at her house when I was their employee and I have such fond memories of those times.

On the way to Waterford and only about one half-hour from Shannon we stopped at Bunratty Creamery Bar across the street from Bunratty Castle for scones and coffee. Across the street by the castle is Durty Nellies Pub the oldest pub in Ireland established in 1620. There are a lot of "knock off's" of Durty Nellies in this country. The next stop, about an hour later was the Rock of Cashel to tour the old 4th Century castle. This was the seat of kings and mediaeval bishops for 900 years and flourished until the early 17th century. In 1101 Muircheartach O'Brien granted the Rock to the Church and in 1127, the bishop Cormac MacCarthy, started work on a Chapel which survives to this day and is the most remarkable Romanesque church in the country. The next stop was just down the street for a Hot Irish Coffee to take the chill off the morning.

One thing we found interesting is the temperature in Ireland is controlled by the Gulf Stream and it rarely gets below 40 degrees. Every morning it is usually misty but by the afternoon the sun is out and with this moisture and sun you end up with the Emerald Isle as Ireland is known.

We were going to spend a couple nights in Waterford, the home of Waterford Crystal that we would tour. From there we would venture out and see some things like the Jameson Distillery where I would become an "Official Irish Whiskey Taster" complete with certificate. No trip would be complete without kissing the Blarney Stone at Blarney Castle. Mary was hesitant of going up the small four-foot wide spiral staircase in the old castle but after a couple stops to get air into her shaking body she was all right.

Mary Kissing the Blarney Stone high up in Blarney Castle

We toured the town of Kilkenny and came across a place called "Roots & Fruits" which we thought was a neat name. Then there was "Paris Texas" that we would visit on another trip to Ireland and the Kilkenny Castle. It was then on to Killarney for a couple of wonderful days. The Ross hotel was truly an Old Irish Hotel with all of the charm we would expect. The days we spent on tours, like the Muckross house, then the evenings in the Ross Hotel Pub or other Pubs. One evening while out walking and shopping we passed a Local Irishman coming at us. He saw us and spoke "Yanks" and we answered that we were. He raised his hand and made the victory sign and said "God Bless America." This seemed such a nice gesture since we had suffered the terrible 9-11 tragedy. The Irish people love Americans.

Another thing that struck close to home was when Mary was in the Ladies room and overheard a couple of Irish women talking about how much fun the Yanks had. We were in the Pub of the Waterford hotel and just having our normal fun, drinking, dancing and laughing. Mary stayed in the privy until the ladies left then came and told us what had happened. She got Steve and me to go ask the ladies to dance. They were at the table next to us but had a male friend at the table. When I asked one of the ladies to dance she seemed delighted and as we danced she commented that we really knew how to have fun. She told me that she had just lost her husband and said they had save a

284

little "bob" (money) and were hoping to live a dream or two when he suddenly had passed away at the age of 55 immediately after retiring. What a shame that the couple had never realized any of their dreams. I am now a firm believer that you must go after your dream *everyday* and not let time pass you by. If your dream is a cruise, foreign country, or fishing put it on a credit card and pay it out, but *make your dream come true*. Time waits for one and life at it very longest is way too short.

The Pubs in Ireland are an institution along with the meeting place to have a "pint" before going home after work or for a fun evening. A place to socialize and relax, to laugh, to dream and share with family and friends.

The Norway
After we got back from Ireland we decided that since dreams really could come true we would dream some more. We both might have accepted the first cruise as meeting all of our dreams and expectations but when you do that you stagnate. When you accomplish one dream it is time to dream further and our dreams were just beginning. With the Ireland trip now behind us we started dreaming of two good vacations a year. You cannot count on "someday" because it may never come.

The SS Norway formerly SS France – Ocean going liner

Since I had really done well on selecting the first cruise on the Internet I started looking for another. Soon I found a cruise for seven days on the Norway for $257 for both in the spring of 2002. We upgraded to the higher level cabin but the price was still awesome. The Norway was once a Trans-Atlantic steamer and was the longest cruise ship at the time. It did not have a lot of decks like modern cruise ships but we had a great time. The Norway could not go into many ports because of how much water it drew so we tendered in which was fun. The tenders held about 400 people so it did not take long.

A woman from Las Vegas named Edna sat at our table and ate two of most everything and the desserts that had any liquor she had three. She was a real hoot but a nice lady.

We got to see San Juan and St Thomas again and St Maartens. At St Thomas we went on a 50 passenger Catamaran over to St John. The tour was billed as a Champagne trip and there was plenty of food and drinks. After getting a briefing about the trip and starting out, we had not gone the length of a football field when Mary was sick. The crew had said to let them know if anyone felt ill. They could not believe Mary was ill so fast. The gal crewmember went to the galley and fixed some ginger ale with powdered ginger and shook it back and forth. Mary drank it and again in less than the length of a football field she was fine. When we got back we looked up Ginger on the Internet and found it is good for all kinds of upset stomach.

Ireland for the Second Time

The trip actually started for me a week earlier than for Mary. For a birthday present Mary sent me to the Bahamas for the Shillelagh's 38th Birthday Party. The trip to the Bahamas was to an all-inclusive package in the Grand Bahamas a couple blocks from the famous Atlantis. I got to visit with some members from the old days including our Pilot Bob Hurt and his wife Nan that had been a stewardess in the days of old.

A truly funny story was about one of the members named Joan that tended to drink a little too much. One night she was sitting at the bar and the bartender sent word to Carolyn that Joan needed some help to her room. Carolyn got one of the porters, a large black native, from the hotel and went to help Joan to her room. When they went to help Joan she responded "I don't care what you say I am not having sex with him" she meant the porter. So Carolyn got one of the club members, Steve Huffines, to help Joan to the room. They got her to her room and into bed, clothes and all. The next morning Joan came down for breakfast and sat with Joy, Steve's wife, and was telling the story about being helped to bed by this really handsome gentleman and Carolyn. She went on and on about how nice Steve was and what she didn't know was it was Joy's husband. When Joy said that Steve was nice and he was her husband, Joan didn't know what to say. More about this later.....

The Shillelagh's were going to go back to Ireland for Thanksgiving again so we decided why not? This time we were going to stay at a five-star hotel in Kilkenny and then go to Killarney. The flight over was pretty much as before and a stop at Bun Ratty for scones and coffee on arrival. The hotel in Kilkenny was truly a five-star as advertised. Right up the street from it was the place we had seen before called "Paris Texas." This time we were able to investigate the place and made it a point to have lunch there. We were so impressed with not only the quality but also the quantity and mostly the price. We knew we would have to return the next day for lunch too. We toured the old Castle in Kilkenny again and saw things we did not see the first time around. We also visited a 12th Century church and got the history of it. It mystifies me how these building could be built without the modern equipment of today and yet has square sides and plumb walls. The most amazing thing was that they are standing after 800 to 900 years or more.

While in Kilkenny we wanted to find a Pub that had real traditional Irish music. This was not easy but we found one and got there early. The place was almost empty when we arrived but twenty or so Shillelagh's took over one side of the pub. We had a couple of Paddy's (a whiskey you can not get in the states) and others had some "pints." Soon the band showed up and one of the musicians playing the banjo was missing a couple teeth and looked like something from the "hills of West Virginia." The band was really great and played the type of music we had come to hear. It wasn't long till we were singing the songs with them. By this time the Pub was full and the locals were having a ball watching us have a good time. About six to eight of the lady members got up and sang with the band and got a real ovation from the entire Pub. One of the gals was 80 years old and had been a treasure to be on the trip and get to know.

Again we had to visit the Jameson Distillery and I got to watch another group of members get certified as "Irish Whiskey Tasters." There is not a trip to Ireland complete without visiting the Blarney Castle and Kissing the Blarney Stone. The shopping at Blarney Mills rounds out that trip.

We were off to Killarney and the Ross Hotel that had our favorite water hole pub. It seemed somewhat like "coming home" since we knew our way around town a little. Mary had heard from Carolyn about some "home-made cough syrup" from the local purveyor of medicines. We bought a couple bottles at $7 each and can attest to the quality of the product. We made a tour of the Dingle Peninsula and had a great luncheon in Dingle.

On this trip we got to meet our tour guide and bus driver Dave Spillane's wife Noreen. She is exactly what you would expect of an Irish Lady. Dave is quite the comedian and is always concerned about each member of our club and that is the reason why the club has adopted him.
We were to take a trip around the Ring of Kerry but an auto race interfered with the trip so as good Shillelagh's we adapted and did something else. We visited a renowned jeweler and a shop that specialized in fine woolen and linen. At each stop and sometimes twice or three times a day we had an Irish Coffee break. These stops were all included in the price of the trip. There were a couple of ladies on the trip that did not care for Irish Coffee so I was more than happy to partake in theirs.

We used the pub much as the Irish people do to sit around and swap stories. On one particular evening Joan was telling the story about the week before at the Bahamas and about being put to bed by this really handsome gentleman and going on and on. What was so funny was that Susan was sitting there with us and she added, "Yes he is handsome, he is my dad" to which Joan almost died. Everyone almost died laughing.

We had a great second trip to Ireland and thought it was about time to dream about other places. Little did we know what was in store?

288

Elvis is Alive

A local Houston radio station was advertising an Elvis Cruise to Cozumel for four days leaving from Galveston so we thought we should be on it. Lisa, Mary's daughter, loves Elvis and so does her best friend Jessica. Mary decided to take Lisa and Brett on the cruise since Jessica was going to go with her boyfriend. Bryce got to go too and would celebrate his second birthday on the cruise as my present. He had not talked much until we were on the trip when he started saying "boat in the water" and he has talked a mile a minute since then. It was a fun trip and I got to take Mary to a local bar that I had visited in 1969 with the Shillelagh's. The thing that was different now is the bar is right downtown but in 1969 it was out in the country by the beach. The bar didn't move but the town grew around it. The Los Palmeras has absolutely the best Margarita's in the world. I had told Mary about them so we stopped in and had lunch and a couple of their Margarita's. Mary drank about an inch of hers from the giant fishbowl glass and said she didn't think she could walk. She asked the waiter what was in it and he described the fresh fruit juices and the liquor. They are so smooth and strong and had not changed since I had been there years ago. Mary nursed hers all day while I was working on a second and third.

During the trip the cruise had a Karaoke night and singing a lot of old Elvis songs. Jessica wanted to get up and sing, but not by herself, so she talked Mary into going with her. Mary had a couple of drinks and is always willing to "help a friend." The song they chose was "I like Rock and Roll." Mary took the microphone and said "are you hear to have some fun" the place clapped and Mary said to let it all down 'cause you will never see these people again and to join in. When they started singing they brought the place down, people were trying to get into the club and the place was packed. Everyone loved it and Mark, Jessica's boyfriend, turned to Lisa and said "your mom rocks."

Camping with Janice

My boss, Janice Thompson, from SMU in Plano purchased 60+ acres about 80 miles west of Dallas in what she called 4-Corners. This was in an area where Janice had hunted and knew a few of the property owners. On the property there was an old house and a steel building with the back half turned into living quarters. Janice wanted to remodel the old house and turn it into a Bed and Breakfast. It was going to be a real project because she was going to do most of the work herself. She would have to gut the old house and start new, after leveling the old pier and beam house.

To break the monotony Janice decided to have a camping and cookout over Memorial Day weekend 2003. She would invite friends and fellow workers from SMU. Janice and I had been very close while I worked for her in Plano and Mary and I were invited, even though we had moved to Houston.

Mary had not been camping and the weekend sounded like a great time to spend with old friends. I had purchased an air mattress in Dallas for the couple months before I moved to Houston for the fold-out couch we had. I was positive it had been a queen size air mattress. As we planned the camping trip, we purchased a tent and gathered up the other equipment we might need. Mary kept asking me over and over if we needed another air mattress and I assured her the queen-size would be great for the two of us on the ground.

Mary and Janice as lunch is getting cooked

All went well until we got to Janice's put up the tent and it came time to blow up the air mattress. Mary said it sure didn't look like a queen size and I told her to go look on the box. Sure enough it was not a queen and I was kidded about it all weekend. Turned out it was a Twin mattress. (Not too far off, huh?)

Janice had some friends that were ranchers and she talked them into bringing their chuck wagon to the spot where the cooking was going to take place. By the time we got there on Saturday Robert and Smokey were already preparing some items for the "big meal" that evening. They were busily working on some calf fries, by skinning and cleaning them. There were bags and bags of them and without thinking Mary asked Smokey how they got so many. Without skipping a beat he answered her "Well ma'am there is two per bull". We got a kick out of it and the more we talked the more we convinced Mary to try some at the meal.

That evening there was a big turnout of people from SMU, other friends and neighbors of Janice. A big buffet was served with brisket, hamburgers, ribs and all of the other goodies like potato salad, Cole-slaw and of course the calf fries. Mary did try them and thought they were pretty good. Janice, Robert and Smokey had done a great job turning out a real western cookout which even included a peach cobbler cooked over the open coals. There was music, dancing, lots of talking and even a couple of adult beverages.

Sunday morning we had a breakfast of eggs, bacon, sausage, home-made biscuits, gravy and fried potatoes also all cooked over the open coals.. This was a "real stick to your ribs" breakfast. Shortly after breakfast we headed south for the 6-½ drive back home.

We would repeat the campout the following year of 2004 but we purchased a "queen-size" camping bed with air mattress. We had just as much fun as the year before and saw many of our friends once again. We missed going in 2005 but hope to go this next year.

Norman and Barbara's 50th Wedding Anniversary
What a wonderful life Norm and Barb had for 50 years. Barbara met Norman when she worked for him at the concession stand at the city swimming pool. Norman had bid

on and was granted the contract. He was just home from the Korean War and getting his civilian life moving. Starting out delivering bread, Norman and Barbara were married in 1953. He then changed careers and started selling insurance for Metropolitan Life. Over the years he was always a top producer and Barbara could stay at home and raise their children, Linda and Doug. After his retirement and their move to Broken Arrow, Norman piddled in the yard, made some fantastic wooden Hobby Horses, wooden pens, even a drop leaf table and many other items.

I tried to get Norman excited in computers but his laid-back attitude meant he was only going to use it for what he needed. Being a diabetic for years and years, Norman kept track of all of his medical records on the computer. On one occasion when we were visiting I mentioned how easy it was to find people on the Internet. Norman said he sure wished he could find an old soldier friend from the Korean days. The name was not a real common name and it only took me about five minutes to find his friend out in California. In thirty minutes they were talking on the phone and bringing each other up to date on the past fifty years.

As their golden anniversary approached Norman wanted to have a surprise get together for Barbara. When she found out his plans she put the dampers on that. However in October 2003 there was a family celebration for their fiftieth anniversary but it would be at Doug and Donna's in Lincoln, Nebraska. We flew to Omaha and drove to Lincoln. It was just family being Jim, Sheila (Jim's sweetheart), Linda, Doug, Donna and their children Jessica and Brent and Mary and I. We went out for dinner at the country club and had a great time. There were arrangements for a piano player to come and play for a while before dinner. Linda sang Barbara's favorite song "Peg of my Heart" for her mother. Barbara played and always loved piano music, and I have too, and I think we inherited it from our mother playing as we were children.

Barb and Norm on the Big 50 celebration day – at Doug's

In just two short months we were to have to let go of Norman as his many years of diabetes took its tool. They had fifty wonderful years and each was a compliment to the other, I believe that is why their life worked so well.

Not another trip to Ireland
Our mind had been made up to look for other exciting places to explore and when we got the monthly Shillelagh magazine there was a trip to Ireland to spend New Years in Ashford Castle.

I felt that every Queen should spend a night in a real Castle so my Queen Mary was going to have to make another trip to Ireland. I looked for air fares to Baltimore for the week before Christmas 2003 and saw a lot of flights and told Mary we would decide on one when she got home from work. In just the eight hours she was at work all of the flights were sold except Christmas Day. We flew in and spent a couple days with Laura and then went to visit my cousin Lois while she had all of her family in to celebrate their Christmas and open presents. Janice came up from Manassas and brought Stephanie, Mary Beth's daughter. Lois had not seen Laura or Janice for some 30-35 years.

We left Baltimore for Boston and on to Shannon with a time schedule we were getting use to. We headed for Killarney and a stay at the Killarney Plaza hotel where we would spend a couple days touring and celebrate New Year's Eve before heading for Ashford Castle on New Year's Day.

The time in Killarney was convenient to touring the southern part of Ireland. Some of the most popular places like Blarney Castle and the Jameson Distillery are pretty much a given on most of the trips, we didn't mind seeing them again. Naturally there were the usual stops for some Irish Coffee to warm the innards. We had a couple members, Carole and Marcia that had been on a previous trip with us that were apprehensive about climbing up to the top of Blarney Castle to kiss the Blarney Stone. We explained that Mary was a little unsure when she first tried it but it ended up not being too bad. Mary and I told them we would guide them up and take our time. Pauline's grandchildren and two other members went with us to climb the round stairways and Kiss the Blarney Stone to receive "The Gift of Gab." I had hoped since I had kissed the stone I might receive more of the "gift." Carole and Marcia were so happy after they completed the excursion they thanked us several times during the trip.

A Shillelagh member, Pauline brought her grandchildren a brother 21 and sister 20 on the trip. They were two of the nicest, sweetest and most considerate young people any of us had ever met. We would have all adopted them at any time. Pauline is a pushing 80 and is quite a lady and wonderful person in her own right.

New Years Eve was a party complete with noisemakers, hats and live band at the Plaza Hotel. This hotel is located right on the square near the Ross that was closed for gutting and remodeling. The band was really pretty good and played some slow tunes so Mary and I got to dance a couple times. The rock 'n roll music was decent and Mary always had a member of the club to get out on the floor with her. The local Irish population that was at the celebration was having a good time and some of them asked members to dance. They did not feel like we were crashing their party. The fact that the Irish people like "Yanks" and are so friendly helps to make all of the trips enjoyable.

On New Year's Day we slept in a little but were on the road by 10am and headed for Ashford Castle where we would spend two nights. We were really looking forward to the castle and the history of the area.

We made a potty stop at the Creamery Bar near Bunratty Castle, which is familiar territory and maybe only 20 miles from Shannon. Further on with the drive we stopped for lunch at a place that had great seafood and soups. We have never had bad soup in Ireland but the chowder at this place was superb. Finally after a big part of the day we were within sight of Ashford Castle.

Ashford Castle in Ireland has been open since 1222

We arrived at Ashford Castle to learn that Mel Gibson had left that morning. Ashford castle has been open since the year 1222 and most anyone that is anyone has spent time there. Now "My Queen Mary" and her humble servant (me) have can be added to the list of important people. Ashford Castle is "The Castle" in Ireland and is located about three-quarters of a mile of the village of Cong and has a lot of 11th and 12th Century history around it including old churches and historic graveyards. Cong is also where John Wayne and Maureen O'Hara filmed "the Quiet Man" and is more famous for this at present. If you have not seen the movie it is worth renting and watching.

We did get to see and photograph the "Quiet Man House" and we even visited some of the pubs that John Wayne and Maureen had visited years ago.

Ashford Castle was everything we expected with the thick six to nine-foot thick walls. The Castle had been remodeled in the late 1930's to add plumbing and bathrooms. What had been the dungeon is now a pub complete with music, shows and orators. The Castle grounds are immaculate and the view from our room was spectacular looking out on the lake behind the Castle. A stream passes in front of the castle with a bridge across it. The food and service we received was fitting of the King's and Queen's. The normal room rate for a visit is over $500 a night however; as always the Shillelagh's negotiate special rates.

After our two nights in Ashford Castle we were off to Galway and the famous Galway Bay. Along the way we stopped at a pub that was famous for their seafood. We were not disappointed and the break from the riding on the bus was welcomed. The hotel in Galway was right on the main square and afforded a nice place to venture out and do a walking tour of the town. Several of us headed out on foot and one of the first things we saw as we crossed the main square was a pub called "Fibber Magees." Remembering the old radio program of Fibber Magee and Molly the pub just looked like one they would visit. Later the pub would be in the news for trying not to comply with the non-smoking ordinance, but they capitulated after one day. The four of us walked all over the downtown area and by the port where many persons left for the New World. On the way back to the hotel we found a neat little pub that we would explore later in the evening before heading home the next day.

We were sure this would be our last trip to Ireland for quite some time since we had now been there three times, but another **Dream** had come true with spending a couple nights in a real Castle from the times of Kings, Queens, Knights and Empire building. Little did we know what was in store for us?

The flight home was uneventful but we did chat with other members about the cruise later in the month that we had signed up with the Shillelagh's.

The Navigator of the Sea
The end of January 2004 saw us headed for Miami and a seven-day cruise on the Royal Caribbean's Navigator of the

Sea cruise ship. The ship was almost new and the second largest cruise ship afloat. We flew in the day before the cruise, as is our normal routine, but on arrival at the hotel we found some other Shillelagh's that we knew. Where do members congregate to spread tales except at the pub? Sandy and Nancy as well as some others had been on the Ireland trips and we had lots to talk about.

The next morning it was up, have breakfast and head for the ship. On arrival we had to check out the room and Mary was ready to upgrade because of the size. The trip was over Super Bowl weekend and Mary thought it would be a somewhat empty cruise. We went to the Purser's office and were told that all of the rooms were that size and in fact the cruise was sold out as are all Super Bowl cruises. We had just gotten spoiled on other ships with larger rooms but since we only sleep there it was not a problem.

The ports of call were some that we had been to before but nothing of real excitement on any of the stops. However, this did not stop the fun on board with the Shillelagh's. The shows on the cruise were top notch, the food and service were great and we found a little place to hangout. Yep it was a piano bar and most evenings the club owned the bar. The piano player had a great time with the sing a long and the lack of quality of the singer's abilities. He loved to pick on someone and it was a great time.

The days in the hot tubs at poolside were nice since the tubs were just under the edge of another deck and thus not in the real hot sun. The ship has a center Promenade that is six stories high and like a shopping mall on both sides.

The cruise was a great time for relaxing since we were not under pressure to see this or that.

Mary's Family Reunion
Mary comes from a large family of six brothers and one sister. She spent most of her growing up life in Missouri near Fort Leonard Wood. As a child growing up times were hard for the family so we can relate some things together. The only difference is that her family was not as close with each other as might have been liked. When Mary's father passed away in

January 1998 we attended the funeral and it was the first time all of the children had been together for quite some time. A lot of talking and visiting was done and it was decided that any disagreements needed to be put aside and there should be a family picnic.

Mary and her brother Frank did most of the planning and put together a weekend in 1999 at campgrounds called Boiling Springs, convenient to everyone but us. Mary's brother, John lived in Vicksburg, MS and also had some distance to travel but not quite as much as we did.

Mary and I produced a newsletter for several months prior to the time of the picnic and the turnout was great. Most of us stayed at a motel about 15 miles from the campsite because only one cabin was available. All but her sister and one of the brothers came. Frank did most of the cooking since he had been a chef and the rest of us talked, ate well and strolled down to the creek.

We all talked about having another reunion soon but it turned out to be 5 years. So over Labor Day weekend of 2004 we headed back to Boiling Springs. This time we had planned far enough in advance that we were able to rent some of the cabins for those that planned to attend. By this time John had moved to the Washington, DC area so he was the distance traveler. He flew into St Louis and met up with Frank and we all gathered at a diner close to the campgrounds for lunch before setting up camp.

Again, Mary and Frank had been the instrumental players in the reunion. Frank had planned every meal with precision and brought a friend to help cook. He had arranged for a large pick-up load of wood to be delivered for the campfire. The cabin we stayed in was a three-plex and the cooking would be done inside for the most part.

This time many of the nieces and nephews came from as far as Ohio. Lisa surprised her mother by driving up with Bryce and surprising us on Saturday morning. She had not seen some of her cousins for many years as they were just not a close knit family. This time however, two of the brothers did not show but her sister did. There was a lot of cooking by Frank and his buddy since there was about 30 in attendance.

On Monday there was a canoe trip scheduled and we would be taken by van about 5 miles up the stream where we would float the stream back to near the campgrounds. There were a few spots that the canoes scrapped bottom and we had to get out and pull them through those areas. The time of the year we were there the water is at its lowest however it turned out to be fun. Mary had never been in a canoe or done much paddling but caught on so fast and learned to steer and read the deep spots with little trouble. The canoe trip was a lot of fun but was also a lot of physical work. A good time was had by all in attendance.

Ireland – to Celebrate Dave's 40th Birthday

Not long after we got back from the cruise the word was spread that Dave Spillane, our guide in Ireland wanted a select group to please come and share his 40th Birthday the following year. Because Dave, Noreen and the kids are dear to us we decided "what the heck" why not go one more time. There were some members that Dave particularly wanted to come celebrate.

Since the club goes six or eight times a year to Ireland there were many members that also wanted to be there so it was going to require two trips in a month just to accommodate those that wanted to go. Most of the special "invites" would go on the second trip leaving March 28 and coming back April 4th 2005. Joy and Steve Huffines had been asking us to spend time with them coming and/or going to Ireland and this would be the chance. We flew in to Baltimore on Saturday before we were to leave on Monday so we could attend the "pre-trip" party at Carolyn's. Another couple that was coming from Florida would arrive about the same time so we would take them from the airport to Carolyn's where they were going to stay until leaving for the trip. It worked out that Walt and Linda were waiting for us as we got off the plane.

We headed for a quick brunch and then off to Carolyn's for the late afternoon party. We got to Carolyn's about an hour early so it gave us a chance to share some gossip before everyone started to arrive. Carolyn is the epitome of the perfect hostess. Joy and Steve were coming and also a couple that have been a good friend of theirs for years that were also going on the trip. It was a great get together and lasted well into the evening. We had to bail out and head for Maryland to be able to see Mary's Brother John on Sunday morning, which we did.

Sunday afternoon we met Steve at the Baltimore airport and returned the car and headed for their house. That evening we headed for the Fleet Club in Annapolis and got to meet Torre the man that stole Susan's (Joy's daughter) heart. It was a great evening with Carolyn, John, Walt, Linda as well as Steve and Joy. Torre called Susan in Ireland while we were all at the table and we got to convey our thoughts of him to Susan. The next morning would see us up and on the way again to JFK airport via the Shillelagh bus for the trip to Ireland.

One of Mary's good friends from the days of working in Canton, TX also named Linda would meet us at JFK along with her sister and another friend to make the trip. We all met up at the airport and checked in early as required, then went off to have a snack and wait for the flight to be called. The trip over was nice and saw us arrive right on time at Shannon. As we had done in the past we got to Creamery Bar in Bunratty and breakfast was ready and waiting.

Bunratty Castle

We were then off to Killarney to spend four days in very familiar territory. This time we stayed in a different hotel but right next to our favorite Ross hotel. It had now been gutted except for the front wall and was in the process of being rebuilt. This would mean that now we had stayed at three of the four hotels on the main square of town. We were familiar with the Pubs in Killarney and looked forward to hearing some Irish music.

One of the highlights of the trip was a young 17-year-old girl named Jodie. She started saving her money from babysitting and other jobs starting at the age of 12 to be able to make this trip and also have spending money. After she had saved her money she then talked her grandmother into chaperoning her on the trip. Both were a delight and we enjoyed showing them the Pub scene. Jodie enjoyed the night at the pub and purchased a couple of CD's of the band to take home. I asked her if she had the band sign them, which she did not. So I went and talked to the band and they were more than happy to sign the CD's and also to have a photograph taken with Jodie. This really made her day.

We also did our tours from our base in Killarney such as the Dingle Peninsula and seeing the old stone huts again that monks built in the 11th Century.

One of the 11th Century Bee-hive huts used by monks

Irish Celtic Monks assembled these beehive-shaped stone huts no mortar was used--- even today these stone huts are still perfectly water-tight.

Also along the trip there was a number of what are referred to as "potato famine houses". They are very small and sometimes held more than one family trying to survive. After the ride around the Peninsula we ended in Dingle for a good lunch. The seafood, soups, stews and breads are always outstanding throughout Ireland.

Mary and me on the dolphin in Dingle Square

Mary and I were walking down the street in Killarney doing a little bit of window-shopping when Noreen and the kids, Jack & Laura walked by. It was like being back home walking and seeing someone you know. Noreen did not see me until she was just past and I spoke her name. It was really neat since the next day the Shillelagh's would celebrate Dave's big 40th Birthday. We had the party at the hotel and were joined by Noreen and the kids for the dinner and somewhat of a roast.

Dave is an avid golf player and one of the guys took a putter, bent it and put it back together with Band-Aid's as a present for Dave. Some of the members like Steve, John and Howard got to play a couple rounds of golf the day before the party with Dave. We all had a great time at the party and Dave didn't look a year older than when we first met him four years ago.

After our time in Killarney and the sightseeing we headed for the town of Cobh which is pronounced "Cove." At one time it was known as Queenstown and was the last stop of the Titanic on that fateful voyage. Also the town was known as a place the survivors of the Lusitania were brought when the German U-boat sank it in 1917. The town is famous as well as the sailing port for all of the Irish people that left during the potato famine to immigrate to America.

Our hotel was right on the bay and our room looked out upon it and the small park across the street. We went on a guided walking tour known as the Titanic trail which covered a good part of the city and ended with a "pint" at a pub on the top of the hill overlooking the seaport. This tour was excellent and our guide had done all of the research and also was responsible for getting plaques put in important history locations. The hotel was first class but the trip had to end after being in Cobh for four days.

The building the last passengers boarding the Titanic left from (in rear)

The next few months were quiet around the home front except for enjoying the hot tub with its new surroundings and my re-doing the kitchen counters. The kitchen job was estimated to be a two-week job but as I got into it would find that it would be a six- week project. Once it was done with new Formica tops and new tile we would have no trouble cleaning it like the old rough tile.

50th High School Reunion

August of 2005 saw me headed for Ohio via Clarksburg to attend my 50th High School Reunion. I would have to make the trip without my partner Mary since she could not get a day off without pay. My buddy Dave from high school was also going to be there without his wife and sweetie, Jane.

I flew in to Pittsburgh and headed for Clarksburg on Thursday to see Aunt Frances and hear about the finalization of the plans for the BIG 100th birthday party to be held the last weekend in October. Late that evening I headed part way to Steubenville. Friday morning I got up and drove the rest of the way into my old hometown. I checked into the hotel and then took a quick drive up on the hilltop where I grew up. What a depressing sight the area is and how it has turned into a depressing and dilapidated area. The LaBelle View as it was known when I was growing up was once prime property and a proud place to live. I hated to see the yards uncut, houses needing paint and fixing up, and looking like a slum area. Aunt Lil's house up on the corner where I used to cut the grass was the best looking house in the area.

I headed back to the hotel to meet Dave who was coming in from Virginia. We sat around and caught up on the last few years of life and talked of old times. Soon it was time to go to the Friday evening class get together. We checked in and got to see many of our old, literally classmates. Dave and I convinced ourselves that we must have been eight or nine when we graduated from High School since we looked pretty well for our age compared to many of the others.

I did get to see Sam, who I had not seen for 50 years. We worked in Kinney shoes together. He mentioned about the "girls" and the way we used to tilt the mirror to see up their dresses (no panties). I had totally forgotten about this, we laughed and laughed.

Saturday morning saw us at the old High School for a tour of our old stomping grounds. We met and were given the tour by the assistant Principal. We use to put up signs on the first day with arrows pointing to "Elevator" for the freshmen. The school now has an elevator, which it never had while we were in school, and some of our "old" classmates did use it on the tour.

After walking around the three floors, we headed back to the new addition. While we were standing near the athletic office and the group of us was swapping stories, the current Athletic Director was listening and laughing. I told the story about being on the golf team and after we had played all of our matches the coach wanted us to play one more for a "school champion." The golf course is very hilly and we had walked it so much the team decided to draw straws, make up scorecards and turn them in. When we did the coach said, "You didn't play because I was over at the course." We never dreamed he would ever show up at the course. He canned the whole team and none of us got our Varsity Letters. We all laughed about it and headed into the new gym. While we were looking at the gym I got a tap on the shoulder and the Athletic Director said, "Here is your letter." I darn near fainted and I gave big thanks and everyone thought it was way too cool.

Saturday evening was the big reunion dinner and there was a good turnout. Dave had been a Navy Photographer and so the two of us took lots of photos for ourselves but we decided to share them with some of our friends. I was to combine the photos and put them on a CD.

Old buddy Dave Davis that was my HS best friend - hard to think 50 years gone by – Yep we were only 9 when we graduated – we look good

Sunday morning saw us at the new Jr. High that was built on the site of our old one. We had breakfast at the school and a tour that was really neat. We told some stories there and the assistant principal of that school showed us around. He pointed to one room and told Dave and I it was something new and if there had been one in our days we would have probably spent a lot of time in it. The room was a "time out" room for troublesome students. I was surprised with the security built into the new school. Once the last bell rang the school was in "lock down" where no one can get in, but the doors open from the inside. There is a camera at the door and if someone needs to get in they can be let in from the office. There were cameras in every room and all halls.

Disney Cruise

Mary had promised Bryce two years ago a Disney cruise if he would just get potty trained. I guess it is a boy thing because he just wasn't in a hurry to do this in our timetable. We worked on him and he finally, at almost three was doing pretty well. Early this year it was time to start living up to her promise. In early September we were off to Orlando via Southwest airlines. On the trip we sat in the second row and I tried to get Bryce to have his picture taken with the Flight Attendants. I had spent a lot of time trying to teach Bryce to kiss a ladies hand when introduced but he was not having anything to do with the two gals.

After much coaxing and a promise to take my photo with the Flight Attendants he reluctantly gave in. I got a couple photos and then the two Attendants came to have their photo taken by Mary and Bryce. Then they sat one on each side and Mary took the first picture. Next Bryce said "don't tell my Pawpaw that he is cute", as they had told him. That broke them up. For the second photo the two Attendants gave me a kiss on the side of the head. Bryce immediately came over and started rubbing it off. One of the gals said, "Are you rubbing it in" to which Bryce answered he was rubbing it OFF. We were to visit Cousin Charlotte and Gene then to spend the night at the Wingate hotel near the airport. We would get up early the next morning for the trip to Port Canaveral and to board the Disney Wonder.

306

We got to the cruise ship early and had lunch, checked out our room and had a little while to relax before the "lifeboat drill." We left about 4pm and were headed for Nassau for the next morning. Our seating was at a table with a lady, her mother, her son and two nephews who were from upper Pennsylvania. The food on the cruise was great and the shows were outstanding.

We visited the Atlantis hotel in the Grand Bahamas and the Disney Island of Castaway Cay. There was a good time had by all three of us and Bryce did well for being away from his parents for almost a week. We got home late on Thursday evening and Mary had to work on Friday.

Bryce surrounded by Mary, Me (his Paw Paw) my cousin Charlotte and her beau Gene Lang the night before the cruise

Fun times on the cruise

Chapter 30 – Family

Norman is Gone

In October of 2003, after celebrating a wonderful fifty years together with Barbara, who would have imagined that Norman would not be here at Christmas time. Norman had such a wonderful time in Lincoln at Doug and Donna's celebrating with family and seemed to be in excellent health despite his diabetes. He had an opportunity to chat with family, hug on his beautiful grand-daughter, watch his football playing grandson and celebrate the time with Barbara.

All of this seemed to fall apart in early December when Norman was not feeling well and went into the hospital. As the days went on things turned for the worse and I received a phone call that I should make a trip to Tulsa. I flew to Tulsa to be with Barbara, Jim and Doug. As it turned out things did not improve and Norman drifted off into a coma. His vital signs did not look good and after much discussion with family and physicians it was clear that Norman would not improve and could not sustain life on his own. Barbara, Linda and Doug made the decision that the life support should be disconnected.

It was a very traumatic time for me and even though I knew deep in my heart it was the correct thing to do, it was hard watching Norman go to his Maker. In my opinion it is not the right thing to do to prolong a person's existence if there is not Quality of Life or if the vital signs show no response. To simply have a person on a feeding tube and life support when there is no chance of recovery is not fair to the person. So the family made the correct decision, but a very difficult one at that.

Norman was the perfect match for Barbara in his easy-go style and willingness to please in any way he could. Their life, which I am sure had bumps in the road, was a fantastic one as far as I have ever been able to ascertain. Norman worked very hard and loved his mate Barbara and their children and grandchildren. I can never remember Norman being anything other than the perfect Brother-in-law. I am so thankful that my sister knew 50 wonderful years together with Norman and their family.

Barbara Passes to be with Norman

Late Friday evening I received a call about my sister Barbara not doing well. We hurried and made plane reservations to get to Ohio but could not get out until Saturday at 8am. Before we left the house for the airport on Saturday I received the sad news that Barbara had gone to join Norman and my parents.

This was a very hard time for me to cope with. I am so lucky that I had Mary to be with me and her strong faith in God has helped me immensely. I am very aware that we do not all go on forever but sometimes we just don't understand "why now."

I am so thankful that Barbara and myself had been so close all of our years and especially the last eight or ten years when we talked weekly if not more often. Linda and Doug were such comfort and I am so proud to have them for a niece and nephew. They are both very classy individuals.

At the funeral I did get to see Ruth Ann, Barbara's best friend and out next door neighbor. She is still the sweet gal that I have always remembered. Another of Barbara's friends Josie McPherson was there and I had not seen her in some 50 years. She had skydived on her 70th birthday two years ago. She was looking great and it was wonderful to see her. Laura came to be with me, which I appreciated. Aunt Frances came up also and we talked about more pleasant things like the pending 100th birthday party.

Frances Celebrates 100th Birthday

The weekend was almost a year in the planning as excitement raged, the menu planned, guests lists and reservations made. All of this led up for the Friday thru Sunday, the last weekend in October 2005. We would be just a couple days short of being there for the actual birthday on November first.

Celebrating your hundredth birthday is no small achievement. If you were to know Aunt Frances you would know she wanted it to be perfect, and it ended up to be that and more.

Frances started coordinating the party with Barbara and when she passed away then Jim had to pick up where Barbara left off. Even though Frances was almost a hundred years old, she played an active role in the planning by visiting the options of

310

places that might host the party. Her favorite restaurant in Clarksburg would wind up the winner in the selection for places to hold the party. The main dining room would just hold the invited 47 people. Some of the other options were just "too cold and no atmosphere" even though they were big enough.

Once Julio's was the final choice the menu had to be decided. Originally Frances and her two "ladies in waiting that take care of her", sisters Willie and Billie had decided on a couple items for choice of on the menu but it was expanded to contain something for everyone. Frances ordered napkins, book marks and got her guest book in her choice of Burgundy which is a Royal color as it should be for her.

The guest list was prepared and Jim printed, with Frances' approval, the invitations and got them in the mail. He then started coordinating with Julio's for the event. Jim prepared and printed the Menu, while I prepared a Power Point slide presentation to be shown during the entire evening.

When we were growing up we knew that Frances had been married and that her husband had been killed as a Maryland State Trooper. He was killed on Christmas Day 1927 but I had not known until the last few months that Frances had in fact been engaged to another person that died in a swimming accident. Last year on a visit to Frances she had given me a box of old photos and I went through it, putting names on the photographs. There were several photos of James Noon and Frances, whom she had married just 14 months before his death.

We were enlightened to some of the stories of her youth.   The trips she had made, most of which we were familiar with, were repeated for the show.

Frances decided to give all of the ladies a yellow rose in remembrance of Barbara but as time went on she changed it to a yellow rose corsage. They were beautiful rosebuds with baby's breath and such a reminder. We felt Barbara there all evening.

As plane reservations were made we were able to meet in Dallas to fly on to Pittsburgh with Jim, Sheila, Bryan and Cyndi who were coming from Tulsa. We arrived in Dallas about the time we were to board the flight and had no trouble meeting the Tulsa gang. After we arrived in Pittsburgh and piled into the van that Jim had reserved, it was a little less than two hours we were in Clarksburg.

Linda was already there and we went to see Frances for a short visit. Soon Mike, Laura, Joy and Luke would arrive. The Manassas gang of Janice, Mary Beth, Jason and Stephanie would arrive about midnight after a long day of work for Janice. We waited up for them and met them in the lobby, but it was soon bedtime for all.

Saturday, after a breakfast in the lobby, some of us headed for Julio's to set up the sound system, the projector screen and talk with Pam, the owner about the layout of the room.

Then it was out to visit Frances for a short time and back to get ready. Doug and Donna would arrive with the projector so we would go back to Julio's a little early to get it set up. Joy and Stephanie were to give out the name tags and have the guests sign the register book while Janice gave out the corsages.

The first cousins of Frances, Ralph and LeRoy came from Waterford, OH escorted by one of the youngest twin daughters, Bobbie. Linda's husband Dale and his mother arrived, as well as Chuck Chapman and daughters Carol and Susan with her husband.

Frances wanted everyone to join in and sing "Take me Out to the Ballgame" to get the party in a festive mood. She also requested that Linda sing "Thanks for the Memories" at the party as Frances had a lot of memories to be thankful for. Linda treated us with one more song reminding us that God is always looking out for our good. He sure has where Frances is concerned.

Some of the friends Frances invited we already knew but there was quite a few we met for the first time. Everyone that wanted a chance to "tell on or about" Frances was given the opportunity. Linda Gimmel the daughter of one of Frances' best friends, Ruth Gimmel told the story of the Las Vegas trip that six of the ladies took and carried 106 pairs of shoes for a

312

weekend trip. Some of the other friends told stories and all agreed that it was Frances' motto that "it only cost a nickel more to go first class". Janice, Mary Beth and Laura created a memory using each letter of Frances to start a remembrance and Janice read it to Frances. The evening ended with a short visit back at the hotel by Frances for some last moments before her bedtime. The rest of us stayed and visited well passed our bedtime but enjoyed every minute seeing the relatives we had not seen often enough. It was decided that Bryan and Cyndi had not seen Janice, Mary Beth and Laura for more than 25 years, way too long for cousins.

Brother Jim, Aunt Frances and myself on the evening of the party

Everyone got up early Sunday morning and after a quick visit to Frances' for a pepperoni roll we would start heading home. Linda and Laura snuck out of the motel and went to check on the rolls and Linda ordered some warm to eat at the house and then 10 dozen more for each family to have a dozen to take home. All was cool till the lady said it was almost $170 but Linda made the generous gift to all of us of a dozen to take home. Thanks Linda, what a special lady you are to all.

After saying our good-byes to everyone it was time for us to head south to Dallas via a quick trip to Pittsburgh. In Dallas we said bye to Jim, Sheila, Bryan and Cyndi and got on to our plane for Houston.

I can assure you that in the last couple of years Frances has just dreamed of the day she could celebrate being a Centenarian. I am sure that dream has given her the strength to go on through several falls and other medical problems.

The weekend was a great time and affords a wonderful place for me to stop and get this into print.

Cyndi, Doug, Frances, Janice, Linda, Mary Beth Laura & Brian (Kneeling)

It is pretty hard to imagine life any more fun than that during the time of Aunt Frances' 100th Birthday party. Getting together with so many family members, relatives and friends was such a pleasure.

The rest of the year 2005 passed without any more great events. The upcoming year had a few things to look forward to. There was an Irish cruise and my 70th birthday ahead, but surely I can't be anywhere near seventy years old.

Chapter 31 – 2006 Cruises in

What a year this turns out to be

Cruise on the Carnival Legend

After a quiet welcoming in of the New Year we started to get excited about our upcoming cruise in January. This cruise was to be with our *Shillelagh Travel Club* friends and with many performers of Irish music. Our tour guide from Ireland, Dave Spillane, was going to come and enjoy a vacation on the cruise.

The end of January we flew to Florida for the seven-day cruise on the Carnival Legend headed for St Maarten, Barbados and Martinique. We got to the hotel the night before the cruise and already in the lobby were many of our friends enjoying chatting so we joined in.

We were up early the next morning for breakfast and to catch the bus to the ship. Next was an easy check in, then we were off to explore and do some necessary such as registering for the Irish entertainment. Our tour guide from Ireland, Dave Spillane, had come to enjoy a vacation on the cruise.

Dave Spillane & Mary at Lifeboat drill

The Dady Brothers

There were some great entertainers performing such as a young group of kids from Northern Virginia doing Irish dancing. They performed almost every night and the energy they had was something only to wish for. All in all the performers were great but one pair of brothers called "The Dady Brothers" was outstanding. We made sure to see their performance every time.

The cruise was a good one but our visit to Barbados and Martinique was somewhat of a disappointment. I had always heard great things of both places and I think that if you flew in and spent at least three days they could be nice. To visit by cruise ship is not worth the effort. St Maarten Island is different and always a great place to visit. Carolyn, John, Mary and I took Dave for a trip around the island. We found a great little place for lunch at an outside eatery.
Naturally, we had to stop by the nude beach to get Dave's expression.

It is always great to go on a cruise but it is nice to get home. The one thing bad about taking vacation so early in the year is Mary using part of her vacation time so soon.

Memorial Day with Janice

We missed the 2005 Memorial Day campout at the "Four Corners" ranch with my boss Janice Thompson. Janice is a very special and fun person so we decided to make the long drive again. I mapped a direct route through back roads of Texas all the way to Mineral Wells.

After picking Mary up from work we headed off on the six and half hour drive only to find few rooms available for Friday night. Two years earlier they couldn't give away hotel rooms since Mineral Wells was drying up. Something happened and the hotels were full but we finally found a place.

Mary with out tent

Saturday morning, up and breakfast then head the last twenty miles to the ranch. It was great to see Janice as well as some other old friends. Our camping spot was ready for us and the tent went up quickly, but with a lot of sweat. We got to meet a few new friends and had a great chuck wagon type cookout. A lot of swapping tales till late into the night and then off to our tent to sleep. Early Sunday morning meant packing up the tent, getting some breakfasts and head back home for the long drive.

Alfred and Ashlie's Wedding

Update: As mentioned earlier on, (pg 272) I had a favorite student in Plano named Alfred Delshad that was getting married in Sherman, TX. I was asked to be his Best Man so I headed there on Saturday June 10, 2006 to perform the honor. I was made to feel right at home and part of the family. The wedding was held at the Chapel on Austin College. Their wedding was scheduled for the next day, Sunday the 11th and I was honored when asked to be his best man. I had a chance to meet Ashlie and her family, including her 100-year old Great Grandmother.

Me with Ashlie and Alfred (Al-2)

Saturday was a cookout at her grandmother's and a fun time. The wedding went off without a hitch at the Austin College Chapel.

Ashlie had graduated and completed the four-year program in three years while working full time. She received a full scholarship to Perdue for her graduate school, pretty awesome.

An odd bit of news I found out prior to the wedding was Alfred (Al2) had been in charge of the food service at Austin College for some six plus years before going to SMU. This period was during the time Lesley was at Austin College. Al 2 said that he must have gotten to know her but not by name. What a coincident that he was there at the time Lesley was in school.

I did take time to look at the class plaques of Karen and Lesley. I thought back of the time of getting to see Karen graduate and then for "Lesley and her family" to not allow me to watch her graduate, sad time in my life.

Chapter 32

Surprise Birthday Season

Early August started with what would turn out to be later a surprise when Carole Jacoby called and told me that she and Marcia, two Shillelagh friends, were coming to Houston, from Maryland, on their way to Dallas to visit relatives. She said she was coming on Thursday Aug 24th and wondered if we could get together on Friday, as that was Carole's birthday. I told her that would be great and I would give them a short tour and even fix supper of ribs.

August 23rd (Wed) came in as the official beginning of the "Birthday Season" for me unknowingly. I received a phone call from LaRita Mason a very dear friend from Amarillo/Phoenix. She stated she was going to be in town for a presentation by a friend and wondered if Mary and I could get together with her. One of her favorite places to eat is in Galveston and that happened to be where her friend was giving the presentation. I indicated I would check with Mary and get back to her, and all was a go.

LaRita asked about getting a ride to Galveston from the Galleria area or she could catch a shuttle. I told her I would pick her up and we would be back to the house by the time Mary got home from work. What I didn't know was she and Mary had already talked about going to dinner.

After picking her up, chatting and Mary coming home, we headed for Gaidos for some seafood. A great evening of company but LaRita wanted to know what Mary had planned for my birthday. I told her that we were going to dinner with her daughter and friends. I should have caught on since she asked me several times what we were going to do and that she wanted a complete history of the weekend.

LaRita is on the road almost constantly and periodically she sends an email of her travels, visits and dinning experiences of the previous happenings. These are fun to read and informative so when she asked me to let her know about the party I thought nothing of it. We had a great visit and parted with the hope of seeing her the next time she was in the area. Little did I know what she was up to?

Carole and Marcia arrived on schedule Thursday evening August 24th and we arranged to get together the next morning. Friday morning I arrived at the hotel to pick them up and give the gals a nickel tour of the area. We headed off to Kemah, which is one of the tourist areas near here with lots of eateries and amusements for kids. After a couple hours of walking and some good ice cream from Marble Slab we had seen enough. From there we were off to drive past NASA and to LaMadelaine's for a leisurely late lunch. The next stop was back to the hotel and they insisted they would drive to our house for a cookout that evening. I gave directions and they were to come over in an hour or two.

I headed for the house and got some of my baby back ribs cooking and some veggie lasagna baking. I also baked some Irish soda bread that I had come to enjoy on our trips. Carole and Marcia arrived and were excited about the bread. Carole said she had never perfected making the bread at home but I had purchased a mix while in Ireland and always had great success with it.

Carole's Birthday cake and Irish Paddy's

322

Marcia

Carole

This was Carole's birthday and a cake was ready for dessert after dinner. A great evening of friendship with supper passed too quickly. Carole had said she was going to go to Dallas to see relatives and we talked about other possible sightseeing areas of the state. Because Carole and Marcia had enjoyed the soda bread so much I decided to send the remaining half loaf with them to share with relatives. What I did not know was they were not going to Dallas but had come to share my birthday with me.

Saturday morning and afternoon August 26th was uneventful. Late in the afternoon it was time to get ready for what I thought was going to be supper with Lisa, Brett, Jessica and Mark to celebrate my birthday here.

We headed for the Hilton hotel where Mary said we were going to have some drinks and look out over the bay and it made sense to me. When we arrived we headed down to the lower level. As we rounded the corner in the hall there was a group of friends for a surprise party.

As I rounded the corner this is what I saw.....

I had tried to get Brother Jim to visit me for five years and he and Sheila were standing there. Doug and Donna came from Lincoln, NE, Walt and Linda came from Florida. Also there were Carole and Marcia, who were supposed to be in Dallas, I thought.

Also many other friends from all over including three gals I went to High School with, Mary Alice, Barbara and Joan. Janice Thompson, my boss at SMU was standing there with Betsy also from my days at SMU. La Rita and Dr Ray Battin were there along with Rueben and Lori. Linda and Virginia came from Tyler, Rick and Linda came from Dallas, Debbie, Mack, Barbara and Juan were standing in the group. Scott was taking movies and Brett was taking still shots as I just was in shock. Of course Lisa, Jessica and Mark that we were to have supper with were laughing their heads off. They had decorated the room for a '50s Sock Hop and it was complete with an awesome DJ. Needless to say it was a night that could never be outdone no matter what.

324

The Big 70 Birthday Cake

The DJ – Jessica – Lisa – Mary – Debbie – Barbara – Marcia

Barbara – Donna – Sheila – Doug – Janice   Janice Thompson (old Boss)

Donna and Doug   Sheila and Jim

Lisa – DJ - Jessica

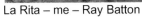

La Rita – me – Ray Batton   They Made me dance or try

Mary plays me a song   My Sweetie and me

My real birthday present from Mary was supposed to be the following weekend on my actual birthday with a visit to Virginia and my girls.

Off to Virginia

We headed for BWI on Friday knowing there was a hurricane lurking. The flight was pretty good until we were on approach to land. It was a fairly bumpy landing but the main part of the storm had not reached the airport. The drive to Virginia was in a lot of rain and Mary does not do well in rain.

Saturday morning we had scheduled to meet with the girls for breakfast. When we arrived whom do we see but Jim, Sheila and niece Linda along with the girls, again surprised by the happenings. After a slow breakfast we headed for Mary Beth's home and just visited for a while.

In the early afternoon we had cake and the girls presented me with a beautiful scrapbook of my life. The scrapbook is awesome and so much appreciated. This trip was just icing on the previous weekend party.

Birthday cake at Mary Beth's

A meal had been planned months earlier at an Italian restaurant but just days before we left Mary found out it had unexpectedly closed after many years. A different place to eat was found and Mary just wanted to check in and when she started to call no answer. All afternoon there was no answer. As we decided to go back to the motel to change we decided to go by and see if they were open and why no answer on the phone. When we got there we found out the hurricane had knocked out the phone and they couldn't get it fixed until the following week. We then headed back to the motel to get changed and get back to the restaurant.

Mary Beth – me – Dick Spalding – Janice – Laura

Dick has known the girls since they were babies and even babysat them in Arlington.

Jim (has known Dick some 40+ yrs) – Mary – me – Dick and Bernice

Mary's brother John was going to join us as was an old friend, Dick and Bernice Spalding. Dick had been in Asmara and at Arlington Hall with me and stayed with us for several months after he got out of the service.

Mary and John   Jim – me – Linda

The evening went well and was a lot of reminiscing. Sunday morning was breakfast with family again and we were off to Delaware in the afternoon.

The immediate family at the party in Virginia

Off to Delaware to Carolyn & John's

My longtime friend Carolyn had been trying to get us to come and see her new beach house for a long time. Since it is difficult to get back east often we decided to work both time with the kids and Carolyn on this long weekend.

A three hours drive from Virginia got us to Carolyn's and she had the fixin's of a party started. That evening about 40 friends showed up, many old-time Shillelagh members, and everyone had a great time.

Carolyn my bud   Another Birthday Cake

Mary & Steve my friend since 68   Sandy we go back to '68

Monday, Labor Day, there was to be a Jazz Funeral at Bethany Beach a couple miles away and we were prepared. We wore the traditional black and a Jazz band led the parade complete with a casket of "summer". It was a lot of fun and about 100 people were in the parade with several thousand spectators.

Sandy (Carolyn's cousin) John and Carolyn

That evening a gal (Marilyn) that had been on a 1969 Shillelagh camping trip to Jamaica that I was trip director had a party at her house. Tuesday morning we headed back to BWI and home to Houston. This was the climax to a real birthday season of a couple weeks and I still hadn't come down from the "high".

Mary's Family Reunion
The next upcoming event to look forward to was Mary's family reunion the first weekend of October. Mary has seven siblings and older brother Joe had some heart problems during the past year. The reunion was moved up a couple years for this reason.

Time went by so fast the next thing we knew it was Thursday and we were on the plane for Tulsa. We were supposed to go on a late evening flight but managed to get on an earlier flight. This was great since we planned to drive to Springfield, MO to meet up with Scott and family. We managed to arrive in Springfield by 10:30, which was about the time we would have been landing had we stayed on the late flight. Friday morning we got up and had breakfast with Scott, Jen, & Joshua and headed for Boiling Springs.

The drive was a couple hours and we arrived shortly after Frank. Before long all of those that had committed to attend arrived.

Lisa surprised all of us by showing up Friday and we found out that originally she booked the same flight we did and when she found out she changed to the earlier flight. Then when we changed to the earlier flight she had to change to an even still earlier flight in order to surprise everyone.

Mary's family – Gene – Mary – Pete – Frank – Joyce – Joe (2 missing)

Scott made peach cobbler on the ground like the cookout we had

It was a great couple days visiting with all of Mary's relatives who have always made me feel part of the family. Saturday was the "official" big day and plenty of food was available. Hearing some of the old family tales was great and we even got some recorded on the movies.

Sunday morning we were off headed back to Tulsa. Things went smooth so there was time to visit with Jim, Sheila, Cyndi, little Nate and Bryan. A couple hours later and we were back on the plane heading home.

The Wreck

October 27th saw us coming home from a fundraiser at Bryce's school in our pickup. Less than a mile from the house a guy ran a red light and hit us in the right front corner. We were pushed about 50 feet because he was most likely going 30-40 mph. Mary was banged against the door and I was caught by the seat belt across the chest. I had thought there were some broken ribs but later determined there were none. I was really sore for a couple weeks and the first week could barely move without a lot of pain. We had plans for a cruise and I needed to get better so I did very little for the next couple weeks.

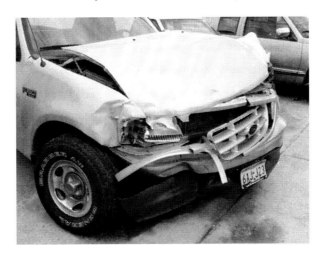

The pickup was a total loss and even though it was four years old it only had 15k miles on it. We had bought it at a really good price and we got almost as much as we paid, it would be hard to replace at anywhere near the price.

Ecstasy Cruise gone bad

The next event for the year is a four-day cruise to Cozumel and back in early November. Earlier in the year I questioned Carnival why they never had specials from Galveston. The representative emailed by immediately requesting my phone number. When I sent her the phone number I had no more than pressed the "send" button when she called.

As we talked I was informed about a special program for Active, Retired and all Veterans where up to three rooms could be at a special price. I inquired about dates and found out there was a time that would work for us. She told me that she would put a hold on three for a couple days for me to check with family and friends.

Mary had wanted to take Scott and family on a cruise since we had taken Lisa and family a couple years earlier. That night I called my old friend Barry Ross about a travel trailer question. He asked about going on a cruise and I told him what I had found out, to which his response was "book it". So November 9th was going to be the cruise beginning. We had gotten a three-cabin upgrade so our rooms were on the deck we entered the ship on, right in the center of the ship for smooth riding, perfect rooms.

As we got through the birthday parties and the trip to Mary's reunion the cruise time got closer. The time has been flying by at break neck speed. Barry and Jane arrived on Wednesday the 8th and we enjoyed the evening catching up on things since our last visit.

I took the opportunity to present Barry with a 2007 Calendar of our 1962 Sudan Hunting Trip Photos I had made for him. We were up fairly early on D-Day (Thursday) and after a quick breakfast we got loaded for the trip to Galveston and the cruise. A call to Scott and we met on the highway.

Jane and Barry check out the calendar

We always like to arrive at the ship no later than 11:30 am since in most cases we can board early and this was the case. The terminal was almost deserted prior to the real crowd arriving. We checked in and had to wait about ten minutes before boarding.

We headed to our room to see if we could drop off our carryon bags. Normally you cannot get in the rooms until around 2pm but our rooms were ready. Next stop was the Lido deck to the lunch buffet. With a nice lunch it was time to explore the ship and show Barry and Jane some of the amenities of the ship. We had to kill some time until the mandatory fire drill at 4pm. We departed during the fire drill and were on our way.

On Friday we were to learn we were going to be docking at Progresso, Mexico instead of Cozumel. This port is one we simply do not like and we had booked the cruise because we really like Cozumel and wanted to enjoy the port and excursions. We were all really disappointed but we would make the best of it. As the cruise went on we learned of this happening a couple other times recently. The propulsion of the ship was supposed to be the problem.

Me with Barry in Progresso – so far 46 years of friends forever

Me with Barry and Jane Ross – long time friends

We did have a decent cruise, the food was great and the company of family and friends was excellent. Just unhappy since it was Barry and Jane's first cruise for it to go wrong, but they took it in stride. All in all we really had a great time. They are truly great friends and we look forward to more trips.

Mary with son Scott

Thanksgiving

It was decided that instead of spending Turkey day on the scheduled Thursday we would have a get together on the Saturday prior. Lisa and Brett's home was going to be the place and Scott and family and Jessica, Mark and Sterling would attend. A great meal would be consumed.

On the next day we had a commitment for brunch at a friend Malisa's to meet her new beau. I woke up with my left arm sore at the shoulder and down the arm. I figured I had slept on it wrong. After getting home a couple aspirins seemed to cure the problem. Tuesday morning at 3:30 I woke up with my shoulder, but not my arm, hurting so much I could barely stand it. Again a couple aspirins and after sitting up a couple hours I was OK.

I decided, along with prompting from Mary, to call and see if I could get into the VA. This started a chain of events leading to me spending the actual Thanksgiving in the hospital.

A blood test indicated a higher level of an enzyme than normal indicating a possible heart problem. A stress test showed a small blockage but not serious enough for immediate surgery.

As time passed and seeing the cardiologist it has been felt that the blockage could have come from the wreck and not a heart attack. Time will tell how things go but care needs to be a keyword.

As we progressed closer to the New Year the pain was pretty much gone. There were some more tests, EEG, EKG, CT scan, CAT scans, visits to the VA and finally in February the news the problems with the blockage had pretty much for sure been from the wreck and did not seem to be permanent damage.

I think the care from the VA was better than any other hospital. I sensed the caring every time I have visited.

Chapter 33

The New Year 2007 rolls in

We attended a New Year's Eve party at a friend from Mary's work. It was a fun time and seeing some friends from New Years, past.

Without much other fanfare or exciting happenings the 2007 is here.

Time started to become a reality, as the New Year began, a cruise in December 2007 with many family members attending was being planned by Donna and Doug. Things got underway and it looks like it should be a fun time. The ship was almost booked full even though it was twelve months down the road.

Downsizing

For several years we have been trying to downsize and place items of interest with our children. Trying to ship a lot of "stuff" either by mail or truck has gotten so expensive that I have been trying to encourage some of my kids to take a vacation and leave room to haul stuff back East.

As things turned out Laura was selected to go to Dallas to teach a class on the TabletPC for Nestle division there. Over the last few years she has started to feel uncomfortable about flying so driving was an option. Even though it was to end up a 3.5k round trip for her she could visit along the way. She was going to bring Luke and leave him with me while she was in Dallas.

For several years we have been trying to downsize and place items of interest with our children. Trying to ship a lot of "stuff" either by mail or truck has gotten so expensive that I have been trying to encourage some of my kids to take a vacation and leave room to haul stuff back East.

She arrived on schedule on January 21st via Montgomery, AL. I had promised to cook some of my special Baby Back Ribs on Monday and it would just be an "R&R" day.

Me cooking my "famous" ribs

Luke and Bryce eating their fill

Laura was scheduled to leave about 6:30 am on Tuesday. I got up, fixed her breakfast and got her on the way. Normally I would have stayed up but Luke was still fast asleep, so I decided to go back to bed. I went off into a really deep sleep and the next thing I knew it was 9:30 and the phone was ringing.

The phone call was a real shocker. The voice on the other end said it was Bruna and she was in the states, in Baltimore. She said her childhood friend married a GI and was in NJ. Bruna had gone to NJ to visit her old friend and Luciana told her about the Kagnew Website and when they got on it and went to the "Then and Now" page Bruna saw my photo and just had to call me.

Bruna has always been special to me since I was stationed at Kagnew Station the first time in 1958. She is mentioned earlier on in the book on page 59. I was appointed NCOIC of the Photo Lab. Along with photographers and lab technicians and getting the darkrooms completed I was assigned a pretty young lady, Bruna, to be the secretary for the photo lab. This young girl had a father that worked at the QM site off base to the right at the bottom of the hill leading into the main gate.

Bruna became like a little sister to all of the people in the Post Signal section. She was just learning English and would often over hear the guys talking and come and ask what a "slang"

342

word meant and also some cuss words. We would explain the slang words and then on the cuss words tell her never to use them. I went over to Kagnew with an 18-month-old and had two more daughters born there. Bruna would come over to our house and play with the girls on a regular basis and became a fixture of our family.

When I departed for my first tour I got her promoted to the office of the Post Signal to where she collected for phone charges. Because of this many people will remember her. I went back in '61 to '64 and she was still part of the family.

Bruna in 1962 as a Teenager   Bruna 1969 (pregnant)

I made a trip back as a civilian in 1969 and was going to make a trip from Cairo to Capetown but was unable to buy a 4-wheel vehicle in Cairo because of the '67 war. I just went back to Asmara and visited. At this time Bruna had married and was 7 months pregnant. It was a great time and of course Lee and Vera Ruebush were there on their third tour between Kagnew and Iran so I had lots to visit about.

Thoughts of Bruna never left my mind in all the years and I often wondered how she was and even if she was alive because of the trouble in Eritrea. I had inquired many times about her and once even gotten an email address in Addis Ababa, but the email was returned as not a good address. This was truly another Wildest Dream coming true in getting to talk to her and subsequently seeing her.

Laura was still on the road headed for Dallas. I called her after talking with Bruna, and her first words were that I should drive back with her and Luke and see Bruna. She was coming back on Thursday the 25th and head home on Friday the 26th. Well I ended up driving back with her and the Van full of "downsizing".

Some of the things I had cherished needed to be passed on to other generations. There was my mother's cedar chest, Winterling Bavarian China, quilts, some animal heads for Luke, Elephant foot for Janice, and assorted other items.

We headed for Montgomery, AL to spend the night with Laura's best friend Cyndi and her family. Then up and on the way for the 13 hour drive to Manassas. Late in the evening we unloaded the stuff and I got to spend the night at Janice's. Sunday morning after a great breakfast we made the last leg of the trip to PA to Laura's home.

The plan was to spend the day, January 31st, with Bruna and two daughters Janice (oldest) and Laura (youngest), and then the evening with her daughter Daniela, my cousin Ginny and her triplets.

What a wonderful time it was to see her. Some interesting facts were that in 1980 Bruna and her Husband went to Addis. There they raised the two boys and later had Daniela while opening a furniture factory. They have done very well, in that one son is an Architect and the other son is an Engineer.

They paid for Daniela to go to "the American School" in Addis and then she came to the states and graduated from Old Dominion University in Norfolk, VA. Daniela got a degree in International Relations and has been working her since then. What a beautiful girl Daniela is and just as sweet as her mother always was and is.

The real problem is that her visa will run out in 2008 and she needs a sponsor and a job. The contract was supposed to be an indefinite contract which would have provided Daniela the necessary paperwork to stay and eventually get citizenship. So Daniela has a job for a year but after that would have to go back to Addis.

To me, this would be a shame since she wants to stay here and her grandfather worked for Kagnew for over 25 years and Bruna for 17 years.

The moment we see each other – How wonderful

Me with Bruna Jan 31st 2007

Laura, Janice, Me, Bruna and Daniela

Anyhow it makes for a great story since I have tried for many years to find Bruna and now to know she is well, and has such a beautiful and wonderful daughter is heart warming. It is heard to believe she is now 65 years old.

Time sure flies but Dreams and Prayers do come true.

Luke and Eagle Scouts

While we were back at Laura's to meet up with Bruna on Wednesday we had an exciting couple days first.

On Monday, the 29th of January Luke had to appear before a board to answer a battery of questions for his efforts in becoming an Eagle Scout. It was a stressful evening as I joined Mike and waited while Luke was grilled. After what seemed like several hours, but really only one hour, the board made their decision and Luke would be inducted as an Eagle Scout. The Official Ceremony would be later after all the paperwork was completed. April 28th would be the date of the Ceremony. There is a lot of paperwork, invitations and time required to put the historic event together. Luke had wanted to complete everything prior to his fifteenth birthday in May. Most young men do not complete the requirements until just before the deadline which is their eighteenth birthday.

The last weekend in April I would get to see as Luke receives the honor, which was a very proud time for me also. I flew back east and Janice, Mary Beth, Eagle Scout Jason, and Stephanie would drive from Manassas to Laura's.

Luke after receiving the Eagle Scout Award

Luke also received recognition from State and National leaders and even President and Laura Bush. A flag that flew over the State and Federal Governments Capitols just some of the items Luke received. All in all it was quite an afternoon and was topped of with some snacks for everyone.

I think it is pretty awesome to have both grandsons as receivers of the highest Scouting award, I am so proud of both of them.

Chuck Wagon Cookout

Mary's son Scott had been hearing how much fun we have had at the ranch of my boss with the camping and chuck wagon meals. He got the idea we should have a chuck wagon cookout in our yard, complete with camping. The weekend of Apr 13th, 06 was selected. I got the things together we were going to need during the previous couple weeks. I thought we should have a "real chuck wagon" so I built one and covered it with Formica.

Using the basic design of a real ranch wagon I made ours smaller and compact but practical. We needed a counter to cut up the supplies we were going to prepare.

My home made Chuck Wagon

Everyone but me slept outside the night before in the tents. The day of the "big cookout" I got up and got a fire started to make coffee, the old fashioned way. Our goal was to do all of the cooking in authentic chuck wagon style. No store bought charcoal, but real wood coals. I had purchased a half-cord of Mesquite wood which was perfect and produces great hot coals.

Both Scott and I had searched the Internet about this type of cooking and had found a wealth of information. The way the old ranch chefs judged the heat was by how long they could hold their hand over the fire.

With flat top "Dutch-oven" cookers, and cast iron skillets we got breakfast started. Scott made biscuits and both of us cooked bacon, sausage and eggs along with potatoes. This first batch of biscuits came out good but not perfect. A little too much coals on the bottom. Just a tiny tad burned, but salvageable.

As soon as the breakfast was done it was time to start the evening meal. I made a pot of beans that would need to cook all day, Scott started on the stew and later in the day a peach cobbler and more biscuits.

Scott with our cook area

Keeping a close eye on our masterpieces all day long the evening approached. The meal was nothing short of fantastic. The biscuits this time were absolutely perfect, the beans good, and the stew could have won a blue ribbon. The peach cobbler topped off a meal to make history.

It is now history since we both decided this was way too much work and it would be a long time before we did it again. We had learned so much, had so much fun and eaten so well.

07 – Carnival Conquest Cruise
Early in the year Mary and I decided that since the last cruise was sort of a bust we needed another cruise. We had discovered a website called Cruise Critic. When we decided the dates and ship we would sail we joined what is known as the "roll call" for that sailing.

This turned out to be one of the most fun things we had done. Because we were sailing without any friends it gave us a chance to talk to others that would be on our cruise.

The more we got into the roll call the more fun we had. We met about 65 people that would be on the cruise. There were some school teachers from Maine, a couple from OKC, another couple from Lubbock as well as a couple of gals from WA.

The cruise was from Galveston to Jamaica, Grand Cayman and Cozumel and back to Galveston.

The real fun started as soon as we came up the escalator at the terminal at 10:30am. We rounded the corner and two gals (from WA) said *"you must be Mary and Al"*. They recognized us from the description we mentioned on the board, me as Santa and Mary as Phyllis Diller. Everyone was in agreement that Mary did not look like Phyllis Diller.

We met about a dozen or so of the people from the "roll call" at check-in. We were going to have a little get together at three in the afternoon but we were so late starting to board (2:30) that the plans got out of kilter. We did get together later and met even more of the group.

Jamaica is not really a safe place to go wandering around town so we spent the day at Sunset Beach and had a great time. Mary had fun on the water slides and on the beach while I tried to stay pretty much in the shade because of past skin problems.

Grand Cayman the next day and since we are not snorkeler's, even though I love to swim, but ear problems keep me away from that fun too.

The Carnival Conquest in Grand Cayman

Cozumel, the port we missed in November, was a big disappointment to us. A big hurricane had destroyed a large part of the docks and downtown. We were told that the storm only moved a couple miles an hour and took three days to pass. We wanted to visit Las Palmeras a restaurant I had been fond of since 1968. The food was always great and the Margarita was the best in the world. We order the drinks and looked at the menu. I commented the menu was not the same and one sip of the drinks and I asked the waiter "has this place changed hands". In a look of shock he admitted that the place had been destroyed and the old owner sold out.

We did a tour on the "Sub Ocean View" which is a boat that has windows below the water line and you can sit on the benches and look out the big glass windows at the fish etc. It was a good time and Mary did not panic like she thought she would. The top of the boat remains out of the water.

We really got to know two couples from Maine pretty well on the cruise. The two gals, Lynn and Tina are school teachers and husbands in construction type work. Even though they were younger, we had a lot of fun on this trip. I guess that my idea of "age being only a state of mind" is true. We had such a great time we have since signed up for a cruise in April 2008 with two of the couples we met on the Conquest cruise.

Mary, me, Lynn & Tina (school teachers from Maine)

We returned back to Galveston and enjoyed the long "sea day" with our new found friends. We had such a great time we have since signed up for a cruise in April 2008 with two of the couples we met on the Conquest cruise.

Memorial Day at Janice's

After thinking long and hard we decided to make the long ride up to Janice's for Memorial Day. This time we would "camp out" in the motel. We would go up on Friday and back on Sunday so the 400 mile drive, each way, is a lot for a weekend, especially in the rain both ways.

Janice had done wonders on the guest house she has been working on for over three years and is about 95% completed. Doing all the work herself was no easy task.

I had built a "chuck wagon" for the cookout we had at home and since it was way too much work I decided Janice needed it to use at her ranch.

The cookout was not as much fun as usual because the weather scared off a lot of guests. The weather broke early Saturday morning and stayed clear and sunny till Sunday so those of us that went got time to enjoy. The drive home was a long seven hour drive in the rain. The new truck performed well and was better riding than the truck that got wrecked.

Long time no see...

The beginning of July came and I received a phone call from a cousin Butch Robinson. I had received email from him once in a while over the past several years. Before Barbara passed she had written Butch while working on family history.

Barbara was close to Butch's sister Sally Lou, the same age as Barb, who has passed a number of years ago.

Butch was a little younger than I was and we never really were as close. It was a nice surprise to get the phone call and hear that Butch was in the Houston area. He has a daughter in a suburb of Houston and was wondering about getting together for dinner. We set the time and place and what a great visit. His daughter and her new husband, wife Carol joined us in Galveston for dinner.

I carried a copy of "the book" to give to Butch since it had a fair amount of history in this. Carol was looking through the book when Butch started talking about my roller skating days with Barb and Sally Lou. I showed them the photo of Hannah and myself in the book. Carol was very surprised and announced that her first husband had been married to Hannah. Small world isn't it?

Cousin Butch Robinson (brother of Sally Lou) and Me

July 07 visit to see Frances

For the last year or so we have wondered how long Frances would hang on in good health, so after a lot of talking Jim and I decided to make a visit while she was still doing well. The last weekend in July was chosen as the time for me to meet Jim in Dallas and on to Pittsburgh to visit Frances.

We detoured on the way to Clarksburg to go by Mom and Dad's grave, as well as Barb and Norm and pay our respects.

Then before we headed down the road we needed to get something to eat, so we decided on Naples Restaurant which was *"the"* place when we were in High School. They always had a *"heel"* which was a meatball sandwich in the heel of D'Carlo's Italian bread. The waitress came and I said "I would like to have something I hadn't had for some 50 years" to which her response was ***"you want a heel"*** and that was correct.

The sandwich was not the same size as I remembered. It had grown quite a bit or my ability for intake had shrunk. It was great as a remembrance and I finished the meatballs but not all the bread.

Frances – Linda – Jim – Laura in Jul 2007

Frances still sharp in Jul 2007

Frank Taylor (Minister) & Frances

354

During our visit with Frances, niece Linda came down and we had a great visit. Laura and Luke drove in from Pennsylvania. Frances was still very sharp but did on occasion have to stop to think about something. Heck, I do that too....

We made a visit to the Church that Frances was a member and truly enjoyed visiting with the minister. He worked during the week as a Chaplin at a hospital and was the minister on the weekend.

Memorial Window in memory of Grandpa and Grandma

We made a visit to the Church that Frances was a member and truly enjoyed visiting with the minister. He worked during the week as a Chaplin at a hospital and was the minister on the weekend. He was from the Richmond, OH area and was actually related to my first real squeeze Hannah Grimm, small, small world.

THESE DOORS WERE GIVEN
TO THE CHURCH IN
LOVING MEMORY OF
THE RAYL FAMILY
By LINZY AND FRANCES RAYL

Doors donated by Linzy & Frances   Plaque for doors

The weekend ended and we had to head back home feeling good that we had gone. Since it was a long trip we wondered if this would be the last visit or not.

Trip to San Antonio

Throughout the summer not much was happening except waiting for the December cruise with twenty family members and friends.

However, the market was falling out of the housing business and the end of September saw Mary getting her walking papers from the company she had worked for during the last four-plus years. Mary had been in the title business for over 23 years but not enough seniority at her last employer to protect her.

Needing a break in her life, we thought it would be fun to fly up to Maine and see our school teacher friends. Mary had several leads on possible jobs and as we waited to see if one of those would pan out the cheap fares disappeared. Our next thought for a get away we would check on a cheap cruise out of Galveston. We thought since there were no children out of school, the ships would need passengers. Wrong, they were full and not a room available. COULD ALL THIS BE A SIGN???

356

It this was a sign we couldn't read it. Lisa and Brett had promised Bryce a trip to Sea World in San Antonio and were going the last weekend in September so we thought getting away for the weekend would be fun and decided to tag along.

I had not been real wild about Sea World but as it turned out the entry price was in line for the entertainment available. We had a great time and prior to one of the shows we had been talking to some couples sitting right in front of us. After the show started the MC came up and got Mary and Myself and took us to the front for a little skit they did. He then got a little girl about six or seven and brought her up with us. Bryce got upset and said "she is not their granddaughter".

The MC then put her back with her family and took Mary off to the side. Next he went back up in the audience and got the wife of one of the couples sitting in front of us and brought her down as a trade for his taking Mary. She was a good sport and quite good looking. The MC then took some photos with a water-proof camera, then sent my new friend and myself back to our seats, and gave me the camera. The skit was nice as he joked with Mary.

The next show was the Shamu show. At Sea World all active duty military get in Free as a tribute to our service people. We had remarked this was an awesome thing especially with the military bases located in San Antonio.

At the beginning of the show the announcer asked all Active duty military and all veterans to please stand while they played the Star Spangled Banner. I stood up as did at least a hundred others. I had been looking down and when I looked up I see myself on the big screen that they project the show on. The gal that had been with me in the previous show was a couple rows in front again. She turned to me and said "you will be famous by the time you leave here" and then smiled.

We enjoyed the trip and would recommend it for anyone of any age group.

Frances joins Barbara

Early in October we received some phone calls from Frances' care-givers, Willie and Billie that she was not doing well at all. As it ended up on Saturday the 12th I would fly to Tulsa and drive back to Clarksburg with Jim.

When we arrived at noon on Sunday the sight was what I did not want to see. Frances was just on her bed with her mouth open and not really communicative. Linda joined us on Monday as we knew the end of a great life was near.

Frances joined Barb on the 16th of October and just 14 days shy of being 102 years old.

Janice, Mary Beth and Laura and family, their mother (Joy) joined us late Thursday night. The funeral was held on Friday the 19th and the minister came home to do the services. What a great life Frances had enjoyed. Jim spoke at the service and mentioned the number of place Frances had been to as shown by the visas in her Passport as well as some that did not require visas. She now is at peace and with Family again.

The next several days were spent going through the items that Frances wanted different member of the family to have. She had always been a "class act" and had many nice things for a remembrance of her.

The drive back to Tulsa allowed Jim and me to reminisce a lot. The flight then to Houston was uneventful.

Closing out 2007

The "family and friends" cruise had been in the planning for some eleven months and was about to really happen. The cruise was to be on Royal Caribbean's newest and largest ship the Freedom of the Seas.

Our group would be made up from nine different states. The cruise would include, Doug, Donna, Jessica and fiancé (James), Brent and girlfriend (Kayla), Donnas' parents Jim and Nancy, Linda and friend Marie, Jim and Sheila, Janice, Ginny (cousin), Les and Betty – (Norman's brother and wife), Barry and Jane (friends since Asmara), along with Mary and myself.

The plan was to try to arrive in Ft Lauderdale/Miami about the same time on Dec 15th. I had organized some transportation to get groups from Ft Lauderdale to our hotel in Miami. I had also got "a deal" on the Radisson hotel by using Hotwire.

The first two groups arrived at the hotel, got settled in and met back in the lobby bar to wait on the last group to arrive. When all were located we were going to get some supper and to meet at Bubba Gump's. We walked to the free monorail for the bay area and with directions headed for Bubba's. With everyone getting to meet and know each other we had a great time and great meal.

Sunday the 16th meant it was time got get going and get to the ship

Front – Ginny, Linda, Marie, Jim, Sheila, Mary, Jane
Back – Al, Janice, Barry, Les, Betty

Left – James, Brent, Donna, Jim
Right – Jessica, Kayla, Doug, Nancy

Arriving at the terminal we had a swift check-in and boarding. As always we try to go by the room, head for the lunch buffet and explore the ship. We checked out our dinning room tables and had two great tables for 10 each. Having tried numerous times to get Jim to go on a vacation or cruise with us, he had finally given in on this trip. Jim was going to go more or less to shut all the relatives up. He really wasn't expecting to have a great time. By the time we got to Miami Jim was starting to weaken and have FUN....

When we got on the Ship and having talked, joked and chatted with all the friends and family Jim was starting to show enjoyment.

One many more smiles on Jim's face – great to see it

The cruise was to the ports of San Juan, St Thomas and St Maarten. The first stop of San Juan the group went off in different directions. Some were looking for Coach Purses, some looking at the Historic sites and some just walking. We all met up at the courtyard where the Pina Colada was first created.

The second stop of St Thomas was one of our favorite places to stop. We toured the island with Sunny Liston. The trip included a couple hours to shop, a trip around the island and a stop at the beach with all of it taking the whole day. The tour was $25 per person and a great time.

Mary and I had done most of the research on the tour and we had heard of a great drink that is famous to St Thomas, called the Bushwhacker. Mary and I were walking down the street and saw this classy lady holding up a sign advertising the Bushwhacker. We thought it was only really available on top of the mountain so Mary asked the lady where we could get one. She was standing in front of the bar her and her husband owned. DAH!!! We went in and had an awesome drink and a lot of wonderful conversation. Seems the couple had move to St Thomas some 17 years before from the Carolina's and loved the island. We told them we would be back in April and bring another group by to see them.

Our next stop was back towards the pickup place and over to Jen's place. We found more of our party back at the pick-up point and with Jen's just across the street we all headed over there. Mary and I had been there before but I think it had changed hands but was still a place to get something to eat.

Mary – Janice – Jane Ross

Jen's turned out to be a highlight of the island stop. The waiter "PJ" with his very dry sense of humor turned out to be a hoot and everyone enjoyed him. Jen's had a drink called "Voodoo Juice" so several tried that bucket of juice. After a bite to eat we headed back to meet the tour to the top of the mountain. We had a great view and everyone loved the tour, the island and the stop at the beach.

Janice – PJ and Ginny at Jen's Cafe

Jessica on the Flowrider

The meals on the cruise were all excellent and the shows were all great. During the sea days the younger members had a great time on the Flowrider.

Ginny does the boggy board

Mary, Janice and myself in St Thomas

Two happy brothers – Al & Jim

The whole gang
Jim, Nancy, Les, Betty, Jane, Linda, Barry, Marie, Mary, James, Ginny
Jessica, Sheila, Jim, Janice, Doug, Donna, Brent, Kayla, Al

St Maarten was equally as much fun, with Doug and family going on Segway rides. Janice, Ginny and a bunch went to the beach and we just toured the city.

Chapter 34
Year 2008 comes in quickly - A busy year

08 – Cruise on Ecstasy

With the awesome family and friends cruise now history then surviving Christmas and New Years Mary had a Brainstorm.

Mary said "well while I am still out of work we should take another cruise". My response was "it hasn't even been a month since the last one". But she has a way to get me to check thing out. I made a call to Carnival about what was going out of Galveston that was reasonable. As it turned out we were offered a deal for a five-day cruise on the Ecstasy and with the military discount that we couldn't refuse. The five-day cruise was actually cheaper than a four day cruise.

Mary on deck in Galveston   Formal night on ship

The cruise was to Progresso and Cozumel. At the stop in Progresso we went into town and looked around and did a little shopping. It is probably our least favorite port to visit.

We really looked forward to Cozumel since the last time we had been on the Ecstasy we got detoured to Progresso and never made Cozumel. It was the trip with Barry & Jane and Scott and family. We really had wanted to show the place to Barry & Jane.

A place Las Palmeras I had been going to since 1968 and where I took Mary on our first Cozumel cruise has great food and the world's best Margarita. We were looking forward to one of the adult beverages with anticipation but were totally shocked when we got there. Mary and I took a sip of our Margaritas and both said, almost in unison, the place must have changed hands. I call the waiter over and asked if the place had changed hands. He had a total look of shock and explained after the Hurricane the building had been totally destroyed and the former owner sold out. It was beyond my comprehension why someone would change their trademark famous recipe. It was no longer the smooth mixture but tart and acidic like many. So we were totally disappointed.

Mary with waiters – Iwayn and Rudolpho

We did have fun on the cruise and Mary got me picked for one of the skits on the cruise, which was fun. It was a story of the Three Pigs and we had to run around our group competing against the other team when our name was mentioned. Later on the cruise the guy on the other team told us he was totally blown away with my movements since I was about twice his age and I beat him every time. We had to get the video.

After returning from the cruise Mary was offered a job and the worry was on the decline.

Planning the Veteran's Cruise

After returning from the cruise on the Ecstasy I noticed that someone was trying to put together a cruise for Veterans. I could quickly see that he was trying to do it for profit rather than really Saluting the Veterans. He was planning the trip from the East coast.

I thought, why not one out of Galveston? So I wrote to the Cruise Critic (CC) Bulletin Board, powers that be, and asked about an Official CC trip. I explained that I wanted it to be a real Salute to Veterans cruise and in a couple weeks I got a reply that it was approved. The cruise being planned was some 18 months off and scheduled for the 8-15th of November 2009, over Veterans Day.

I posted the details on the Cruise Critic board and the response has been very positive, so as time goes on we expect a great turn out.

Carnival Freedom

We had met two couples, Lynn and Ronnie and Tina and Scott, on our cruise on the Conquest in April 2007, as mentioned early. We had a lot of fun and during the following summer and winter we emailed a lot and even Instant messaged a lot. We became true friends and they asked us to join them on a cruise on the Carnival Freedom for a cruise in April 2008.

The Carnival Freedom was a brand new addition to the fleet of Carnival Fun Ships so the more we thought about it we decided to go.

We booked the cruise as part of a group for the special prices. The group was put together really for the purpose of the leader getting a free room and not for being a great leader.

Brett – Devin – Ronnie – Lynn – Scott – Tina – Mark – Carrie & me kneeling

We met in Miami and Lynn and Tina's flight was delayed so we ended up babysitting Lynn's son Brett and buddy Devin. These are two awesome young men that were going on the cruise as well. When everyone got in at midnight we did a lot of hugging and went on to bed for the busy next day.

Up early, with breakfast and ready to go Mark (Mary's nephew) and wife Carrie came to our hotel for a ride to the boat.

The planning for the cruise had gone on for months and "the girls" planned a cabin crawl. The people agreed to bring a $5 gift representing their State and if they wanted to they could have drinks and/or snacks in their rooms. We started at the bottom of the ship in the lower grade cabins and worked our way up to the suites.

There were about 19 cabins involved and it was a real blast. One of the cruisers was a liquor distributor and brought samples of Petron Tequila for everyone. Mary and I had Chocolate Martinis in our cabin and they were a real hit.

Mary always does her Vanna thing   We decorated our cabin door

The cruise was to St Thomas, St Maarten and San Juan. We had been to these islands at Christmas time with the "family and friends" cruise and really like them and we had found a couple places we wanted to show our friends.

Tina – Mary – Lynn

There was a drink we had heard about called Bushwhacker and we found it in Dec and a neat little café called Jen's. We took our friends and they loved both places.

Me at the 19th hole with Bushwacker

Back to Jen's Café – Mary – PJ – Tina - Lynn

Our table mates gals – Dawn and Bridgett

Our table mates were really two neat couples. At one point Tina came over to our table and I mentioned that I had a daughter older than her. Bridgett responded "No Way". Once I convinced her it was true, for the rest of the cruise they both talked about "when we grow up I want to be just like YOU".... They were a lot of fun and had a great cruise and we enjoyed them in the piano bar and at meals.

There was a surprise for Lynn that was really hard to contain, **more later on**.

Visit to New Braunfels
Several years ago, on a trip to Austin, Mary and I made a detour there to see where Lesley's in-laws lived. They were having a garage sale and Mary even went up and looked around.

One week, in early spring, Mary said she would like to go somewhere for the weekend. She asked me what I would like to do and/or go. I responded that I would really like to go to New Braunfels and see Lesley's in-laws, and leave a copy of my book, cook book and some other items for Lesley.
When I mentioned what I wanted to do Mary said call them and see if it can be done. I already had the phone number and knew that Patricia liked to be called Trish. I went in my room

and called and said that I was Lesley's father and that I probably wasn't really as bad as the stories she has heard.

I explained what I wanted to do and Trish was most gracious and said she would be home and it would be just fine for us to come by on Saturday after lunch.

Mary and I went to New Braunfels on Friday and spent the night so we would be totally rested when we met Trish on Sat. We got up and had a leisurely breakfast and looked around town a little. We knew exactly where Trish lived so after lunch we arrived.

We had a real enlightening visit; the details of which I think should not be discussed here. I did learn a great deal and left the books, and a wallet that Lesley's grandmother Burrus had made for me that was never used. I thought it should remain on that side of the family and after the discussion I asked Trish to hold it for Lesley's son.

Trish was warm and delightful and even said for us to come by anytime we are in the area. A couple months later, out of the blue, she called me to give me an update on things.

Busy Summer
A busy summer was ahead for me with grand daughter's graduations, wedding, reunion, trip to Maine and then back to DC.

I started off the 30th of May heading for DC to meet Janice and drive up to see Joy Marie graduate from High School. The graduation was the evening we got there and a graduation party scheduled for Saturday.

Joy had earned the Honor of Valedictorian and had to give her speech, which she wouldn't give early. The graduation went great and I got to meet their good friend Robert, Tina and daughter Maggie that I had heard about for years. They were everything I had heard, an awesome family.

Joy Marie

Saturday for the party started out looking like it would not be a good day, rain early but cleared and was perfect. A lot of friends, family and relatives enjoyed the food and party time.

The following week was spent visiting with Laura and Family and a trip to the National Aquarium in Baltimore with Robert and family. On the way home we made a stop at Ginny's for hamburgers and it was great to see her and the triplets again.

That weekend meant time to head to Manassas for Stephanie's party and graduation. While there Janice and I had breakfast with an old friend from Asmara, Clair Deemer. I had sent him a pdf copy of my book and encouraged him to do a book about his life. He said he couldn't come up with 10 pages. I assured him that with a little thought he could do it and his kids and grandkids would enjoy it. I promised to help if he got it in Word format. It became a reality in Sept 08.

Stephanie's turn
Sunday evening was Stephanie's graduation party and held in the teen center of the Church. Mary Beth and gang did a great job with the food and decorations and it was an awesome

event. Joy and Luke had left for Peru and were not able to attend.

Monday evening was the graduation and Stephanie graduated with "honors" and even though Osborn is a really big school it went well.

Tuesday saw me flying back to Houston to get ready to fly on Thursday to Lincoln, Nebraska to attend the wedding of Jessica and James.

Stephanie

Wedding

Jessica has grown into quite a young lady and the time we spent on the "*Family and Friends*" cruise in Dec gave us a chance to meet James. The week spent on the cruise and the observations and we agreed with their choice as life mates.

I flew into Omaha and Jim, Sheila, Bryan and Ashlee picked me up for the hour drive to Lincoln. We arrive in time for a cookout and get together. We got to meet James' family and a lot of friends of families.

I felt attending the wedding was so important especially since Barb and Norm had both passed and would be watching from above and they adored Jessica.

Friday a bunch of us guys went to the Air Museum for the SAC headquarters. It was a surprise with the old birds they had. One awesome thing was as you walked in there was and SR-71 hanging from the ceiling.

Friday evening was the rehearsal dinner at Old Chicago and was a fun time for everyone and plenty of food and drinks to ruin a diet.
The wedding on Saturday was very beautiful and I tried to stay up in the balcony to take photos during the ceremony. The reception was at the hotel and was an awesome event.

Jessica and James

Jerry's Family Reunion
The next item on the agenda for the busy summer was attending the family reunion for a good friend Jerry Sheets. I met Jerry a couple years before I met Mary when I dated his sister-in-law. We have remained very close friends.

In the summer of 2007 Jerry had known of my writing my little book and asked my advice on how to do a booklet about his uncle Leroy.

Jerry – wife Jan – son Tom

Jerry's grandmother was one of 23 children, by the same father and two wives, first wife died. They moved to the Texas Panhandle at the very turn of the century and the land was barren and not worth much of anything. As the family grew and those 23 children settled more land, Oil was discovered. All of the descendents of that original family had a reunion yearly and the 2008 was going to be the "Last Big" reunion.

Prior to WWII some of the members of the different families had a falling out with each other. Leroy being Jerry's uncle enlisted in the Army in July 1941 to save being drafted and thus could select Aircraft maintenance schooling. He left for basic training in August 1941. After only 4 weeks of training the Army told Leroy that he had to ship out to school and he would get more basic training later.

When he got to the school, they informed Leroy he was going to be shipped out to the Philippines and he would get training there. So after receiving shots and transport across the country Leroy departed for the Philippines and arrived there on Nov 19th, 1941. Pearl Harbor was attacked by the Japanese on Dec 7th, 1941 and they attacked the Philippines the same time but because of the International Date Line it was Dec 8th 1941. History tells us a lot about the gallant battle of Bataan. Leroy lived it and was in the infamous Bataan Death March. Leroy passed in a POW camp on June 9th 1942.

When Leroy was brought back to Spearman, TX for burial ALL of the relatives "buried the hatchet" and attended the funeral.

There were letters from Leroy, from some of his friends and survivors and Jerry wanted to put this into some kind of a book. I told him that I would do the formatting if he did all the research and proofreading. The book "The Ultimate Sacrifice" was completed and Jerry was to unveil it at the reunion. Everyone knew about it and they were very excited to have their copy. I attended the Reunion in Altus, OK and was truly treated like "one of the family". I am very proud of Leroy and my having a small part in putting this tribute together.

A Trip to Austin

Because of our love of cruising and the attention on the Cruise Critic Bulletin Board we have gotten to know a group that calls themselves "*Conquest CRAZIES*". They started out watching the Carnival Conquest come into Galveston Harbor on the harbor cameras and then leave again about 8 hours later.

Mary got much enjoyment watch and as they would all watch they would post comments on the board. Next was a guess as to what time the Conquest would get out. It is an awesome site to see such a huge ship depart 3500 people and reload another 3500 people along with fresh food and supplies and be gone in such a short time.

As the months passed the group decided to get together and take a cruise on the Conquest. An ex-Air Force retired fighter pilot (screen name MACH) was selected to be the leader of the pack. He became a Host on the bulletin board and is a really neat guy. They planned their cruise for September 20, 2009, again more than 18 months away. The group grew and in different areas there became some small get-together's. Even though we were not going on the cruise Mary had gotten to know most of the active members. We were invited to join in on the Austin get together.

I really wanted to get to know Mach since he had become very well known with Carnival and the Head Cruise Director of Carnival John Heald. I thought it would be nice to have whatever pull I could manage for our Veterans cruise.

We attended the get-together and had a wonderful time and made many, many new friends.

Carolyn's Surprise 70th Birthday for John
The party started out with a phone call early in the summer to me from my very, very dear friend Carolyn McKenna.

Carolyn and I go back to joining the Shillelagh's way long ago in 1968. The first Shillelagh trip for both of us was to Freeport in the Bahamas in early 1968 and we have remained close thru our each going thru some difficult marriages. Carolyn knew me in the days when I had the photography studios in Manassas, Vienna and Leesburg.

Carolyn – John – Mary – me in Ireland in 2004

Carolyn called me and asked me if my photography talent was booked for the weekend of August 9th and she wanted to "hire me" to come and take photos at a surprise 70th birthday party for her husband John. My response was "I will be there you tell when and where" since Mary and I both think the world of John. We knew that Mary wasn't going to be able to attend having started a new job and the plans for a long weekend, the next weekend after the party, was already in the mills for many months.

I made arrangements to fly to Dulles and Carolyn would have her cousin Sandy meet me up at the airport. I had known Sandy the same time period so we were good friends. Carolyn had told John that Sandy was going to use their other vehicle for a trip and that was the excuse to have the vehicle for me to use for the weekend.

I arrived on Friday as scheduled and Sandy and I had lunch and I took the car and headed for Manassas, via stopping to see Mary Beth and follow her home. I would spend a great time with her. I got the chance to work on her kitchen sink and install a new faucet and then after the party to do a little caulking in the bathrooms.

Saturday morning I headed out for Aldie, VA and the B&B that was to be the location of the Party. Tucker and Mary Ann owned the B&B and are also members of the Shillelagh's. The B&B complex is made up of 6 houses and really nice grounds for the party.

After meeting Tucker I quickly went thru and took some photos before anyone else was there. However, when I got to one of the cabins, Walter and Linda Dickerson were already resting up. They had flown in from Florida as they had done two years earlier for my 70th BD.

Tucker had a whole pig roasting that had been put on the fire late Friday night. The neatest way to cook a pig was the hospital bed that the pig was spread out on. It could be raised, tilted and lowered as needed. The fire was in a pan resting on some upside down angle iron and could easily be moved in and out to add more coals.

Carolyn with John's daughter – son and his wife

The party was a complete surprise to John. He thought the group was just going to dinner and spend the night in the B&B. They had a van bring them to Aldie from Reston and when they got off the van Walter was poking his head with a camera from the end of a building near the front of the van. I took up residence near the back to get some candid photos. John saw Walter and was surprised, then Carolyn told him to "look there" and John saw me with shock. He knew something was up at that point.

The evening was a total success complete with a group playing Irish music and everyone had a great time. I was able to visit with some Shillelagh friends I had not seen in a while and that was great.

The party reminded me of the 70th BD party that Mary had for me that was a total surprise.

Surprise visit to Maine
The weekend after John's surprise party we were scheduled to do a surprise in Maine.

Mary and I were chatting during the previous year with our new friends Lynn and Tina and the subject kept coming up about our possibly visiting Maine. So one evening while talking with

Tina we thought it would be fun to surprise Lynn. Mary had never been to Maine or any of the Northeast. I had been stationed in Massachusetts but never got to Maine.

We really wanted to go during the fall but schedules would not permit so we picked a weekend in August and booked a flight. We did this in March before the April cruise with our new friends. Being very difficult for me to keep secrets it took a lot to keep me quiet.

The couple weeks before we were to go to Maine while we were all on Instant Messaging I would drop hints that I knew only Mary and Tina would pick up on. Lynn was never aware that I was pulling Tina's chain. Tina would privately email me on some of the things I said and was in panic status worrying that I was going to spill the beans. Of course I was just having fun at her expense.

The weekend came and we spent the biggest part of the day flying to Maine via Newark. Up at 3am on Thursday and we got to Maine and Tina's house after a 3 hour drive at about 5 pm.

Mary rises up and Lynn sees her and surprise works

When we got there Tina called Lynn and said she had finally gotten her birthday present in and that she needed to come and pick it up since it wouldn't fit in Tina's car. Tina had been telling Lynn the present was backordered since June.

Lynn said she had grandson Preston and had supper about ready. Tina said to eat and have Ronnie bring her in the truck. Tina was forceful enough that Lynn finally said ok.

So a while later Mary and I got on the back porch and Mary hunkered down in a recliner chair. Lynn was brought to the screened in porch and looked over and saw me but didn't register since they had a friend that had the same barber as I do (bald on the top). Lynn thought it was him and all about that time Mary raises up and Lynn almost went into cardiac arrest. The surprise was a total success.

Friday night we went over to Lynn and Ronnie's house for dinner after a full day of sightseeing. Ronnie cooked and I had carried Bushwhackers pre-mixed and the girls worked on them.

The three Sista's – Lynn – Mary – Tina

The whole weekend was one of the best times of our lives. Tina had been talking about a "pig roast" and had been planning it with Lynn and family. Scott and Tina had them for several years but had not had one in a year or two, so nothing was suspected.

Saturday night lots of friends and neighbors, about 40 or so came and it was an awesome event. It was sort of a pot-luck meal with Scott and Tina doing the Pig. Everyone that came said to Lynn, "where are your friends from TX" to which Lynn would respond "you knew" and of course they all did as well as Lynn's family other than Ronnie. Lynn's daughter was instrumental in helping pull this off with Tina.

Sunday evening Ronnie and Scott cooked fresh Maine Lobster complete with corn on the cob and potatoes and it was a great evening.

Ronnie does Lobster - Awesome

I get sugar from Lynn and Tina

The friendship we have with these two couples is something only dreams are made of. They are truly genuine caring people and we are so proud to have made them our friends.

Carnival Ecstasy – Oct 08

Mary had a worked long enough now to have a couple days vacation so in September after coming from Maine our thoughts went back to the water.

I called my sweetie at Carnival and inquired about pricing for late October or early November. There were some military discounts for the weekend of Oct 23d. Just for the heck of it I decided to call my buddy Barry and Jane that live out in Alpine, TX to see if they might have any desire to venture to the seas again. When I called their cell phone they were still in Wyoming hunting prairie dogs.

Barry's normal answer followed "book it". They were due home the first week of October and that would work. We talked about their coming on Amtrak but it ended up that they drove.

The cruise was scheduled from the 23d to 27th and a simple four day cruise to Cozumel and back. Barry and Jane arrived on the 22nd and as always such a great time. Mary had to work a half day on Thursday so she got home about 10am and we departed for the terminal.

Barry – Jane & Mary – ready to go

Because of Hurricane IKE the cruise terminal in Galveston had suffered a lot of damage but there was the brand new terminal in Houston sitting empty. It was quickly put in shape and only three or four days of sailings were interrupted.

All went great, since it was only 13 miles from the house we were there in no time at all. We processed and soon were on board having lunch.

This is the same ship that was Barry and Jane's first cruise which was detoured to the port of Progresso instead of making Cozumel.

Me – Mary – Jane and Barry watching show

Well, guess what we had propulsions problems again. This time all that was going to happen was we would just be a couple hours late in getting to Cozumel. Barry and Jane had signed up for the submarine cruise before and wanted to do it this time. All went well and they got the submarine cruise down to about a hundred feet.

All in all it was a great cruise with our best friends. Mary and Jane have become like sisters and share lots with each other. Barry and I have been friends now for some 47 years. We have the coming April 2009 and the November 2009 Veterans Cruise booked with Barry and Jane. We love 'em.

Me and our dinning room hostess Eva – what a doll

It is a Small World

With having put together the Veterans Cruise I did something I had been meaning to do for a great long time. I joined the American Legion in Pasadena in the summer of 2008 but really didn't do much for a couple months. The reason partly was that the building took a big hit from the hurricane IKE and did almost a million dollars damage. With the current events of this country going to "hell in a hand-basket" I figure this was one group I could associate with and maybe have some political power on the country.

When I joined I explained about the Veterans cruise and one of the things we were going to do is have a brochure on self-publishing a book like this one. I had an extra copy of the Hunting part of this book so I left it. I volunteered to even come and teach a class for the members and also offered to help with some computer classes.

In November I went by the Post one day to see how the rebuilding was coming along. The repairs hadn't begun but as I walked in the door a guy sitting in the temporary office says "I know you". He didn't look like anyone I remembered but then he responded "I am reading your book". His name is Paul and he stated the Post Commander had given him the hunting book to read since he said he had been in Asmara.

It turns out that he had been there in early 1960's when the Congo War was starting (as mentioned on pg 74).

Paul mentioned he had been there in civilian clothes waiting for the rest of his "team". Paul was a member of an ASA Special Forces Team #6. He casually mentioned a few things that I knew only someone that had been there would know. With the clearances we had and in the Photo Lab we "were in the know" on a lot of stuff.

Part of my ordering the photo equipment for the Class "A" Lab was because the government expected the Congo and Angola to be another Viet Nam. Castro had sent a battalion of military to the Congo and this did make the news. What didn't make the news is what happened to them. When they disembarked from the ship they arrived in the Congo on they were placed in trucks. The Cubans had their weapons but NO ammunition and were supposed to get that when they got to their base about 25 miles inland.

What they didn't expect was to get ambushed. Paul and his six-man team ambushed them – not knowing they had no ammo and killed 166 of the Cubans. This was probably a real turning point in the Congo not escalating. Paul and his team later went on to Angola.

Paul is from Pasadena and retired from the Army in 1984 and immediately went to work for the NSA in Maryland. He retired in 1994 by combining his military and civil service time into 30 years.

Now the strange part – Paul had loved motorcycles all his life. One night after an American Legion meeting he and I talked about bikes etc. Paul also got medical disability from being exposed to Agent Orange in Viet Nam and is not allowed to ride motorcycles anymore. He still loves them and gave his collection to his boys. About early 2008 he stopped in the motorcycle shop to shoot the breeze and kind of smell the bikes. The owner realized he really knew his bikes and pleaded with Paul to work the front counter. Paul committed to three days a week or so. A couple months later a middle aged guy comes into the shop and had a jacket with something about the Congo. (I don't remember what it was) Paul said something about the Congo and the guy pulled open his jacket and a lot of his side was gone. Without stopping the guy explained that many years ago he was in the Cuban army and sent to the Congo and they got ambushed and he even knew it was Special Ops #6. Paul looked at him and said "that was me". The guy came around the counter and Hugged and Hugged Paul. Paul had thought the guy was Mexican originally. The guy had not wanted to be there in the Congo and held no ill will towards Paul. Paul said it was like two long lost brothers seeing each other.

Then topping it all off was the fact that he was reading my book, and I had been in Asmara, and had been putting in the photo lab because of the Congo problems. After we talked a good while we both knew the other was vastly aware of what was going on.

It surely is a small world....

Thanksgiving time

Because holidays have always been a problem we were going to celebrate Thanksgiving with Lisa, Brett and Bryce along with friends on November 22nd. We were scheduled to celebrate Thanksgiving at Scotts on Thanksgiving Day.

On Saturday morning as we had breakfast as part of our prayers, Mary asked that somehow the kids could patch their differences before Mary died.

A little before we were to leave Scott called me and asked some cooking questions for the turkey for Thanksgiving and asked what we were doing and said going to Lisa's. He said that was nice and that Joshua was at his grandparents.

When we arrived at Lisa's and had just got settled, the doorbell rang and it was Scott, Jennifer and Jacob. Mary's prayers had been answered. She told both of the kids that if she died that night she was happy. Of course the next morning she emailed them to say she was still alive, but she was very happy they are working things out.

A couple weeks prior, when we were visiting, Scott mentioned that Lisa had been in a Christian book store and heard a song, called "I Apologize" and had called Scott and asked his forgiveness for all in the past. Scott had not said anything more about it but we figured it was a great start and nothing was ever mentioned to Lisa of what Scott had said.

Chapter 35

Perspective of things to come

Some of my thoughts on what the future holds are not optimistic. As for the Country itself – I think we are in for some sorry times.

When we look back at history we learn that the Crusades back in the 11th – 12th Centuries were really aimed at the fanatic Muslim believers. Those crusaders had their supply lines spread so far it was impossible to continue eastward to finish the job. Travel in those days on horse took years.

Today it is hours away and the fanatical Muslim believers have grown thousands fold. Countries can be conquered from within and the Muslim belief is "if you are not a true Muslim you should be killed". As what once was the Free World is allowing immigration and these other believers get power it is the end for some of these once great countries. France has an exploding Muslim population and France's end is in sight.

Politics have really ruined a big part of the future for this country and I personally feel the only way around the demise is to "clean house". At some point this might even include a revolution. "War is hell" but look at our cities with the shootings, robberies, crime of all kinds and much of it done by gangs and many here illegally. Sometimes it is necessary to "go to War"…

What is lacking in many homes today are two parents, or two parents that agree on how to raise children. Quite often we see the teenager getting pregnant and not being married but expecting the "handout" from the government. Illegal aliens come to this country to have children so they can be US citizens and then getting the healthcare system in total shutdown. We can not afford to be everything to everyone.

The political views of educator's presents a problem in that the average student is subjected to heavy indoctrination of "Liberal" ideas. Sure, it is good to "help thy neighbor" but that applies only to certain circumstances. Not to the influx of "illegal immigration" and handouts for all.

Our borders need to be secured, the business owners need to be fined or jailed for hiring those illegally in our country. This would bring an immediate a lot of the illegal immigrants and if they cannot get welfare, jobs, healthcare they would GO HOME.

One of the most pressing problems with the younger generation is the effort parents put forth to raise them. Far too many parents are so lax in seeing their children complete schoolwork and school itself. The national dropout rate from kindergarten thru high school is an alarming 35%. Those students that do graduate are not prepared for the future partly because of the study habits and the schools *"teaching for tests"* and not *"why"* the student needs to learn something.

So many jobs have been farmed overseas for cost savings to companies these countries are growing at our expense. One of the reasons these jobs have gone overseas is the lack work ethics being taught the children of today. Far too many parents try to provide "everything" for their children and this prepares them for the "handout" society.

Bashing – "I guess"

With the close of 2008 I have felt some hard times as far as children. Have I been a perfect parent – No. We tend to learn parenting from our parents, and then trying to correct those things we thought were wrong in the way we were raised.

There are a lot of things I would have done differently, but hindsight is 20/20 and all we can do is to offer our help to the generations coming along, as we get smarter ourselves.

I do know that in my marriages I always put working hard on the top of the priority list. Working hard and long hours is not always *"working smart"*. I always had a goal to try to provide for the family and children and some times I may have expected too much in loyalty and not invested enough time with the family. For this I have many regrets.

The lack of vacations, the time doing chores and not having fun with the family was a big price to pay. I attribute some of my faults in growing up as I did, always working even from a young age back to carrying papers. I do not ever remember a "family vacation" at all growing up, but the kids always visited grand parents and relatives without our parents.

Families growing up with divorces and children involved are in for some horrible times. Blame – who gets the blame and how much goes where? Nothing, to the children, is ever seen as it really happens; they are too young and in most cases should not be privy to all that is happening. Bashing one parent by the other in a divorce or "playing mind games" is totally wrong.

I have tried to connect numerous times with Karen and Lesley to no avail. I have made contact with Lesley's in-laws for which I am eternally grateful. They are wonderful people. I have learned many things about Karen and Lesley and their mother that has helped me realize even more the fault was not "All" mine.

However both of these two girls are now adults. Both Karen and Lesley are really old enough to make their own decisions and maybe can put 2+2 together and come up with something close to four.

As I close out this year of 2008 and having tried again and again to make contact with both girls I am at the point of not wanting to try any more. Does this mean I don't Love them – absolutely not. I will **Always** Love them, but they have choices in life. One of my favorite sayings is "***Good Judgment comes from Experience and Experience comes from Bad Judgment***".

My Wishes

I do want this known here and now. When I die I do not want Karen or Lesley to be informed of my passing. The only exception to this is if things have changed and a good relationship is rekindled between us. This is my wish – and I hope my three older girls, all related to me, those who know me, will abide by my wishes.

Aside from the dreams that I have accomplished I am very proud of the rest of our family for all the wonderful journeys in life they have pursued, and accomplished. Everyone has been, and is, a winner.......

I am so very proud of all five of my children. The three oldest have brought so much happiness and joy to my life I will be eternally thankful.

This record of highlights of my life may get some updates but I am so thankful to GOD for the life I have been given. I have had my share of challenges, overcome most of them and truly have the greatest of families and relatives.

Thank you all, and especially my sweetheart Mary for having me and being part of your family too.

The Family Tree for Harold & Mary Susan Rayl

The Ashbee Family History

This side produces Grandma Rayl

Stephen Ashbee married Deliah Knicely

Children:
George
George - First wife Lydia Pethtel
Was the father of **Dora Matilda**
Occupation: Farmer
Joe
Harriet - married a Thomas

Second wife Hannah
Children to second wife:
Lawrence - wife Hazel

Glen - wife **Lucy** Cox born in Mannington, WV
Occupation: Goodyear - Akron, OH
Glen and wife **Lucy**
Children:
Clarence - died in infancy

Bobby - was in Army during WWII and died in an accident

Edward - was in Marines and served at Guadalcanal - later died

Ruth - married Charles Chapman
Children:
Linda
Susan
Carol

Daughter: Georgie - Married a Marsh

Dora Matilda married **William Fillmore Rayl** - April 6, 1903

The Rayl Family History

This side produces Grandma Rayl

Great – Great – Great Grandfather
George Rayl
    Born in Marshall County, West Virginia
    Married to: Elizabeth Durbin

Great – Great Grandfather
Joseph Rayl
    Born in Marshall County, West Virginia
    Buried: Fork Ridge, Marshall County
Brothers:

Thomas	William
James	Lewis
Samuel	Benjamin
Linz	Cass
George	

Sisters:
    Hannah
    Mary Jane

Great - Great Grandmother
Katherine Arminda Fish
    Born at Big Run West Virginia
    Died: November 20, 1919
        Father: Jeremiah Fish
        Mother: Jane Lucy Pelly – Pethel *(Not certain name was Pethel)*
        Brothers: Jeremiah, John, William, Jim
        Sisters: Jane, Jenny, Lydia, Sarah, Minnie

Joseph Rayl married Katherine Arminda Fish on April 22, 1877
    Children:
        Harl – married two times -   second wife
            Florence
            2 sons and 2 daughters –
            Sons: Charles and Rodney
            Daughter: Frances died
        Encil – Died January 29, 1919
        William

Velmia - married Clyde Smith – Dec. 16, 1906
Died January 28, 1976

Great Grandfather **William Fillmore Rayl**

Born: Wolf Run – Marshall County, W V on March 6, 1879
Died: September 11, 1970
Also related to Goshorn and Ingram
   Occupation: Farmer, Foreman at Phillips
   Sheet & Tin, Clarksburg &
   Weirton Steel
   32nd degree Mason

Great Grandmother **Dora Matilda Ashbee**
Born: Green County Pennsylvania on March 24, 1884
Died: August 22, 1974

William Fillmore Rayl married Dora Matilda Ashbee on April 6,
1903 in Wheeling, West Virginia

Children:
Harold Fillmore
Born: January 31, 1904
Died: December 17, 1980

Frances Arminda
Born: November 1, 1905
Died:
   Occupation: partner, later Owner of Haught
   & Rayl, Clarksburg, WV,
   married James Sidney Noon - He was a Maryland
   State Trooper killed in the line of duty on
   December 25, 1927

John Linzy
   Born: May 24, 1911
   Died: August 30, 1991
   Married Vera Fountain Rule
   Died: June 25, 1985
   Occupation: Vice-President - Tuller Engineering -
   Columbus, OH

William Albert -
    Born: June 5, 1914
    Died: February 23, 1966
Married Marjorie Nuzum –
    1 son: William Edward
    Occupation: Fairmont Foods

Grandfather
Harold Fillmore
    Born: January 31, 1904 Wheeling, West Virginia
    Died: December 17, 1980
    Occupation: Electrolytic Office - Weirton
    Steel

Grandmother
Mary Susan Hooton
    Born: June 25, 1909 Monongah, West Virginia
    Died: March 4, 1964

Harold Fillmore Rayl married Mary Susan Hooton on May 4,
1933

    Children:
    Barbara Jane
        Born: January 19, 1934
        Died: September 17, 2005
        Married Norman Lee Gritton on October 25, 1953
        Died: December 18, 2003
            Children:
            Linda Kay
            Born: October 2, 1954 -
            married Dale Alan Kanary on May 19,1984

            Barry Douglas
            Born: December 4, 1956 -
            married Donna Sargent on July 12, 1980

                Children:
                Jessica Lynn
                Born: April 22, 1984
                Brent Douglas
                Born: March 28, 1987

Albert Franklin
Born: September 2, 1936
Married Joy Reed on March 16, 1956 at Ayer MA

Children:
Janice Lynn
Born: April 22, 1957 in Massachusetts

Mary Elizabeth
Born: January 5, 1959 in Asmara, Eritrea,
  Ethiopia
married Charles Sisk

Children:
  Jason
  Born: Dec. 4, 1983
  Stephanie
  Born: January 9, 1990

Laura Sue
Born: February 27, 1960 in Asmara, Eritrea,
  Ethiopia
married Mike Bucknam

Children:
  Joy Marie
  Born: May 11, 1990

  Luke
  Born: May 5, 1992

Albert Married Sheila Burrus on July 31, 1970

Children: <u>BOTH ESTRANGED</u>
Karen
Born: Feb 3, 1971
Married Brian Toonen

Lesley
Born: May 25, 1978
Married Bryan Saunders
2 children

James Lee
Born: May 13, 1942
Married Bonnie Beatrice Pack on July 25, 1964

Children:
James Brian
Born: February 8, 1969
Married Kimberlee England on August 5, 1995

Children:
Ashlee Dawn
Born: Dec 11, 1995

Cynthia Renée
Born: January 5, 1971
Married Shaun Adams on Sept 26, 2003

Children
Nathan Gregory Adams
Born April 16, 2004

The Hooton Family History

Charles Morgan Hooton
Born: July 22, 1850
Died: February 19, 1916

Brother: Benjamin Franklin Hooton
Born: April 12, 1827
Died: January 20, 1902

Sister: Priscilla Hooton Knotts
Born: February 25, 1826
Married August 30, 1849
Died: January 23, 1906

William Knotts – The son of Priscilla Knotts (?)
Died: 1937
Wife: Eloise
Son: **Don Knotts**
Born: July 21, 1924

Wife: Kay   Married in 1947

W. M. Funk - Was in Company H, 12th WV Infantry
Born: 1820
Wife: Nancy
Died: 1907
      Daughter: Sarah M.
      Born: March 29, 1855
      Died: September 9, 1898

Charles Morgan Hooton and Sarah M. Funk were united in marriage by John W. Carrico on Aug 1, 1875

Buried Knotts Ridge Cemetery - off Route 50 - Rowlesburg, West Virginia

      Children:
      Charles Warren
      Born: December 17, 1876
      Died: March 11, 1967

      Carlos Raymond
      Born: Sept 12, 1878 in Rowlesburg, WV
      Died: September 30, 1964
      Occupation: Coal Miner in Clarksburg and Jordan, WV

      Elva Leo
      Born: January 21, 1885
      Died: September 24, 1978
      Married to: Riley Himelrick

Carlos Raymond Hooton and Mary Etta Vance
Were married in Oakland, Maryland on January 20, 1903

      Children:
      Charles Nathaniel
      Born: June 4, 1904
      Died: June 29, 1994

      Charles Nathaniel married Velma Love
      (Velma died October 10, 1975)

Charles' Occupation: Union Carbide, Clarksburg, WV
32nd degree Mason

Children:
Thomas
Born: December 7, 1934
Arthur Raymond (Bob)
Born: February 18, 1944

Charles Nathaniel married widow of Bernard, Hazel Hooton on
November 26, 1976

Bernard Duncan
Born: January 20, 1906
Died: June 26, 1973
Bernard Duncan married Hazel Boyles

Bernard's Occupation: Mechanical engineer for
Baltimore & Ohio Railroad, Baltimore - assisted in
drawing plans for the "Cincinnatian," a crack B&O
passenger train between Cincinnati and Baltimore

Children:
Lois
Born: October 2, 1934
  Children:
  Patty
  Lee
  Ginny

Charlotte
Born: September 4, 1938
  Children:
  Susan
  Sharon

Margaret Frances
Born: November 21, 1907
Died: January 1983
Margaret Frances married Ray Woody
(Ray Woody died May 15, 1937)

Margaret's Occupation: Hair dresser - Social
Security Office - Baltimore

Children:
Charles Morgan
Born: March 1, 1931
  Children:
  Sheila
  Charlene
Margaret Frances married Wilbur F. McCartin
(Wilbur died May 19, 1977)

Mary Susan
Born: June 25, 1909
Died: March 4, 1964

Mary Susan married Harold Fillmore Rayl May 4, 1933

Mary Susan's Occupation: Housewife
  Children:
  Barbara Jane
  Born: January 19, 1934

  Albert Franklin
  Born: September 2, 1936

  James Lee
  Born: May 13, 1942

The Vance Family

Silas Nathaniel Vance married Mary Susan Harris

Mary Susan Harris died December 12, 1930
She was a daughter of Thomas D. and Jane Harris of
Gallipolis, Ohio - The family lived on a houseboat in
Portsmouth, Ohio
Brothers:

Sisters:
Thomas Harris
     Mrs. Charles Clendenning
William Harris
      of Charleston, West Virginia
James Harris
       Mrs. Ann Johnson
Oscar Harris
      of Logan, West Virginia
Frank Harris

Silas Nathaniel Vance died January 17, 1927
12 Children:
    Bertie
    Born: May 24, 1878
    Died: May 20, 1959
    Married Lew Lewis from Wales
        Children:
        Loretta
        Thelma - married Arthur Robinson - had 3 children
            Sallie Lou
            Butch
            Charles

    Lillie - Born: September 12, 1879
    Married William F. Rogers
        Children:
        William F. Rogers - married Bess - 1 son
        William Rogers (Billy) - married Francine Collinger

            2 children
            Harry
            George - married Lillian - 1 son

George (Cookie) married Kathy
2 daughters Susan, Jane

Vivian - married to owner of a casket company around Toledo or Cleveland - 1 son – Alvin

Harry
Born: June 12, 1881
Died: October 15, 1890

Thomas D.
 Born May 12, 1883
Died: September 28, 1943
Wife: Verdie

Nathan (Silas Nathaniel)
 Born: January 21, 1885
Died: November 17, 1951
   Was a pioneer in Central West Virginia coal development
   Was a Mason and native of Pomeroy, Ohio

Mary Etta
Born: February 21, 1887
Died: December 3, 1976
Was born in Nelsonville, Ohio - Married **Carlos Raymond Hooton**

Jane
Born: October 26, 1888
Died: September 8, 1945
Married to Clyde Leonard

Isaac
Born: April 3, 1889
Died: September 19, 1890

Ida
Born: September 28, 1890
Died: April 30, 1938
Married to Hayward Snider
   1 son: Enoch Givens
   Enoch married Eleanor

2 sons
Charles
Born: March 25, 1893
Died: January 2, 1894

Son - Stillborn on May 29, 1894

Celina
Born: February 10, 1896
Died: 197?
Married Henry McCormick - Several children

Just remember – You too can accomplish your dreams, if you really try hard enough and never ever give up.

Quitting is the same as failure and **FAILURE IS NOT AN OPTION....**

Start dreaming NOW if you have not already done so..